'Total Germany'

'Total Germany'

The Royal Navy's War against the Axis Powers 1939-45

David Wragg

Pen & Sword
MARITIME

First published in Great Britain in 2015 by
Pen & Sword Maritime
An imprint of
Pen & Sword Books Ltd
47 Church Street
Barnsley
South Yorkshire
S70 2AS

ISBN 978 1 47384 464 3

A CIP catalogue record for this book is
available from the British Library.

Typeset in Palatino by
Replika Press Pvt Ltd, India
Printed and bound in England
by CPI Group (UK) Ltd, Croydon, CR0 4YY

Pen & Sword Books Ltd incorporates the Imprints of Pen & Sword
Aviation, Pen & Sword Family History, Pen & Sword Maritime, Pen
& Sword Military, Pen & Sword Discovery, Pen & Sword Politics, Pen
& Sword Atlas, Pen & Sword Archaeology, Wharncliffe Local History,
Wharncliffe True Crime, Wharncliffe Transport, Pen & Sword Select,
Pen & Sword Military Classics, Leo Cooper, The Praetorian Press,
Claymore Press, Remember When, Seaforth Publishing and Frontline
Publishing.

For a complete list of Pen & Sword titles please contact
PEN & SWORD BOOKS LIMITED
47 Church Street, Barnsley, South Yorkshire, S70 2AS, England
E-mail: enquiries@pen-and-sword.co.uk
Website: www.pen-and-sword.co.uk

Contents

Acknowledgements

In writing any book, an author is grateful for the help and assistance of many others, and especially those who have placed on record their wartime achievements, many of them in the invaluable Imperial War Museum Sound Archive.

No work on something as vast as our wartime navy can cover every inch of ground, and for those whose appetite has been whetted by this book, I hope that the bibliography at the back is helpful. This text concentrates mainly on the Royal Navy's war against Germany and Italy, but it is impossible to ignore events in the Far East and the Pacific as this was truly a world war.

David Wragg
Edinburgh
Spring 2015

Introduction

Neither the United Kingdom nor Germany was in a position to fight a major war in 1939 but the reality was that the former was better prepared, having put the time bought by the Munich Agreement the previous year to much better use. The imbalance was most marked at sea but although the Royal Navy was by far the larger, better-equipped and more balanced force, it was also thinly spread across the world, as in 1914.

The Germans had very ambitious plans for a much-expanded and modernized navy – so ambitious that many doubted their practicality – and these were hardly even started in 1939. Priority had been given to creating the Luftwaffe, a large and modern air force, and the army. Even here, there were weaknesses. The Luftwaffe was not a strategic air force, although Hitler's war plans assumed that it would act as one. It lacked heavy bombers. The Germany army, unlike the British army, had not mechanized between the wars and was heavily dependent on horses for transport.

The German navy, the *Kriegsmarine*, lacked aircraft carriers or even adequate numbers of destroyers and, contrary to popular belief, had very few ocean-going U-boats in 1939. Yet, senior officers were secure in Hitler's assurances that war would not break out until 1944. Chamberlain's speech to the British people on 3 September, followed by the Admiralty signal 'Total Germany. Total Germany' declaring all-out war against that nation came as a shock to the *Kriegsmarine's* leaders.

Glossary

Allies: A term dating back at least to the early nineteenth century but used commonly during the First World War to describe the members of the Triple Entente, more properly known as the 'Entente Powers', which were the United Kingdom, France and Imperial Russia. During the Second World War it was used for just the UK and France initially, later including the Soviet Union and then the United States.

ASDIC: Derived from the initials for the Anti-Submarine Detection Investigation Committee originating in the First World War and today known as sonar. Such equipment emits audible pings and then traces submerged objects through their echoes.

Auxiliary carrier: Term applied by the Royal Navy to what are commonly called escort carriers; see below.

Auxiliary cruiser: Merchant vessel taken up from trade and armed with a naval crew. The British used these as convoy escorts, but the Germans used them as surface raiders. In neither case could they survive contact with major warships.

Axis Powers: The alliance formed by Germany, Italy and Japan. Unlike the Allies, there was very little co-ordination at times, especially between Japan and Germany or Italy, or cross-fertilization of ideas or technical developments.

BARBAROSSA: Code-name for Germany's invasion of the Soviet Union.

Battle-cruiser: A warship usually with battleship-calibre armament, but in which armour was sacrificed to give greater speed. The German battle-cruisers *Scharnhorst* and *Gneisenau* had guns of just 11in calibre; these were supposed to be replaced by guns of 15in calibre, although this never happened.

Battleship: Designation given to large heavily-armed and heavily-armoured ships. Second World War battleships generally had guns of 15in calibre, but some British battleships had 14in or 16in and some Japanese ships had 18in guns.

CAM ship: Catapult-armed merchantman, a merchant vessel with a fighter aircraft that could be catapulted off to shoot down enemy aircraft. The fighter pilot was usually from the RAF, but a number of Fleet Air Arm personnel also flew such aircraft. The weakness of the concept was that the aircraft had to be sacrificed at the end of a single sortie unless within sight of land, and this meant that there was always a reluctance to use it in case a greater need came later in the voyage.

Capital ship: A major warship such as a battleship or battle-cruiser, but by the end of the war the aircraft carrier had joined these as a capital ship and many would say had even usurped their position.

Case White (*Fall Weiss*): German code-name for the invasion of Poland.

Coastal Command: Royal Air Force command that provided maritime-reconnaissance and anti-submarine patrols as well as search and rescue (SAR) in the open seas, and was generally meant to be tasked by the Admiralty. SAR in coastal waters was provided by RAF Fighter Command.

Corvette: During the Second World War this term was adopted for a warship specifically designed for convoy escort duties, smaller than a frigate or destroyer and also slower and of broader bream than the latter, as well as less heavily-armed.

Cruiser: Warship smaller than a battleship or battle-cruiser but much larger than a destroyer. The Washington Naval Treaty of 1922 laid down that light cruisers had a main armament of 6in guns and heavy cruisers a main armament of 8in guns (displacement tonnage was not taken into account). The Royal Navy's Town-class cruisers had up to twelve 6in guns in four turrets but were classified by the service as 'heavy'. In addition there were auxiliary (see above) or armed merchant cruisers, and anti-aircraft cruisers that were usually older ships modified to allow continued use.

Cruiser war: A term sometimes used for commerce raiding.

Destroyer: Small fast warship, and by the Second World War much larger than its First World War counterpart. Armament varied between 4in and 4.5in on British ships, but some German ships were larger and the French had their *contre-torpilleur* destroyers with 5.5in armament.

DYNAMO: code-name for the evacuation of British and French forces from Dunkirk.

E-boat: Enemy fast motor gunboat or motor torpedo-boat, known to the *Kriegsmarine* as *S-Boot* for *Schnellboot* or 'fast boat'.

Electro U-boat: German U-boat development that appeared from 1943 onwards, with an enlarged hull to enable additional batteries to be fitted for higher underwater speeds.

Empire: A prefix given to the name of a merchant vessel owned by the British government but managed and crewed by a commercial ship-owner. Such ships included enemy vessels seized either on the high seas or caught in an Allied port on the outbreak of war; ships that were built at government expense to compensate for losses or ships taken up for use by the armed services; or US-built 'Liberty' vessels supplied to the United Kingdom under the Lend-Lease Programme.

Enigma: Code used by all the German armed forces, but broken once a machine and codebooks fell into British hands. The breaking of the Enigma codes was a major factor in the Allied victory and especially in countering the U-boat threat to Atlantic and Arctic convoys.

Escort carrier: small aircraft carriers sometimes converted from merchant vessels, but later increasingly using merchant vessel hulls to allow conversion to a merchant vessel post-war. Limited in the number of aircraft that could be carried and in operational speed. Sometimes known as 'auxiliary carriers' and indeed, many were used as aircraft transports, maintenance carriers and as carriers for aircraft providing cover for invading troops.

FELIX: Code-name for a planned invasion of Gibraltar should Spain have seized the territory; however, it soon became clear that Spain intended to be neutral, although much used as a base by German agents.

Fleet Air Arm: Originally that part of the Royal Air Force deployed aboard British warships, but it reverted to Admiralty control in May 1939 and naval airmen gradually replaced their RAF counterparts, although a large number of RAF personnel transferred to the Royal Navy.

Flotilla: A command of smaller warships such as destroyers, corvettes or submarines. No definition of the number of ships, but usually it would be between six and nine.

Frigate: Originally a general-purpose sailing warship much smaller than a ship of the line (predecessor of the battleship). Frigates disappeared from the world's navies during the late nineteenth century. They were reinvented during the Second World War as a convoy escort larger than a corvette and slower than a destroyer, and were usually dedicated to anti-submarine or anti-aircraft duties. In more recent times, they have reverted to their general-purpose role.

JUDGEMENT: code-name for the Fleet Air Arm attack on the Italian Fleet in its major base at Taranto.

Kaiserliche Marine: 'Imperial Navy', the old name for the German navy.

Kriegsmarine: 'War Navy', the official name given by Adolf Hitler to the German navy in 1935 to replace the post-First World War name of *Reichsmarine* or 'State Navy'.

Lend-Lease: A programme under which the United States provided ships, aircraft and other war matériel without payment from the British government and on condition that the equipment be returned to the United States at the end of the war (naturally, anything that had been lost on war service could not be returned). In return, the United States armed forces were allowed to use bases in British colonies, mainly in the Caribbean.

Luftwaffe: German Air Force or Air Arm that controlled all German service aviation from the early 1930s to the end of the Second World War. Although autonomous, it developed as primarily a tactical air force without long-range heavy bombers until too late in the war for them to make an impact.

MAC-ship: Merchant aircraft carrier, a ship that continued as a grain carrier or oil tanker with a Merchant Navy crew, but with a wooden flight deck built over the cargo areas and the superstructure moved to starboard so that naval personnel could fly Fairey Swordfish on anti-submarine patrols around a convoy. Most were British-manned, but two were manned by Dutch personnel including air-crew and maintainers from the Royal Netherlands Navy.

NAS: A suffix following a squadron number to denote 'naval air squadron'.

Reich: The German state ('realm').

Reichsmarine: Official name of the German navy after the abdication of the Kaiser and the creation of a republic or 'Reich'.

Reverse Lend-Lease: Equipment provided by the United Kingdom to the United States. While much smaller in quantity than that received by the UK, this included some warships equipped with ASDIC and radar.

RMS: Royal Mail Ship, a designation allowed the fast ocean liners that, as well as conveying passengers in comfort, also carried the mails. Not to be confused with the Royal Mail Line, a shipping company; ships prefixed 'RMS' always belonged to ship-owners, i.e. private enterprises.

Squadron: In naval use, a command of major warships such as battleships, battle-cruisers, cruisers or aircraft carriers, sometimes comprising as few as two ships.

U-boat: In German, *Unterseeboot*, a submarine.

Wardroom: Royal Navy name for the officers' mess, also used by some merchant shipping lines such as P&O.

Wolf pack: A group of submarines deployed against a convoy.

Chapter 1

'Total Germany. Total Germany.'

'Total Germany. Total Germany.' The message was short and succinct. It was also uncoded. It was the signal from the Admiralty in London to all warships, naval bases, fleets, flotillas and stations that war had broken out between the United Kingdom and Germany.

Communications are rarely secure. Some were not expected to be: they were public. That fateful morning of 3 September 1939, at 11.15, millions listened to British Prime Minister Neville Chamberlain when he broadcast to the British people telling them that the Anglo-French ultimatum to Germany demanding that she withdraw her forces from Poland had expired and that none of the assurances demanded from Germany had been received. He told them that this country was now at war with Germany. The signal sent out from the Admiralty was transmitted throughout the world. It was a simple message. The Germans picked up both the radio, or as it would have been known at the time, wireless broadcast, and the signal.

Immediately, the news was passed to the senior officers of the Germany navy, the *Kriegsmarine* or 'War Navy', as Adolf Hitler had renamed it in 1935, changing the title from *Reichsmarine* or 'State Navy', just over fourteen years after it had changed from *Kaiserliche Marine* or 'Imperial Navy'.

Two of the recipients were *Grossadmiral* Erich Raeder, the chief of the *Kriegsmarine*, and his *Führer der U-Boote*, Admiral Karl Dönitz. The two men were not together at the time, but they were both at meetings. On reading the message, Raeder was so moved that he had to leave the room. Minutes later, Dönitz also received the message. Holding the signal in his hand he paced backwards and forwards, muttering to himself in consternation: *'Mein Gott! Also wieder Krieg gegen England!'* ('My God! So it's war against England again!'). He too then left the room to compose his thoughts.

Later, Raeder noted in a memorandum that:

Today the war breaks out against England-France which, according to the Führer we need not have reckoned with before about 1944 and which until the last minute the Führer believed he should prevent... [the *Kriegsmarine*] could only show that it understood how to die with honour in order to create the foundations for later reconstruction.

Many in the United Kingdom listened to Chamberlain speaking over the radio with an air of resignation. Others were bitterly disappointed. Appeasement, in which the United Kingdom and France sacrificed the Czech Sudetenland in 1938 for another year of peace after tense negotiations with the German Chancellor Adolf Hitler at Munich, has since been criticized. Nevertheless, Mass Observation, which had started its polling of British public opinion in the late 1930s, found that appeasement was very much in tune with public attitudes. Those who remembered the First World War were prepared to pay almost any price to avoid another conflict.

Neither the United Kingdom nor Germany was in a position to fight in 1938. The UK put the extra year of peace to better use than did Germany, which was already having problems financing its massive expansion of the armed forces. Among the most important measures that the UK completed was the 'Chain Home' air defence radar network. Appeasement has frequently been misunderstood by later generations as there were other factors at work. Before going to Munich, Chamberlain had informed King George VI that he saw Great Britain and Germany as the two pillars in a defence against the spread of Russian Communism. Some today present Chamberlain as being sympathetic to the peace movement within the British establishment that would have collaborated with Nazi Germany, but his strenuous efforts to improve Britain's defences indicate that this was not the case.

The *Kriegsmarine* in 1939

Why were these two senior German naval officers so concerned that war had broken out? After all, their country had gone to war against Poland, something which they knew about. Germany had also been asserting her rights, real or imagined, for a year or so before the invasion of Poland. The country had claimed the Czech Sudetenland on the grounds that its population were ethnic Germans; had annexed Austria; and finally taken the rest of Czechoslovakia. All this had been without much more than a murmur of protest from the British and the French.

The lack of protest was fundamental to the problem. In 1936, Britain and France had stood by while the Italians had ravaged Abyssinia (present-day Ethiopia), despite the United Kingdom preparing for war against Italy. The League of Nations had refused to act because of French reluctance to enter a war against Italy, even though the Abyssinian problem could have been brought under control by barring use of the Suez Canal to Italian shipping. The British had considered this, and had even prepared plans for an attack on the major Italian naval base of Taranto in the 'instep' of Italy, using aircraft from the Mediterranean Fleet's aircraft carrier. Neither had the Western Powers done anything when Japan had invaded China.

Although the League of Nations had been proposed by an American president after the First World War, the United States was not a member. The League of Nations was toothless: in its entire existence, it did not intervene effectively and was never supported by its members. There was no such thing as a 'League of Nations Peace-Keeping Force', in contrast to a number of efforts by the United Nations in recent years.

In short, the Germans from Adolf Hitler downwards believed that they could invade Poland without any reaction from the United Kingdom or France. The secret Molotov-Ribbentrop Pact of August 1939 had meant that there would be no challenge from the Soviet Union, and in fact the Soviets would soon join the invasion, taking the eastern areas of Poland. The Germans also believed that they could once again argue their way out of trouble. The invasion of Poland was popular with many Germans, not all of them supporters of the Nazi regime, as it meant Germany regaining territory lost after the First World War when the boundaries of Poland and Russia both moved westwards.

This complacent view had led Hitler to assure his naval commanders that they could not expect a war with the United Kingdom until 1943 at the earliest, and more possibly 1944 or 1945. Raeder had been assured by Hitler that war with 'England', as they put it, was not imminent as recently as that fateful morning.

This was crucial to the *Kriegsmarine*. The German navy was not prepared for war, despite its aggressive-sounding title. Hitler had given priority to the creation of the Luftwaffe and the rebuilding of the German army. The *Kriegsmarine* had not been neglected completely, but it was still far short of what Raeder, and more especially Dönitz, wanted it to be. The planners had come up with a scheme for a navy that would be able to compete with the Royal Navy: this was known as 'Plan X', later replaced by 'Plan Y', which called for a stronger navy still, and next came 'Plan Z'. When they first worked together, Raeder and Dönitz had much the same aims and aspirations for the *Kriegsmarine*, but Raeder doubted whether any future war would see the submarines – the famed and feared U-boats – playing an important role because of improvements in anti-submarine detection, known at the time as ASDIC. Dönitz disagreed strongly, and was able to modify Plan Z so that it called for a much-enhanced submarine arm.

The trouble was that this would take time. Plan Z would not be completed until 1944 at the earliest. Germany lacked the manpower, the materials and most of all the money to do better. Indeed, many believe that Plan Z was beyond the nation's capabilities. While Germany was an advanced industrial nation able to match any other country in Europe in output, quality and innovation, it was also a country with few natural resources. The only fuel available was coal. The growth of the German war machine was such that even in 1939 the budget was stretched. Germany could afford only two out of three of her armed services and had spent all it could on both of them, leaving the navy at the end of the line. Raeder and Dönitz knew all of this, especially the former, who realized that Germany could not win a new war.

Ironically, this pessimistic outlook was shared by his counterpart in the Imperial Japanese Navy, although in his case, rather than considering the UK, it was the knowledge that Japan could not match the strength of the United States Navy or the industrial output of the United States.

The Italians had no need for such pessimism in 1939. Belatedly, the Italian dictator Benito Mussolini had made it clear to Adolf Hitler that Italy would not enter the Second World War in 1939. The new Spanish leader Franco knew that his country, still suffering from the effects of a bloody civil war, was unable to enter the war and could not endure the strains it would impose on a still-divided population. Across the other side of the world in the Far East, Japan was still preparing to go to war with the United States. In any event, once the war became global, Japan was too far distant for any joint operations with the Axis.

So in 1939, Germany was on her own.

Plan Z

Raeder believed that there was a danger of war between Germany and both the United Kingdom and France even before the Munich crisis of 1938. This possibility was not discussed officially. Nevertheless, the belief among senior German naval officers at the time was that any war would see the *Kriegsmarine* operating against British and French shipping rather than seeking a major fleet action as at Jutland, which had so concerned their predecessors during the First World War.

The German naval staff appreciated that the location of the British Isles hindered German access to the open sea, but the First World War had also shown that the UK's strategic weakness was the country's heavy dependence on overseas trade. The German position could be improved if Norway, Denmark, The Netherlands, Belgium and northern France as far south as Brest were to be occupied, giving unrestricted German access to the North Atlantic. The Luftwaffe would also benefit, being able to attack British convoys in the Atlantic including the Bay of Biscay and the Western Approaches, while British ports on the south coast from Dover to Plymouth, including the major naval base of Portsmouth and the major merchant port of Southampton, would also be exposed to attack from the air and from the sea.

Admiral Hellmuth Heye prepared a paper, 'Seekriegführung gegen England', 'Sea Warfare against England', on 25 October 1938. The paper was more interesting for what it did not say, and indeed it gave very little idea of how the war would be conducted at sea, but it was very dismissive of the potential for the U-boat. Like Raeder, Heye believed that British anti-submarine measures were so sophisticated that there would be little scope for submarine warfare. The one concession that he did make in giving the U-boat a role was the use of the 'cruiser U-boat'. He envisaged a small fleet of large cruiser U-boats that would each have four 12.7cm (5in) guns and a high surface speed of 25 knots, which could engage British merchant shipping on the surface. Even so, the paper expressed concerns that once forced to dive, the slow speed of the submarine would mean that these large U-boats would be at the mercy of the Royal Navy's anti-submarine measures.

Heye's idea was similar to the concept of the cruiser submarine that had been the British M-class and the French Surcouf, but with lower-calibre weapons for the German boats. The cruiser U-boats would be positioned along the main convoy routes and close to major ports, but it was also felt that they would end up playing a sacrificial role because of the concentration of countermeasures at such locations.

The main thrust of the paper was that the Kriegsmarine should engage in commerce raiding using the Panzerschiffe (armoured ships) known to the British and American media as 'pocket battleships', later re-classified by the Germans as heavy cruisers. Each Panzerschiff would be escorted by light cruisers, while a squadron of powerful battleships would be necessary to enable the Panzerschiff to break out into the open seas.

Heye also considered it necessary that the *Kriegsmarine* should have its own aircraft.

Raeder appointed the commander of the fleet, Admiral Carls, to head a planning committee. Carls was enthusiastic about the paper and was among the first to urge that the *Kriegsmarine* should begin planning for war. The naval staff had already drawn up a series of plans for the expansion of the service, starting with Plan X which was superseded by Plan Y, in turn superseded by Plan Z.

Plan Z was very much Raeder's baby. It envisaged big battleships and aircraft carriers, armoured cruisers and many smaller vessels, including 249 U-boats. Finalized in late 1938, it was given Hitler's approval in January 1939. Most of Plan Z would be completed by 1945, but the full plan would not be in place until 1947.

The initial plan called for no fewer than 4 aircraft carriers, although this was intended to rise to 8 later with the addition of some smaller ships; 6 large battleships, known as the H-class; 3 battle-cruisers, known as the O-class, later to be increased to 12; 12 P-class *Panzerschiffe*; 2 heavy cruisers; light cruisers and large destroyers; and 249 U-boats. Given the size of the projected fleet, and especially the number of major surface units including capital ships, it is surprising that there were intended to be only fifty-eight destroyers.

This was an ambitious plan, but Germany did not have the shipbuilding capacity to fulfil it and also lacked the necessary materials. The fuel that this vast fleet would consume exceeded the total fuel consumption of Germany in 1938. Germany was effectively rebuilding her new navy from scratch as there had been no sustained construction of major warships since the end of the First World War, so even the slipways were not available.

The first German aircraft carrier, the *Graf Zeppelin*, had been started in 1936 and she was launched in 1938, after which plans were made to begin work on a second ship, the *Peter Strasser*, although she was never started. Orders were placed in 1939 for carrier versions of the Messerschmitt Bf 109 fighter and the Junkers Ju 87 Stuka dive-bomber, designated as the Bf 109T and the Ju 87C. In the middle of that year, the two battleships *Bismarck* and *Tirpitz* were both launched and the keels laid for the first three of the H-class battleships.

Despite Hitler's approval for Plan Z, the Minister for Air, Hermann Göring, refused to allow the navy to have its own aviation, despite the British having recognized belatedly that combining all service aviation in the Royal Air Force had been a mistake. German inexperience in carrier aviation also meant that the *Graf Zeppelin* was obsolete even before she was launched, with a design on a par with the British *Courageous*-Class and France's sole aircraft carrier, the *Béarn*.

Dönitz, meanwhile, was lobbying for a stronger U-boat arm; this did not please his superior, Raeder, but eventually Plan Z was amended to allow the construction of 300. Early in 1939, Dönitz published a book, *Die U-Bootswaffe*, *The U-boat Arm*, and while it did not mention the wolf pack or group tactics, it made the case that the U-boat was to be the major offensive weapon and that merchant shipping would be a primary target. It took British Naval Intelligence until 1942 to obtain a copy. While Dönitz may have seemed to be stretching the already ambitious Plan Z beyond reason, his ideas were far more realistic than those of Raeder as the U-boats were cheaper to build and required fewer raw materials than the big ships and also made better use of increasingly scarce manpower.

The pessimism of both Raeder and Dönitz at Germany's 'early' entry into the war was, surprisingly enough, shared by senior officers in the Luftwaffe. These men knew that their service had been created as a tactical air force, highly effective in supporting ground troops. This strategy was known as Blitzkrieg, 'lightning war', and meant the use of air power and armoured formations to overwhelm the enemy and ensure a rapid advance. The British use of the term 'Blitz' to describe the air-raids on London and other British cities was nothing more than slang. This policy had left the Luftwaffe with a fundamental weakness: the absence of a longer-range heavy bomber. This programme had been scrapped during the late 1930s in favour of building large numbers of twin-engined medium bombers and single-engined dive-bombers, but dive-bombers were of limited use against hardened targets or those with substantial anti-aircraft defences and well-trained gunners.

War meant that RAF bombers could reach Germany, despite suffering heavy losses, but that the Luftwaffe could not reach the UK unless bases were secured in northern France. This was a direct parallel with the *Kriegsmarine*, as bases in France would ensure that U-boats and surface raiders did not have to take the long passage around the British Isles, using scarce fuel and also exposing the naval vessels to interception by the British. It would also reduce the amount of time that could be spent on the open seas.

Germany went to war with its air force and navy ill-prepared, and everything depending on the army. Even the Germany army, the *Heere*, at this stage was far from impressive. It had faced no resistance in the

Sudetenland or Austria, or indeed when the remains of Czechoslovakia were taken. In Poland it had overwhelming power and faced a country with a small navy, an obsolete air force and an army that, like the other services, fought defiantly and bravely but was also short of armour and artillery. Even so, the Germans had many reservists in 'Case White', the attack on Poland, and senior officers reported that their performance was disappointing.

The problems of the armed services and of Germany going to war too early were not hidden. On 24 May 1939, Major General Thomas of the Wehrmacht's military-economic office drew attention to the fact that the military spending of the USA, France and the UK for 1939-40, once adjusted for differences in spending power, would outspend Germany and Italy combined by at least 2 million reichsmarks. If military spending as a proportion of gross national income was used as a basis for comparison, the contrast was worse: Germany planned to spend 23 per cent, France 17 per cent, the UK 12 per cent, and the USA just 2 per cent.

To Thomas and many other senior officers these statistics suggested that Hitler should be cautious and not rush into war. To Hitler and his inner circle, the figures suggested something else. Germany could not win an arms race. Time was not on her side.

For the *Kriegsmarine* this meant that, as a basis of comparison, Germany would have four aircraft carriers by 1944 if Plan Z went ahead, but the Royal Navy would have six new fast armoured carriers plus the brand-new HMS *Ark Royal*, while France would have two new aircraft carriers. In the air, the RAF would have large numbers of the new Supermarine Spitfire fighter and heavy bombers.

It was clear that Germany had been caught in a trap. War had come too soon. Yet, the British and French were also ill-prepared for war, and assistance from the United States was for the time being so remote as to be almost unthinkable. The loss of France would also leave the British on their own, except for aid from an empire that was far-flung and with which communications were exposed to attack by submarines and surface vessels. By contrast, the Germans had relatively few convoys to defend and at the outset these, mainly of Swedish ore, were shipped along the Norwegian coast as the more direct route from Sweden through the Gulf of Bothnia was impassable in winter due to ice. Later, of course, there would be convoys along the coasts of Belgium and The Netherlands, and across the Mediterranean.

Chapter 2

A Strong Navy but Thinly Spread

In 1914 the Royal Navy was the world's strongest but, according to Admiral of the Fleet Lord Fisher who returned from retirement to become First Sea Lord for the second time in October, it was 'weak everywhere, strong nowhere'. By 1939, the Royal Navy was no longer the world's strongest, but it was still thinly spread. Some of its historic commitments had been cut with Australia, Canada, New Zealand and South Africa having created navies of their own, something that had already happened in Australia and Canada before the First World War and had developed further in the late 1930s. Nevertheless, there was still much for the Royal Navy to do and it remained based around the globe.

Despite the severe economic depression that in reality had dominated most of the interwar years, in 1939 the Royal Navy and Royal Marines totalled 129,000 men and on mobilization this figure rose to 202,000 men as members of the Royal Naval Reserve (RNR) and Royal Naval Volunteer Reserve (RNVR) were called up. Many of the RNR members were serving in the Merchant Navy and brought good navigational and engineering skills to the expanded wartime navy, while the RNVR consisted of many whose experience extended no further than yachting and perhaps not even that.

Each year had seen a flotilla of new destroyers introduced, often replacing older ships with seven, eight or even nine new vessels. Nevertheless, the service had been weakened from its high point of 1914. Lieutenant Commander E.C. Talbot-Booth reminded the readers of his book *All the World's Fighting Fleets*, published almost on the eve of war, that by 1940 the Royal Navy would have just 21 capital ships, meaning battleships and battle-cruisers, as against 68 in 1914; 69 cruisers as against 103; and 190 torpedo craft as against 319. 'With the exception of Germany, every other leading navy will be substantially stronger than before the last war,' he added.

One point he did not make was that the 1939 cruiser was much larger and more capable than its counterpart in 1914 and the same could be said for the destroyers, some of which in 1939 were almost as large as the 1914 light cruiser.

The Royal Navy was still one of the leading navies in 1939, even though the Washington Naval Treaty of 1922 had decreed that the Royal Navy and the United States Navy were to be equal in size and even in composition. The years of recession had seen new ships continue to join the fleet, but not in the numbers required as the threat of war came ever closer. What the recession had done had been to cut the United Kingdom's industrial capacity, not least in shipbuilding. Admiral of the Fleet Sir Ernle Chatfield (later Lord Chatfield), First Sea Lord (the most senior naval officer) from January 1933 to November 1938, knew that a larger navy was needed. New warships were ordered, with a plan to modernize the carrier fleet, but the pace of expansion was stalled by a shortage of slipways and this became the limiting factor in naval shipbuilding from 1937 onwards, once funding for Britain's armed forces was no longer restricted.

A Blue-Water Navy
Navies are generally divided into 'blue-water', ocean-going, or 'brown-water'; the latter defines a service limited to coastal duties, in effect a glorified coastguard, or to operations in a largely enclosed sea such as the Baltic or the Black Sea. The Treaty of Versailles had tried to limit the new *Reichsmarine* to such a role, but even before Hitler's rise to power, senior officers were planning the rebuilding of the German navy to the extent that they sought advice on planning and, even more important, managing the political fallout that rearmament was causing among liberal and communist politicians in the *Reichstag* (German parliament).

Before the First World War, the Kaiser had wanted Germany to have a 'blue-water' navy capable of rivalling the Royal Navy and indeed, by 1914 the Imperial German Navy was the world's second-largest. It was no longer to be the junior service but to be on a par with the army. Those days had not been forgotten.

The Royal Navy was the consummate blue-water navy, spread around the world but also retaining the less prestigious but important tasks such as fisheries protection and keeping ports open during times of war by minesweeping. The United States Navy was also a blue-water navy, but it had the United States Coast Guard (USCG) for many of the more mundane home-based tasks. In wartime, the USCG passed under USN control.

By 1939, the Royal Navy had been through a number of reorganizations. The Grand Fleet of the First World War, the result of a policy of bringing home as many major fleet units as possible ready for a war with Germany, had become first the Atlantic Fleet and later the Home Fleet. The Inskip Award of 1937 handed naval aviation back to the Admiralty, which took control of the Fleet Air Arm in May 1939.

The main organization of the Royal Navy in 1939 was on a series of fleets and overseas stations. The largest of these was the Home Fleet with bases at Devonport, Portsmouth and Chatham, although these were also available for ships returning from overseas, and a forward base at Scapa Flow in Orkney. Then there was the Mediterranean Fleet with its main base at Malta and other bases at Gibraltar and Alexandria, which was probably the most popular posting of all. In the Far East there was the China Station based on Hong Kong, and the East Indies Station based on Singapore. In the west there was the American Station based on Bermuda, and the West Indies Station. Finally, there was the African Station based on Simonstown, the naval base near Cape Town.

One big difference between the Royal Navy and the British army and the Royal Air Force was that the sponsoring department, the Admiralty, was not just a government department but an operational headquarters as well. It could, and did, send orders direct; not just to the commanders of the two major fleets, but to individual ships when necessary. The First Lord of the Admiralty was a civilian, a politician and a government minister with a seat in the Cabinet. The service head was the First Sea Lord, with the Second Sea Lord being responsible for personnel. The major fleets were headed by a commander-in-chief, while the stations would have a flag officer, the title being, for example, 'Flag Officer, East Indies'. The major fleets would have a number of flag officers such as flag officer, carriers, or flag officer, submarines.

In 1939 Commander-in-Chief, Home Fleet was Admiral Sir Charles Forbes. His command included 5 battleships, 2 battle-cruisers, 2 aircraft carriers, 3 squadrons with a total of 15 cruisers between them, 2 flotillas each with 8 or 9 destroyers, and some 20 or so submarines. In addition, also in home waters, another 2 battleships and 2 aircraft carriers were based in the English Channel with 3 cruisers and a destroyer flotilla; and another 2 cruisers and a destroyer flotilla were based on the Humber. Additional escort vessels, meaning destroyers and sloops, were based on Devonport, the naval base at Plymouth, and at Portsmouth.

Wartime started to change the structure of the Royal Navy. New commands were created for the North Atlantic and the South Atlantic. Six home commands were also created: Orkney and Shetland, which included Scapa Flow; Rosyth; Nore; Dover; Portsmouth; and, finally, the Western Approaches, originally based on Plymouth but under the pressure of heavy German bombing, moved to Liverpool. On 2 December 1941, the China Station evolved into the British Eastern Fleet with a commander-in-chief, and after the fall of Singapore it moved first to Ceylon (now Sri Lanka), and once that was attacked, to Kilindini (or Mombasa) in British East Africa (now Kenya).

The Royal Navy in 1939 had far closer links with the navies of the British Empire than is the case today. The relationships varied, with the Canadians taking a far more independent view than the Australians or New Zealanders. The four main Empire navies were the Royal Australian Navy, the Royal Canadian Navy and the Royal Indian Navy, which had been known as the Royal Indian Marine as late as 1935; there was also the New Zealand Division, which in wartime grew to become the Royal New Zealand Navy. In addition, the Royal Egyptian Navy was commanded by a British admiral as even though officially Egypt was an independent kingdom and not part of the Empire, it was heavily influenced by the UK.

No other navy had such a wide spread of responsibilities. It could be fairly said that where the Royal Navy had fleets, the French navy – the *Marine Nationale* – had squadrons.

Imposing Limitations on the Royal Navy

Of course, there were a number of reasons for this, of which the poor state of the economy was just one. Another was the inclination of British politicians to do more in the way of reducing defence expenditure than was required by international efforts to encourage disarmament. This went down well with an electorate that was determined to avoid war at almost any price. After the First World War, a major conference convened in Washington also introduced limits on the size of the main navies. No longer could the United Kingdom strive to maintain a navy that was the equivalent of any two other navies, the so-called 'Two-Power Standard'. The Washington Naval Treaty of 1922 stipulated that the Royal Navy and the United States Navy were to be the same size, with not only the total tonnage of ships defined but also the maximum tonnage of each type of warship and limits placed on the maximum size of any type of warship.

Cruisers, for example, could not be heavier than 10,000 tons displacement; battleships and battle-cruisers were limited to 35,000 tons; and aircraft carriers could not be more than 27,000 tons, although as a concession the RN and USN were each allowed two carriers of up to 35,000 tons. These two navies were limited to a total warship tonnage of 525,000 tons each, with Japan, a First World War ally, limited to 315,000 tons, while France and Italy were both limited to 175,000 tons.

This was all very well, but each of the three largest navies had battleships and battle-cruisers in excess of their permitted tonnage, and all three took the same option: that of each converting two battle-cruisers to aircraft carriers. The Imperial Japanese Navy lost one of its battle-cruisers while under conversion as the shipyard was devastated in an earthquake, so a battleship was converted instead.

The British government decided that new cruisers should have a maximum tonnage of 8,500 tons rather than 10,000 tons, and that aircraft carriers should be no heavier than 23,000 tons. While this was happening – and some ships were built with weaknesses as a result – the future Axis powers adopted the opposite course, consistently understating the tonnage of new ships and even building two ships unofficially while stating that just one was under construction. The UK, despite having battleships of First World War vintage with main armament of 15in calibre and two more modern ships with main armament of 16in calibre, decided that the *King George V*-class battleships should be built with a main armament of just 14in calibre. Reducing the calibre of the guns not only meant that they packed less of a punch, but also had a slightly shorter range.

At the London Naval Conference of 1930, Japan pressed for a total tonnage that was the same size as that allocated to the Royal Navy and the United States Navy. When this did not happen, in 1934 the country formally notified the other Washington Naval Treaty signatories that she no longer considered herself bound by the restrictions.

Germany was also increasingly concerned with rebuilding her military strength. The Paris Air Agreement of 1926 allowed the country to build commercial aircraft and operate air services, but after Hitler came to power in 1933 work on building a new air force started, while the six elderly coastal battleships allowed under the Treaty of Versailles started to be replaced by modern *Panzerschiffe*. The London Naval Treaty of 1936 allowed the reconstruction of the German navy, granting the country a total tonnage of 35 per cent of that of the Royal Navy but, inexplicably, allowing parity with the Royal Navy in submarines!

No longer limited to having a coastal defence force, the Germans started to prepare, laying down new battleships and battle-cruisers, including building one battle-cruiser, *Gneisenau*, sister of *Scharnhorst*, secretly. Two aircraft carriers were planned but only one, the *Graf Zeppelin*, was actually built and never entered service. At headquarters, the German navy started to plan for expansion far beyond what was permitted by the London Naval Treaty. As previously described, first came Plan X which was superseded by Plan Y, and the latter overtaken by Plan Z; even this last plan was modified to allow for an increase in the number of U-boats.

As also mentioned above, after the First World War and the abdication of the Kaiser, the German navy went through a process of renaming. It was no longer the *Kaiserliche Marine* or Imperial German Navy, but instead became the *Reichsmarine* or State Navy. Hitler then changed this to *Kriegsmarine* or War Navy.

The Royal Navy of 1914 had its own aircraft, with the Royal Naval Air Service growing throughout the war, but on 1 April 1918 this was transferred with the Army's Royal Flying Corps to form the new Royal Air Force. The RNAS had by this time grown to 55,000 personnel and 2,500 aircraft. This meant that the navy that had invented the aircraft carrier and conducted trials with catapult-launching found itself with just the few aircraft that could be launched from battleships, battle-cruisers and cruisers, and was providing aircraft carriers for an air force to use. The RAF even invented the Fleet Air Arm as part of RAF Coastal Area, which later became Coastal Command.

Nevertheless, this anomaly was being rectified. In 1937, it was decided that the Royal Navy should have the Fleet Air Arm, although the change did not actually happen until May 1939. Many of the RAF personnel serving with the RN volunteered to remain, becoming the Royal Navy's Air Branch.

This was not simply a matter of administration or of which budget naval aviation was funded from, but of denying the Royal Navy senior officers with any practical knowledge of aviation and how to use air power effectively at sea. By contrast, the United States Navy had progressed to the point where only a naval aviator could command an aircraft carrier. It was only the Royal Navy whose senior officers believed that high-performance aircraft could not operate from an aircraft carrier; the Japanese and the Americans knew differently.

To many, it seemed that the Admiralty and the rest of the government had forgotten Lord Fisher's dictum that the future of naval warfare would be in the air and under the sea. By the air, Fisher had meant airships, but when he became First Sea Lord for the first time in 1904, it was still not known that the Wright brothers had been making their first flights and this did not become public knowledge until 1908. In the early 1920s, the magazine *Punch* ran a cartoon showing Britannia 'in holiday mood' at her ease on a seashore, asking Mr Punch what the wild waves were saying. He replied: 'They are saying, ma'am, that if you want to rule them you must rule the skies above them as well.'

In short, the Royal Navy still clung to the belief that any future war would consist of major fleet actions dominated by the battleship, and officers continued to be taught the 'lessons' of Jutland. The lessons of Jutland, or rather the mistakes, were to be of little value as the war that lay ahead was indeed going to be fought largely beneath the waves and above them.

The British government had seen that the Royal Navy had played fair between the wars and abided by international treaties, and indeed had them enforced on it ever more strictly by successive governments that had drawn the strings of the public purse tight and suffered from an unnecessary and dangerous desire to reduce the size of ships and the quality of their armament. In 1939, it was expected to face opponents who had treated their treaty obligations with contempt and whose expansion plans had never been limited by money – even if, as in the case of Germany, their economies were failing – but only by shipbuilding capacity and the availability of raw materials.

The stresses of the interwar depression had reached right down from the top of the Royal Navy to the bottom. Ill-thought-out across-the-board pay cuts during the financial crisis of 1931 had resulted in a mutiny among ratings aboard the ships of the Atlantic Fleet at Invergordon on the east coast of Scotland. Senior officers were desperate to get a sea-going command as there were so few. An officer without a ship or a posting ashore awaiting him all too frequently saw their careers interrupted by a spell on half-pay, and this unpleasant aspect of service life and family finances was a danger for officers as senior as rear admiral.

It was not until the realities of the deteriorating international situation began to dawn on the British government that half-pay was abolished in 1938, the same year that officers over the age of 30 received a marriage allowance for the first time. As a further sign that a time of great national danger was coming, the Women's Royal Naval Service (WRNS or 'Wrens') was also reintroduced after having been abandoned after the end of the First World War. Other actions were taken as well, with volunteers sought from those already serving in the Royal Navy to allow expansion of the Fleet Air Arm and of the Submarine Service, with both always kept separate from the rest of the RN or the 'General Service'.

War Looms

Few, if any, in the Royal Navy were surprised as war approached. Many in the service had expected war as early as October 1935, after Italy had invaded Abyssinia. The League of Nations was expected to sanction war against Italy but this did not happen, partly because the United States was not a member and at the time was also more interested in isolationism than interventionism, but even more importantly because France did not want to face up to a war in the Mediterranean and on one of her borders.

Tensions had also been increased by the crisis over Czechoslovakia and then Italy's seizure of Albania. Having been granted leave to take the Czech Sudetenland in 1938, Germany finished the job by taking the rest of Czechoslovakia in 1939, by which time it had also absorbed Austria.

Chapter 3

The Belligerent Navies

In 1939 the Royal Navy was one of the world's largest navies but, as noted in the previous chapter, it was thinly spread. The French navy, the *Marine Nationale*, was also thinly spread, but partly because it was a smaller navy than the Royal Navy and usually had squadrons where the Royal Navy had fleets. Nevertheless, France had been engaged in an arms race with Italy between the two world wars and it is surprising that this did not result in a larger fleet. In 1939, for example, the French had just one elderly aircraft carrier.

Germany and Italy had also been preparing for war but the German navy, the *Kriegsmarine*, was at the back of the queue when it came to allocating funding for modernization and expansion or, to be more accurate, creation of a true 'blue-water' navy from the post-Versailles coastal defence force. Germany's continental instincts had prevailed and priority had been given to the army and the air force. Italy also showed a marked disregard for sea power, although she started from a stronger base than Germany having been among the victors in the First World War.

The country that showed the highest regard for sea power was Japan, and the Imperial Japanese Navy had grown considerably. In the immediate post-war period, the Japanese had been helped by a British naval mission who not only introduced the Imperial Japanese Navy to the value and possibilities of naval air power, but had also boosted the country's aircraft design and production capabilities with licences to build British combat aircraft in Japan.

Of these navies, the one with most combat experience in the run-up to the Second World War was Japan, which had used its naval power to further its aggression in China, with aircraft carriers sometimes simply acting as aircraft transports but on other occasions providing highly mobile bases for operational sorties over China. Of course, the Chinese were technically and numerically inferior to the Japanese air and sea power that they faced; nevertheless this was useful training for the Japanese. Yet Japanese aircraft carrier design was poor, dated and wasted that most precious commodity aboard a ship: space.

As this book is primarily concerned with the war in Europe and on the North Atlantic and Mediterranean, the United States Navy does not feature as prominently as it did in the Far East, where it was the service that enabled the United States to take the war to Japan and also reverse the Japanese advance across the Pacific. The United States Army worked wonders in landings on islands in the Far East, as did the United States Marine Corps, but it was the USN that got the troops and marines onto the beaches and it was not until comparatively late in the campaign that the United States Army Air Force (USAAF) gained bases within reach of Japanese targets.

The popular perception of the war in the Pacific was that it was a war between opposing naval air power, but the USN's submariners played their part in breaking communications between Japan and its newly-acquired empire on which it relied for fuel, raw materials such as rubber, and food. By the time the atomic bombs were dropped on Hiroshima and Nagasaki on 6 and 9 August 1945 respectively, the Japanese people were starving; there was only enough fuel left for one final mass suicide attack when the expected Allied invasion came; and the American submariners had so gained the upper hand that they could penetrate the Japanese inland sea and sink ships as large as an aircraft carrier at will. Even the Americans could not believe the reports they received from their submarine commanders until the war ended and the evidence was plain to see.

The biggest casualty of the war was the battleship, the type of naval vessel on which so much hope was placed before the First World War. It was clear on the night of 11 November 1940 that air power mattered when three of the Italian navy's six battleships were put out of action at Taranto. The Battle of the Coral Sea in 1942 was the first in which the opposing fleets did not see each other. Shortly afterwards, the Battle of Midway saw the United States Navy in the ascendant and Japanese hopes of victory in ruins.

Yet, as we will see, the irony of the situation was that many senior Japanese naval officers knew that their country could not win a war against the United States, just as Raeder knew that the *Kriegsmarine* was doomed on the day that war was declared.

The Royal Navy

As mentioned in the previous chapter, in 1940 the Royal Navy was planning to have just 21 capital ships, meaning battleships and battle-cruisers, as against 68 in 1914; 69 cruisers as against 103; and 190 torpedo craft as against 319. The one big difference was that it would also have eight aircraft carriers as against none in 1914. Yet four of these ships were elderly and had been conceived at a time when the aircraft carrier and its design were in their infancy and were in fact due to be scrapped when new, fast, armoured carriers joined the fleet. This plan was abandoned when it was realized that every aircraft carrier would be needed, and the plan for four large new carriers was itself extended so that six were on order, plus a maintenance carrier. The aircraft carriers were far more valuable than any battleship or battle-cruiser, but only if they had high-performance aircraft on board.

The primary purpose of the Royal Navy in 1939 was the historic role of protecting trade. The densely-populated United Kingdom only produced half the food needed by its population. It had ample supplies of coal, but only a token amount of home-produced oil. Most of the country's iron ore had too high a sulphur content to produce good quality steel. A secondary role was to protect the UK itself, the Empire and the dominions – Australia, Canada, New Zealand and South Africa – which differed from the colonies in that they were self-governing. The dominion navies played a part in assisting the Royal Navy, and the Royal Canadian Navy and Royal Australian Navy in particular grew both in size and capability during the war years.

The Royal Navy was also expected when necessary to play its part in expeditionary warfare, and had most recently played this role during the Gallipoli campaign of the First World War.

Nevertheless, one of the most blatant signs of overstretch and of political naiveté was that between the wars the government in London assured Australia and New Zealand that in the event of war with Japan, a strong fleet would be sent east to protect them. This pledge ignored the growing possibility of a war in Europe.

In 1939, ignoring those ships planned to enter service by 1940, the Royal Navy had twelve battleships and three battle-cruisers. The battle-cruisers were in the Home Fleet, which also had five battleships; another three battleships were with the Mediterranean Fleet, which was pulled back from Malta to Alexandria in Egypt; a further two battleships were based at Portland in the Channel Force; and two were under repair or refit at Portsmouth.

Aircraft carriers totalled seven, with one used for training, and the pride of the carrier fleet was the new HMS *Ark Royal*. This fine ship with its two hangar decks and three deck lifts had nevertheless been built down to the government's specification that no aircraft carrier should displace more than 23,000 tons. To accommodate the two hangar decks without making her top-heavy, armour-plating was kept to the minimum and the flight deck was very thin; so much so that on one occasion when 20lb practice bombs dropped off an aircraft as it was arrested on landing, they went straight through the flight deck and into the upper hangar, killing several aircraft maintainers.

There were fourteen heavy cruisers, i.e. ships with 8in guns. These were spread between the Home Fleet, which had just one; two were under refit at Portsmouth and another at Chatham; three each were with the Mediterranean Fleet and the China Station; two more each were in the South Atlantic Fleet at Freetown in Sierra Leone and the West Indies Station at Bermuda. Another two heavy cruisers were in the Royal Australian Navy. There were forty-one light cruisers. No fewer than sixteen of these, albeit with two in refit, were at Scapa Flow with ten allocated to the Northern Patrol keeping an eye open for enemy warships breaking out of the Baltic and into the open sea, while another six were with the Home Fleet, for which Scapa was a forward base. Three more were in refit at Portsmouth, as well as one at Chatham, while another two were based on the Humber and three were at Portland. The Mediterranean Fleet had three light cruisers and the China Station had one, but there were six on the South Atlantic Station, two at Gibraltar and three in the East Indies at Trincomalee in Ceylon, while the solitary British light cruiser on the West Indies Station at Bermuda was joined by one from the Royal Australian Navy. The Royal Australian Navy had two more light cruisers, while the Royal New Zealand Navy had a total of two.

Destroyers had grown in size considerably since the First World War and by 1939 were useful ships capable of anti-submarine operations, providing coastal bombardment or torpedoing enemy warships, ideally providing the *coup de grâce* after a battleship or battle-cruiser had crippled an enemy warship. Generally deployed in flotillas that varied between 6 and 10 ships, the Home Fleet at Scapa Flow had 17 destroyers, another 5 were at Portland, 8 were on the Humber, 5 were in reserve at Portsmouth, 6 were at Devonport, 13 at Chatham and 11 at Rosyth in Scotland. Overseas, there were no fewer than 33 with the Mediterranean Fleet, 15 in Hong Kong on the China Station, 4 at Freetown and 9 in Gibraltar. The Royal Canadian Navy was based around six destroyers but was to have many more ships by the end of the war, while the Royal Australian Navy had five.

Corvettes had yet to be invented as a ship better suited for convoy escort duties than the destroyer and frigates had still to be reinvented as anti-submarine or anti-aircraft ships. However, the Royal Navy had a number of sloops, many of which were also capable of mine-sweeping: 5 were with the reserve fleet at Portsmouth, 6 were active at Devonport, another 6 were at Hong Kong, 4 at Freetown, 2 at Bermuda, and there were 12 in Ceylon based at Trincomalee – 'Trinco' in naval slang – of which five were part of the Royal Indian Navy. The Royal Australian Navy and the Royal New Zealand Navy had two sloops apiece.

The French Navy – *Marine Nationale*

France was second only to the United Kingdom as a colonial power, with possession stretching from the Caribbean to the Far East where French Indo-China was jealously watched by the Japanese. In between, France was also strong in much of Africa and especially in the north, as well as in the Middle East. Its possessions in North America and India had been lost.

Less dependent than the British on imported food and with land borders with a number of countries that could provide raw materials such as iron ore, the French nevertheless had many similar expectations of their navy, the *Marine Nationale*, as the British had of the Royal Navy. Greater emphasis was based on defence of the coastline, but the sea lines of communication with the empire were as important, although there was less of a contribution from the French colonies than from the British dominions. The French did not expect their navy to play a part in expeditionary warfare.

As war loomed, the French revised their operational strategy, devising different approaches to the North Atlantic and the Mediterranean. For the North Atlantic, the Atlantic Squadron started to be upgraded to fleet status, with at its core the two new fast battle-cruisers *Dunkerque* and *Strasbourg*, three modern light cruisers and eight of the most up-to-date *contre-torpilleur* super-destroyers that would scout for the new battleships. Although the battleships and French light cruisers would have three Loire 130 reconnaissance floatplanes, this force was not built around an aircraft carrier. Different strategies were required for the Mediterranean, where the war at sea was seen as being short engagements, often conducted at high speed, with raids on enemy shipping and coastal towns, as well as defending ports in France and French North Africa from similar efforts by the enemy. This would be a cruiser battleground.

The structure of the French navy differed from that of the Royal Navy. In 1939 France and French North Africa were organized in five commands or maritime regions, *régions maritimes*, each under a senior admiral who was known as the *préfet maritime* and who reported directly to the navy minister. These were the 1st Maritime Region based on Dunkirk; 2nd Maritime Region based on Brest; 3rd Maritime Region based on Toulon; 4th Maritime Region based on Bizerte in North Africa; and the 5th Maritime Region based on Lorient. On the outbreak of war this structure was changed, merging the 2nd and 5th regions under Admiral West, and the 3rd and 4th under Admiral South. New commands were created to cover the South Atlantic and West Indies. The new structure meant that the commands became North, based on Dunkirk and covering the North Sea and English Channel; West, based on Brest and covering the North Atlantic; South, based on Toulon but later moved to Bizerte and concentrating on the Mediterranean; South Atlantic, based on Casablanca; and Western Atlantic, based on the French Antilles.

Although French naval aviation was no further forward than the British in the sense that they also lacked high-performance aircraft to fly off the single aircraft carrier, the *Béarn*, they had at least had continuous control of naval aviation, even including land-based maritime-reconnaissance squadrons.

During the arms race between France and Italy between the two world wars, the French developed a new type of warship, a super-destroyer known as the *contre-torpilleur*, usually with 5.5in guns and long-range torpedoes, to counter the growing Italian cruiser fleet.

On the outbreak of war the *Marine Nationale* had 3 battleships and 2 battle-cruisers, with another 3 battleships under construction. The service had just one aircraft carrier and another under construction, while a third had been authorized; there were 7 heavy cruisers and 12 light cruisers, with another building and a further 2 authorized; and there were no fewer than 32 *contre-torpilleurs* and another 4 authorized. There were also 26 fleet torpedo boats with another 6 building and 6 more authorized, as well as 12 light torpedo boats, another 4 being built and a further 10 approved. Abroad, there were seven colonial sloops, plus two building and another one authorized.

An unusual submarine was a cruiser variant with a heavy-calibre gun and also an aircraft that could be launched and recovered while on the surface. Cruiser submarines had also been tried by the British. The concept was that gunnery was a cheaper means of sinking enemy merchantmen than torpedoes and, of course, only a limited number of torpedoes could be carried by a submarine.

A substantial submarine force included 39 submarines with 3 under construction and plans approved for a further 2, while there were also 40 coastal submarines with a further 8 under construction and 12 more authorized. Coastal submarines were well-suited to the Mediterranean where larger submarines were easily detected, as well as to the confined waters of the English Channel. The disposition of these ships was mainly between the Atlantic and Mediterranean Fleets, with the remainder mainly in the overseas commands at Beirut, Saigon and Casablanca.

The Atlantic Fleet had four main bases at Brest, Cherbourg, Lorient and Dakar, the latter being in West Africa. Brest had the one aircraft carrier, 3 *contre-torpilleurs* and 12 standard destroyers as well as 12 submarines, while it was also home to the 1st Squadron with 2 battleships, a further 2 elderly battleships that were used for training, 3 light cruisers and 6 *contre-torpilleur* destroyers. Cherbourg had 3 torpedo boats and 4 coastal submarines, while another 3 torpedo boats were at Lorient. Dakar had four light cruisers, of which one was deployed to Casablanca and another to the French Antilles.

The Mediterranean Fleet had three bases at Toulon, Bizerte and Oran. Toulon had 3 *contre-torpilleurs*, 6 torpedo boats, 11 patrol submarines, 8 coastal submarines and another 8 submarines used for training, as well as being home to the 3rd Squadron with 6 heavy cruisers and 12 *contre-torpilleurs*. Bizerte had 6 patrol submarines and 8 coastal submarines, and was home to the 4th Squadron with 4 light cruisers and 6 *contre-torpilleurs*. Oran was the base for the 2nd Squadron, with 3 elderly battleships and 9 destroyers.

Overseas commands showed the MN to be stretched to the limit. Beirut had 3 patrol submarines; Saigon had a heavy cruiser and a light cruiser; Casablanca had 2 destroyers and 4 patrol submarines. These ships would have been augmented by some of the colonial sloops.

The United States Navy
As with the Royal Navy, in 1939 the United States Navy was subject to the limitations imposed by the Washington Naval Treaty of 1922. There were additional problems. American opinion, both political and public, was inclined towards isolationism between the two world wars, which was one of the two main reasons for the United States not becoming a member of the League of Nations. The other reason was

the so-called 'Monroe Doctrine' which had no constitutional or legal basis but which nevertheless was followed closely by many American leaders: the doctrine was that the United States should keep to its own sphere of influence, the Americas, and not interfere elsewhere, while other states should not interfere in the Americas. This was all very well but it ignored the presence of Canada, a dominion within the British Empire, and that the United Kingdom, France and The Netherlands all had colonies in the Caribbean and Latin America.

In 1939 the United States Navy's manpower was not that much greater than that of the Royal Navy, despite both navies having the same Washington Treaty limits. The difference was probably due to the shore-based maritime-reconnaissance that remained a part of the USN's duties, albeit in competition with the USAAF which also had squadrons exercising the same role. In 1939 the authorized strength was 145,000, but by the time of Pearl Harbor in late 1941 this had doubled.

The United States Navy was also thinly spread, for the Monroe Doctrine notwithstanding, American power and influence had spread across the Pacific, including having islands such as Guam and island groups such as Hawaii as non-incorporated states of the union – although Hawaii has since joined – while the Philippines were run almost as a colony. The US relationship with the Philippines was in some ways similar to that between the UK and Egypt.

There were differences between the Royal Navy and the United States Navy. Military aviation in the United States was still divided between the USN and the United States Army, while there was also a strong United States Marine Corps aviation element and the United States Coast Guard had its own aviation but the USCG passed from the Department of Transportation to USN control in wartime. The USN's aviation included shore-based as well as ship-based aircraft, and there was duplication with both the USN and USAAF operating long-range maritime-reconnaissance aircraft. Alone among the belligerent navies, the USN had senior officers with sound aviation experience, and Congress had gone as far as requiring all commanding officers of aircraft carriers to be naval airmen.

The USN maintained three fleets in December 1941 when the country was drawn into the Second World War by the Japanese attack on Pearl Harbor and by Germany's declaration of war on the USA. In peacetime the largest and most important of these was the Pacific Fleet, based on San Diego and Pearl Harbor, but this had been overtaken by the Atlantic Fleet as ships were transferred when the USN became more involved in the Battle of the Atlantic, escorting convoys to a mid-ocean handover point. The Atlantic Fleet's main base was at Norfolk, Virginia. There was also a much smaller Asiatic Fleet, based on Cavite in the Philippines.

In late 1941 the Atlantic Fleet had 8 battleships with one in refit; 4 aircraft carriers and an escort carrier; 5 heavy and 8 light cruisers with another in refit; 99 destroyers; and 58 submarines. The Pacific Fleet was divided into a Scouting Force and a Battle Force. The Scouting Force had 12 heavy cruisers with 2 in refit; a single destroyer; and 24 submarines with 4 in refit. The Battle Force had 9 battleships with 2 in refit; 3 aircraft carriers; 9 light cruisers with 3 in refit; 49 destroyers with 8 in refit; 8 light and 13 fast minelayers. The Asiatic Fleet had a single heavy cruiser and 2 light cruisers on loan from the Pacific Fleet; 13 destroyers with 2 in refit; and 29 submarines.

In addition there were fifteen naval districts. These were Boston with 5 fast minelayers and 2 gunboats; New York; Philadelphia; Norfolk with an additional 2 gunboats over and above the Atlantic Fleet; Charleston; Jacksonville; New Orleans; Chicago; San Juan in Puerto Rico; San Diego with an additional 4 destroyers over and above those of the Pacific Fleet; San Francisco; Seattle with 5 destroyers; Honolulu, which had its own 2 gunboats; Balboa in the Panama Canal Zone with 10 destroyers and a gunboat; and Cavite, which had two gunboats in addition to the Asiatic Fleet.

While the USN recognized the importance of convoys and their necessity, the main approach to warfare was to seek fleet action. Subordinate commanders were expected to refine their own strategy and tactics appropriate to their own area and the approach likely to be taken by a prospective enemy. This was emphasized in an order given by Admiral (later Fleet Admiral) Ernest King in 1941 when in command of the Atlantic Fleet:

I have been concerned for many years over the increasing tendency... of flag officers and other group commanders to issue orders and instructions in which their subordinates are told 'how' as well as 'what' to do...If subordinates are deprived...of that training and experience which will enable them to act 'on their own' – if they do not know, by constant practice, how to exercise 'initiative of the subordinates' – if they are reluctant (afraid) to act because they are accustomed to detailed orders and instruction – if they are not habituated to think, to judge, to decide and to act for themselves in their several echelons of command – we shall be in a sorry case when the time of 'active operations' [war] arrives.

A comparison could be drawn with the state of the Royal Navy many years earlier in the early 1900s, when much of the freedom of action and initiative allowed commanding officers in Nelson's day had been lost.

The German Navy – *Kriegsmarine*
In contrast to the situation in 1914 when the Imperial German Navy or *Kaiserliche Marine* was the world's second-largest, the *Kriegsmarine* or 'War Navy' was weaker than many of the navies it was to confront. In fact, this was the one thing it had in common with the Royal Navy, which was also weaker in 1939 than in 1914. As already mentioned, it suffered from being behind the Luftwaffe and the army in modernization and development. Plans had been drawn up for expansion, resulting in the aforementioned Plan Z, which was further developed to allow for a much larger U-boat force. Hitler authorized the amended version of Plan Z early in 1939, but there was no time to implement it before war broke out. It was not just the lack of time, or Hitler's assurances that war with the UK would not break out until 1943 or 1944; many doubt whether Germany could have provided the industrial raw material and manpower resources to create such a large fleet, and certainly would not have had the fuel to keep it at sea.

The *Kriegsmarine* was no 'brown-water' navy, but it was far from completing its plans for expansion and development. It did not have any aircraft carriers, and the issue of naval aviation was a bone of contention with the Luftwaffe, which successfully persuaded Hitler that all German service aviation should be under its control. The small number of naval pilots flying reconnaissance floatplanes from warships was transferred to the Luftwaffe before the outbreak of war.

The issue of U-boats had also been controversial while Plan Z was being prepared. The head of the *Kriegsmarine*, Raeder, believed that there was little future for the U-boat because of improvements in the Royal Navy's anti-submarine technology, especially ASDIC. Dönitz, his U-boat commander or Führer, disagreed and won the argument. Even so, contrary to popular belief, Germany entered the Second World War with few ocean-going submarines.

It was clear to senior officers on the outbreak of war that a major fleet action such as that at Jutland was out of the question. It was not that the *Kriegsmarine* had turned its back on naval engagements, but that everyone realized such an action would not be possible until around 1945 and only then if Plan Z was implemented in full.

The premature outbreak of war, caused by Hitler wrongly calculating that the United Kingdom and France were not serious about Poland, meant that the German naval strategy reverted to one thing: commerce raiding. As in the First World War, not only warships and submarines but also auxiliary cruisers, i.e. merchantmen taken up from trade and armed, were pressed into service.

Germany suffered from having only a very short coastline on the North Sea, and even this was far from being the open seas. Before the First World War, the Kiel Canal had been constructed and then improved, allowing access between the Baltic and the North Sea at all states of the tide. Once in the North Sea, German warships had a choice of trying to break through the Straits of Dover, which worked very well on one occasion during the 'Channel Dash' episode as Hitler ordered three major warships back to Germany but was clearly fraught with hazard, or going round the north of Scotland. The latter route was also difficult with British air and sea forces based at Orkney and Shetland as well as at bases on the Scottish mainland. This problem was solved when the German army swept through the Low Countries and into France, reaching the Channel coast and taking major naval bases, of which the most significant was Brest. The Germans had already taken Norway by this time, but while having many sheltered fjords, the country lacked naval bases with the dry docks and support facilities that the Germans found in France.

In the late nineteenth century the British government had, without consulting Parliament or Queen Victoria, exchanged the island of Heligoland, off the North Sea coast of Germany, for Zanzibar. Her Majesty was not amused at this, and indeed was indignant that some of her subjects were transferred to a foreign power without her permission. During the Second World War, the *Kriegsmarine* built heavily-fortified concrete submarine pens on the island. This meant that the submarines did not have to use the Kiel Canal but, of course, they still had to pass around the north of Scotland or risk the Straits of Dover to reach the open sea.

Faced with the limitations of the Treaty of Versailles, the Germans had shown considerable ingenuity in developing a new type of warship, the *Panzerschiff* or 'armoured warship', known to the British and American media as a pocket battleship. These were replacements for the elderly coastal battleships permitted by Versailles but were more heavily armed and armoured, and with their diesel engines had a long range without refuelling.

On the outbreak of war, the *Kriegsmarine* had two aircraft carriers on order, but only one of these was actually under construction. Two battle-cruisers were in service, while two battleships were nearing completion. The three *Panzerschiffe* were already in service and were later to be reclassified as armoured cruisers. One heavy cruiser was in service and two more were completing, while there were also six light cruisers. A weakness was the shortage of destroyers with just twenty-one on the outbreak of war, although another nineteen were completed later; essential after the heavy losses of German destroyers in the two naval battles of Narvik. There were eleven torpedo boats and another thirty-six were completed during the war. Just ten escort vessels were available. There were only fifty-seven submarines on the outbreak of war, most being coastal types, but 1,110 were to be built during the conflict. There were also large numbers of motor-torpedo boats and gunboats, or in German *Schnellboote* collectively but known to the Allies as E-boats.

As in the First World War, the main heavy fighting force of the *Kriegsmarine* was known as the High Seas Fleet. This had bases at Wilhelmshaven, Kiel, Swinemünde and Cuxhaven. On 3 September 1939, Wilhelmshaven was home to the two battle-cruisers and the three *Panzerschiffe* or pocket battleships. A scouting force for the High Seas Fleet was based on Kiel with a heavy cruiser and six light cruisers, while Kiel was also the main base for the U-boats with thirty-nine submarines based there and another eighteen at Wilhelmshaven. An escort flotilla was also based at Kiel. Cuxhaven had a fleet escort and two flotillas with a total of fourteen minesweepers.

The Italian Navy – *Regia Marina*
Although Italy had a long seafaring tradition, that was really before the country was united and was part of the history of Genoa and Venice. Even the Ancient Romans had been slow to take to the sea, initially employing mercenary seamen. During the First World War Italy had been one of the allies, but had seen little action at sea other than helping the Royal Navy to keep the Austro-Hungarian fleet bottled up in the Adriatic.

Between the two world wars, Italy and France engaged in an arms race and Italian naval planners worked on the assumption that France would be the enemy in any future conflict. The priorities were to ensure that the *Regia Marina* retained control of the Tyrrhenian and Ionian Seas while keeping open the sea lanes between Italy and Libya and between Italy and the Dodecanese. Traffic had to be maintained with the Black Sea and the Red Sea, especially after Italy intervened in Abyssinia. The *Regia Marina* would also be expected to do its best to interfere with French shipping and raid Corsica.

Old battleships were modernized and new ones built; a fleet of light cruisers was also created. An aircraft carrier was planned, converting a passenger liner, but as in Germany inter-service politics took a hand and work was delayed by infighting with the air force, *Regia Aeronautica*, which demanded and got control of all Italian air power. Both these services trailed behind the army when it came to defence spending.

Of 6 battleships available when Italy entered the Second World War in June 1940, 3 were elderly examples dating from before 1922 and modernized, leaving the Italians with just 3 new battleships. There were 7 heavy cruisers and 14 light cruisers, of which two were pre-1922, and another 3 under construction. Of the 59 destroyers, 2 were elderly, and these were joined by 5 new ships and another 7 captured vessels; the result of Italy's drive into the Balkans. There were 67 torpedo boats and another 16 under construction, as well as a sloop and another one being built. A single corvette was the first of 30 being built on the outbreak of war, while there were 115 submarines and 38 under construction, as well as 3 captured boats. In contrast to the other navies, the torpedo boats were often used as convoy escorts.

There were three fleet commands, one of which was for submarines, and the other two were based at Taranto, home to both the 1st and 2nd Fleet. Other bases were at La Spezia, with 10 torpedo boats; Venice, with just 4 torpedo boats; and Naples, with 35 torpedo boats. Taranto had 2 light cruisers, 6 destroyers and 4 torpedo boats. In Libya, a coast defence cruiser, 4 destroyers, 4 torpedo boats and 10 submarines were divided between Tripoli and Tobruk. Leros in the Aegean had 2 destroyers, 4 torpedo boats and 8 submarines. In Albania a naval base was established at Durazzo, but no ships were permanently assigned to it.

Further afield, a sloop was based at Shanghai, while at Massawa in East Africa a sloop, seven destroyers and two torpedo boats were based with sight submarines. An area command responsible for convoy escorts, MARICOTRAF, had eight torpedo boats.

One feature of the *Regia Marina* was the use of human torpedoes for attacks on enemy shipping while at anchor or in harbour. This was at great risk to the crews, who were always frogmen. The concept so caught the imagination of the Royal Navy that they adopted the idea, having captured Italian human torpedoes and their crews.

The Imperial Japanese Navy – *Teikoku Kaigun*

Another former First World War ally, Japan had the world's third-largest navy at the end of the war and fully expected parity with the Royal Navy and United States Navy from the Washington Naval Treaty of 1922. Nevertheless, the country had already been involved in aggression, occupying Korea, and between the two world wars was actively attempting to seize Manchuria, a large area of China. While the Imperial Japanese Navy had seen little action during the First World War, it had sent destroyers to the Mediterranean to support the Royal Navy.

At Tsushima in 1905, the Imperial Japanese Navy had inflicted a decisive defeat on a large Russian fleet sent to the Far East and so was victorious in the Russo-Japanese War of 1904-05.

Post-war, a British Naval Mission helped the Japanese plan their future navy and also introduced the country to military air power, with many current British designs manufactured in Japan under licence. However, from the early 1920s onwards relations with the British Empire began to deteriorate. The United States was seen as the potential enemy and many Japanese naval officers, who had to select a compulsory foreign language to learn during their training, elected to learn English. Nevertheless, many of those who visited the United States between the wars realized that Japan could not match the manpower, the natural resources or the industrial capability of the United States.

One further problem was that Japan had just two armed services with the navy and the army each having its own air force, but there was serious rivalry between the two and the army was the mainstay of the pro-war faction.

Admiral Sato Tetsutaro, the Imperial Japanese Navy's foremost strategist, formulated the concept of the 'hypothetical enemy', which considered not the likelihood of another nation threatening Japan's security but its ability to do so. Even this created a problem as the Imperial Japanese Navy viewed the United States as the hypothetical enemy, while the Imperial Japanese Army saw the Soviet Union in that role. Tetsutaro's idea was that maintaining a naval strength of approximately 70 per cent of that of the United States would be sufficient to defend Japan against attack. This led to what became known as the 'Six-Six Fleet', meaning the construction of six battleships and six battle-cruisers every six years, but this was replaced by the 'Eight-Eight Fleet' as Tetsutaro convinced his colleagues that a 70 per cent ratio to the United States Navy would be impossible to achieve without it. Even so, until 1910 major Japanese warships had to be built abroad and it was not until 1920 that the Diet, or parliament, finally approved the Eight-Eight Fleet.

Despite so much thought being given to the strategic position and having had observers at the British Admiralty during the First World War, the Imperial Japanese Navy was preoccupied by the prospects of a major naval battle along the lines of Jutland. The true lesson of Jutland, that it was indecisive and that concentrating so much on a major battle was a waste of resources, was ignored. The big lesson of the First World War at sea, that the most cost-effective means of conducting modern warfare was the submarine, was also ignored. Between the wars, the possibility of creating a large submarine arm was largely ignored and, worse, the need to prepare for anti-submarine warfare was also ignored. Frustrated from building more battleships and battle-cruisers by the conditions of the Washington Naval Treaty, the Imperial Japanese Navy concentrated on developing the heavy cruiser and by 1941 possessed some of the best examples of this type of warship.

As with the Royal and United States Navies, the Washington Naval Treaty also furthered the creation of a Japanese aircraft carrier fleet. Unwittingly, as the Japanese Naval Air Force grew, it was preparing the way for a war at sea in which the rival fleets did not come into contact.

In 1936, Japan rejected the Washington Naval Treaty and resumed naval expansion. Even so, the mission was defensive rather than aggressive, although it did propose that Japan should seize the Philippines and Guam. This changed in 1940 when Admiral Yamamoto Isoroku took command of the Combined Fleet. He foresaw that Japan would have difficulty in resisting the full might of the United States Navy and his strategy rested on the elimination of the US Pacific Fleet by a pre-emptive strike on its main base at Pearl Harbor in Hawaii. Yamamoto had spent time in the United States between the wars and spoke good English.

The Imperial Japanese Navy was unusual in that it included a number of seaplane carriers rather than the odd one that appeared in other navies. It was also to the forefront in the number of aircraft carriers, although some were small. On the other hand, its naval aircraft had a far better performance than any in the Royal Navy.

On 7 December 1941 when Japan entered the Second World War, the IJN had 11 battleships and battle-cruisers; 3 seaplane carriers; 6 aircraft carriers and 2 light aircraft carriers; 18 heavy cruisers and 14 light cruisers; 106 destroyers and 12 other escort vessels; 4 torpedo boats and 58 submarines.

Most of these ships were in the Combined Fleet, the main fighting force. The headquarters was at Hiroshima where 3 battleships were based with 3 seaplane carriers, 2 light cruisers and 12 escorts as well as 14 submarines, but this was also the base for the 1st Air Fleet with its 6 aircraft carriers and 2 light carriers plus 12 destroyers. Kure had the 1st Fleet with 8 battleships, 4 heavy and 4 light cruisers as well as 28 destroyers. At Samah the 2nd Fleet's 13 heavy cruisers were based together with 2 light cruisers and 35 destroyers. The 3rd Fleet was based at Takao, with its single heavy cruiser and 3 light cruisers, 8 destroyers, 4 torpedo boats and 4 submarines. At Truk the 4th Fleet had 2 light cruisers, 4 destroyers and 9 submarines. Ominato was home to the 5th Fleet with 2 light cruisers. Kwajalein had the 6th Fleet with a light cruiser and 30 submarines. The 11th Air Fleet was also at Takao with 3 destroyers, while Camranh Bay, in what was then known as French Indo-China, had the Southern Expeditionary Fleet and a light cruiser. A number of warships were also based on Shanghai, known as the China Area Fleet, as well as at the naval districts and strategic ports, of which there were a total of 8, and the 3 guard districts.

Chapter 4

The Royal Navy goes to War

On the eve of war the Royal Navy mobilized its reserves, with the Royal Naval Reserve and the Royal Naval Volunteer Reserve providing a much-needed extra 73,000 officers and men on top of the 129,000 officers and men of the Royal Navy and Royal Marines, while the members of the Royal Fleet Reserve, recently retired officers and ratings, were recalled.

The service had an old saying that Royal Navy officers were 'gentlemen trying to become sailors', RNR officers were 'sailors trying to become gentlemen' and the RNVR were 'neither trying to become both'! No doubt RNR officers from the smarter shipping lines such as P&O would have rejected any suggestion that they were not gentlemen!

Some accounts of the Second World War make much of the contribution made by the countries of the British Empire and the Dominions in particular, but at the outset the contribution was insignificant. None of the Dominion navies had aircraft carriers or battleships, although the Royal Australian Navy had three light cruisers and the Royal New Zealand Navy had two. The Admiralty had a recruiting office in New Zealand, which encouraged many New Zealanders to volunteer for the Royal Navy and in particular the Fleet Air Arm. By the end of the war, these navies had grown in size and capability with the Royal Canadian Navy even manning two auxiliary or escort carriers, although the air-crew were provided by the Royal Navy. Post-war both the Royal Canadian Navy and the Royal Australian Navy created fleet air arms and added aircraft carriers to their fleets, as did the Indian Naval Service after independence.

The Second World War was to change the Royal Navy more than the First World War had done. After the First World War the Royal Marines had seen the Royal Marine Light Infantry, known as the 'red marines' because of the colour of their tunics, merged with the Royal Marine Artillery, or 'blue marines', to simply become the Royal Marines (with blue tunics). On board ship, they would man 'X' and 'Y' turrets, but they also had other duties including security, messmen and bandsmen, while from even before the First World War a small number of RM officers were aircraft pilots.

In 1923 the Admiralty was recommended by the Madden Committee to give the Royal Marines an amphibious role as well as providing a mobile force that could be used to defend overseas bases. These were far-sighted recommendations but they were ignored while peace lasted, possibly due to financial considerations. Nevertheless, the demands of war saw the Royal Marines develop, also the creation of the Royal Marine Commandos, and the seeds were sown for the Special Boat Service (SBS). Some of the traditional roles were doomed as warfare changed: battleships and cruisers began taking second place to the aircraft carrier, so in the event there was little need for 'X' and 'Y' turrets, especially when destroyers and frigates started to have helicopter landing platforms in the 1960s.

The reservists soon proved their worth with many RNVR personnel rising to command minesweepers, corvettes and destroyers, while others took command of naval air squadrons. By mid-1944, the Royal Navy had reached its wartime peak strength of 863,500 personnel, of whom 73,500 were members of the Women's Royal Naval Service. Many of the lower deck personnel, or ratings, were conscripts called up under the National Service Acts for 'hostilities only'. When merchant shipping was taken up from trade, the ships' companies were signed up under special articles so that they became part of the Royal Navy and subject to naval discipline with temporary naval ranks, although they retained certain Merchant Navy terms of service such as danger money for working in a war zone.

One of the big differences between the Royal Navy and the Merchant Navy was that the latter paid its ratings better but once their ship was lost, pay stopped until they could sign on for another ship, which often meant another company. Royal Navy personnel continued to be paid, even while prisoners of war.

During the Second World War, the Royal Navy lost 50,758 men killed, with another 820 posted as missing, presumed dead, and 14,663 wounded. The WRNS lost 102 killed and 22 wounded, mainly in air-raids. The Merchant Navy lost 30,248 men through enemy action.

Many bases had been neglected during the peace years. Singapore was meant to be a strong naval base and fortress, but construction was neglected and completion delayed. It was in reality only a strong base if a strong fleet was deployed, but when this was needed the RN was heavily committed elsewhere. Rosyth was not used between the wars. Many naval officers disliked Rosyth because of its distance from the sea and because the Forth Bridge was in the way and not only a navigational hazard but a potential obstruction if bombed.

There had been no development of combined operations during the years between the two world wars, despite the lessons of Gallipoli, Ostend and Zeebrugge. Some of this was understandable, as it was not until the middle years of the Second World War that purpose-designed landing craft became available; even the Germans planned to invade England using barges and had used caiques for the amphibious phase of the invasion of Crete.

It was not until Churchill came to power that the importance of combined operations was recognized. In July 1940, shortly after he became prime minister, he set up a special directorate to develop combined operations and to develop equipment as well as training personnel, something that was made much easier by Admiralty control of the Royal Marines. Some believe that the outcome of the Norwegian campaign might have been different had these measures been implemented earlier, but the lack of suitable high-performance aircraft aboard the carriers was another factor.

Combined operations were very much in mind before the war when Area Combined Headquarters (ACHQs) were established close to Plymouth, Chatham and Rosyth with officers of all three services involved, but the priority for these was improved co-operation between the Royal Navy and RAF Coastal Command. During the war, such ACHQs were introduced to many foreign stations. In 1941, under the pressures of the Blitz, Western Approaches ACHQ moved from Plymouth to Liverpool.

Despite the glaring omission of high-performance aircraft from its aircraft carriers – the fault of senior naval officers who, lacking aviation experience themselves, believed that such aircraft could not be operated from aircraft carriers – the Royal Navy had many technical advantages over its opponents. The Royal Navy was fitting its warships with radar, which the Italian navy did not have and so did not expect to have to fight a night engagement. Instead it had good quality ASDIC.

The advantages were not just technical. Despite having shrunk by some 12 per cent since 1912, at the time the United Kingdom still had the world's largest merchant fleet, accounting for approximately 33 per cent of the world's merchant shipping tonnage, and also had a substantial fishing fleet including both inshore vessels and deep sea trawlers. This meant that there was a substantial pool of experienced manpower and, when necessary, ships as well. Passenger liners became armed merchant cruisers, fitted in naval dockyards with guns salvaged from warships that had been scrapped in the past. Sadly these ships were a failure as they lacked the speed, armament or armour to withstand an engagement with a German warship. Nevertheless, trawlers were converted for minesweeping, as were some of the smaller ferries, while tugs became rescue tugs picking up survivors from ships sunk while in convoy. Other merchant ships became hospital ships or troopships, with the latter including the duo that were the pride of the British Merchant Navy, the two Cunard liners RMS (Royal Mail Ship) *Queen Mary* and her newer and larger sister, RMS *Queen Elizabeth*. These two ships had been considered for conversion to aircraft carriers before the war as the Admiralty was concerned about the shortage of flight decks and with their size and speed these two would have been very useful as carriers. However, the resources necessary for this would have been extensive, and in any case many thought that they would be more useful as troopships. The decision was the right one, and they were among the few ships able to cross the Atlantic safely without an escort.

Such wholesale requisitioning of the merchant fleet, not just to augment the Royal Navy but to meet the supply and transport needs of the other two armed services as well, was not without cost. The size of the merchant fleet shrunk dramatically, although it was boosted by ships that had fled from the territories occupied by the Germans or diverted to British ports on their homeward voyages rather than steam into occupation. As it happened, three of the countries occupied by the Germans – Norway, Denmark and The Netherlands – had substantial merchant fleets, although on average some 26 per cent of their ships were caught in port by the German invasions. Of course, a number of German ships were caught in ports under British control and these were captured and taken to augment the British fleet, with the ships owned by the British government but managed by merchant ship-owners. These vessels could easily be identified as they were given new names, all of which were prefixed with 'Empire'. Later, ships built to the government's account and again managed by merchant shipping lines were treated in the same way, as were the American Liberty ships provided under the Lend-Lease scheme.

There were still some deficiencies. In 1939 the RN lacked fast craft such as motor gunboats and motor torpedo boats and this was not addressed until after the start of war; even then really only under pressure from the German E-boats after the fall of France presented the enemy with Channel ports. There was also the shortage of flight decks, but with some ingenuity this was soon resolved. More submarines were needed and not just the larger boats of the 'S' and 'T' classes but the smaller craft of the 'U' and 'V' classes, so useful and effective in the Mediterranean where British submariners played their part in reducing supplies for Axis forces in North Africa.

There was much to learn still, but from the start a convoy system was introduced. Even so, losses were heavy at the beginning, and remained heavy on certain routes such as those across the Mediterranean and to Murmansk and Archangel where the weather was as much an enemy as the Germans. For a period, the Royal Navy also deployed small groups of warships on anti-submarine sweeps but after some serious losses, especially the aircraft carrier HMS *Courageous*, this was abandoned until later in the war when, equipped with Ultra intelligence, the locations of U-boats could be detected and successes scored.

The work of Ultra intelligence and the decoding operation at Bletchley Park was made possible when, in August 1941, the Royal Navy gained a decisive advantage when *U-570* was captured south of Iceland together with the books for the German Enigma code, which could then be intercepted by the British Ultra intelligence. The capture was kept secret but *U-570* was commissioned into British service as HMS *Graph*. The British were thus able to exploit the major weakness of the German U-boat campaign, which was that the U-boat commanders sent and received a significant volume of radio transmissions.

Many believed at the outset that the Second World War would follow the pattern of the first, with the Germans coming to a stop in France and Belgium. No one foresaw that France would be forced to surrender, even though not completely overrun; also no one foresaw the invasion of Denmark and Norway, or The Netherlands, all of which had remained neutral during the First World War. At the same time, unlike 1914, no one thought that the war would be over by Christmas, so the RN rapidly changed its training structure, creating new shore establishments and cutting training courses to the necessary minimum.

The pre-war Royal Navy consisted of volunteers. Officers began training as early as 13 years of age, with the Britannia Royal Naval College at Dartmouth acting as a public school*, and expecting to

---

*British readers will be familiar with this term, but it may confuse others as in the USA a 'public school' is a school funded by the taxpayer. In the UK it is a charitable institution, often charging fees and expecting a certain minimum academic standard from its

spend most of their working lives in the service. The ordinary seaman signed up for an initial twelve years, but only once he was at least 18 years old and had already completed shore training in what was known as 'boy service'. At one stage between the wars, in order to maintain recruitment a shorter service option of five years followed by five years in the reserves was introduced, but as the depression began to hit civilian employment prospects recruitment picked up and the five-year service was dropped. After the initial twelve-year engagement, ratings could sign on for another ten years, at the end of which they were eligible for a pension. Most of those who took this option were senior ratings, i.e. petty officers, equivalent to a sergeant in the army or air force, or chief petty officers, equal to a staff sergeant or flight sergeant.

The wartime navy became heavily dependent on conscription, including not just men but women without children. The bulk of those conscripted for active service went into the British army but others were allocated to the Royal Air Force or Royal Navy, while the wise would volunteer for the service of their choice to avoid being sent wherever the demand was strongest. Post-war, conscription continued but only for the armed forces, while in wartime conscripts could be sent to vital industries such as the coal mines.

Those who were educated away from Dartmouth and wished to become naval officers joined at 17 or 18 years of age. Whether they had joined at 13 or later, they left Dartmouth to spend eighteen months as a midshipman aboard a warship. Those who wanted to fly would also train as midshipmen, and under wartime pressures the two-year flying training course was condensed to ten months.

Commissioning ratings, or in naval parlance, those from the lower deck, had been rare in the pre-war navy, but wartime required experienced officers and suitable chief petty officers were able to be commissioned under what was known as the 'Upper Yardman Scheme'. To increase the intake of officer cadets, a special entry scheme was introduced at Dartmouth. After it was bombed in September 1942, it was evacuated to Eaton Hall in Cheshire. Volunteer reserve officers were sent for training at Hove Marina and the nearby public school, Lancing College, renamed HMS *King Alfred*, before later being relocated to Exbury House in the New Forest, Hampshire. By 1942, however, the rating training establishments, including the specialized establishments

---

pupil intake.

such as HMS *Excalibur* which trained communications specialists, and *Gosling* which trained naval airmen, were also trawled for suitable candidates for officer training.

The main shore establishment for mine countermeasures was HMS *Vernon*, a stone frigate or shore establishment on the Old Gunwharf at Portsmouth. This was heavily bombed and on 3 May 1941 the personnel were evacuated to the girls' public school Roedean, near Brighton, whose pupils had in turn been evacuated away from the coast for fear of German invasion. The temporary accommodation became HMS *Vernon* (R). It is claimed that the evacuees from *Vernon* were delighted to find bellpushes labelled 'Ring for Mistress'.

Training of naval airmen as pilots or observers was hampered by the Fleet Air Arm being dependent on the Royal Air Force, which was overwhelmed by its own training requirements. The RAF found relief in the Empire Air Training Scheme, which saw pilots, navigators and flight engineers trained in South Africa and Rhodesia, as well as New Zealand. For the Royal Navy, the relief was provided by the United States Navy which trained many British naval airmen at its large training base at Pensacola in Florida. Graduates from Pensacola completed their training in Canada, where they learned the 'British' way of doing things.

For both services, training air-crew away from the United Kingdom had several advantages. The most obvious one was better weather, so that flying training was not interrupted by bad conditions. Another was safety. Small, slow, training aircraft were vulnerable should an enemy fighter appear, looking for a target of opportunity. The third was that the costs of training were largely borne by the host country, with those in the British Empire seeing it as part of their contribution to the war effort.

Chapter 5

Early Losses and Successes

In both world wars the Royal Navy moved quickly to its planned wartime dispositions, except that during the First World War, in defiance of all that the Royal Navy had learned over the centuries, there was no plan for convoys until the last year of the war. Shipping losses to enemy surface raiders had been countered by either tracking the enemy raiders down or by using decoy ships and while the latter ploy enjoyed many successes, it was not enough to stem the losses, especially those to German submarines, the dreaded U-boats, that nearly brought the United Kingdom to her knees.

All of this changed. Convoys were quickly prepared during the Second World War. Convoys were never compulsory, unless they consisted of ships under contract to the British government or its armed forces. Nevertheless, ship-owners soon realized that the chances of their ships surviving for any period of time depended on their being part of a well-organized and defended convoy. During the First World War the Admiralty had argued that convoys would attract U-boats and surface raiders and while this argument was logical and even right, a convoy was not only the best means of defending merchant shipping but also the best way of bringing enemy warships, including the U-boats, to battle.

Ships that avoided being convoyed were the fast ocean liners such as the still new RMS *Queen Mary* and the most recent pre-war addition to the Cunard White Star Line's fleet, the RMS *Queen Elizabeth*. These were sufficiently fast to be safe from U-boats. Indeed, as previously mentioned, such was the performance of these ships that pre-war the Admiralty had considered converting them to aircraft carriers. Whether this could have been completed in time is questionable; instead it was decided that they would be of more use as troopships, for which many of their luxury fittings were hastily removed and put into storage.

The main convoy routes included those around the coasts of the British Isles, across the North Atlantic to the United States and Canada, through the Bay of Biscay to Gibraltar where convoys either headed east through the Mediterranean or south to the Cape of Good Hope, while others crossed the South Atlantic.

Same as Last Time?

The big difference in British and German attitudes on the outbreak of war, with little action from then until the following spring, was that the British described this period as the 'Phoney War', meaning that everything was on a wartime footing but there was no action, while the Germans described it as the *Sitzkrieg* or 'sitting war', meaning that they were waiting for something to happen.

Few Germans can have been sure of what the ruling elite had in mind for them but for the British, and for that matter the French, the widespread belief was that it would follow the same lines as the previous global conflict. Even so, there were differences. Italy and Japan had been allies of the British and French in the First World War, but Italy was widely and rightly assumed to be an ally of Germany. Japan, like Italy, had been engaged in aggression against its neighbours, attempting to expand its territory and create an empire, but few could have foreseen the attack on the United States Pacific Fleet in its base at Pearl Harbor in Hawaii or the much less well-known attack on the US Asiatic Fleet in the Philippines. This lack of vision was also shared by many senior officers in the United States Navy.

Many were surprised that Italy was not in the war at the beginning, not least the German dictator Adolf Hitler, but it was to be another nine months before Italy declared war on the UK and France.

The belligerent nations were not the only ones who foresaw the conflict following the pattern of the First World War. Belgium expected to be attacked and her neutrality infringed and was not disappointed, but Denmark, The Netherlands and Norway thought that they would once again rest safely in neutrality.

Imperial Russia had been a First World War ally of the United Kingdom and France, but Imperial Russia was by this time long gone and replaced by the Union of Soviet Socialist Republics (USSR), more usually known as the Soviet Union. It can be debated whether the German Nazi regime or the Soviet Communist regime was the more barbaric and brutal. To the outsider they differed politically, but the outsider did not know that the two countries had signed a non-aggression pact, the Molotov-Ribbentrop Pact – officially the German-Soviet Treaty of Non-aggression – on 23 August 1939. This was followed on 28 September by the German-Soviet Treaty of Friendship,

Co-operation and Demarcation, which modified the earlier agreement and lasted until the launch of the German invasion of the Soviet Union, Operation BARBAROSSA, on 22 June 1941.

These treaties were accompanied by a number of protocols to clarify what each nation expected, setting out their respective spheres of influence in East Europe. This gave the USSR the larger part of Poland, the right to all of Bessarabia, Estonia and Latvia, although somehow Lithuania escaped mention, and the dividing line between the two nations was to be approximately along the line of the rivers Vistula, Narew and San.

Even without these treaties, many in the West suspected that while Germany and the Soviet Union might ally themselves against the West at first, the relationship would not stand the test of time. However, no one realized just how abrupt the end would be.

No Phoney War at Sea

The German *Kriegsmarine* wasted no time. On the very day that war broke out, the British liner *Athenia* of 13,500 tons was torpedoed off the Hebrides. The Hague Convention required the U-boat commander to surface and give warning of his intentions, allowing time for those aboard the liner to take to the lifeboats, but no such warning was given. The U-boat commander was later to claim that he had mistaken the vessel for either a Q-ship, set as a decoy to catch him, or an armed merchant cruiser, but 112 people lost their lives, including 28 Americans. The loss of American lives enabled Hitler to claim that the ship had been torpedoed by the Royal Navy in an attempt to sour relations between the United States and Germany. Another claim by the Germans was that a bomb had been planted aboard the ship to give the impression that it had been torpedoed!

The Royal Navy started the war by conducting anti-submarine sweeps as well as patrolling the seas for German raiders. The anti-submarine sweeps were at this stage a waste, and dangerously wasteful at that. The resources devoted to them would have been better spent beefing up the convoy escorts. Later in the war, with the German Enigma codes broken and the Admiralty obtaining details of the positions of the German U-boat packs, anti-submarine sweeps could be directed to those areas where U-boats could be found and destroyed; however, in the beginning, lacking such intelligence, it was akin to hunting for a needle in a haystack.

Two weeks after the loss of the *Athenia*, on 17 September the aircraft carrier HMS *Courageous* was torpedoed by *U-29* while on an anti-submarine sweep. Flying for the day had just ended. One of those on board described the torpedo hitting the ship and creating an explosion as if the earth 'had split from pole to pole'. The ship was plunged into darkness and sank within twenty minutes, taking 500 men with her, trapped below decks in the dark. It had not helped that she was poorly protected with an escort of just two destroyers, far less than the minimum for such a valuable asset as an aircraft carrier.

Courageous was a sister ship of another carrier, *Glorious*, and had been converted after the Washington Naval Treaty of 1922 had left the Royal Navy with battleships and battle-cruisers in excess of the country's limit for such vessels. The treaty did not distinguish between battle-cruisers and battleships, which was wise as the specification varied between navies. These two ships, together with *Furious*, had been a class of light battle-cruisers intended for a planned invasion of Germany in the First World War, with an invasion of Pomerania on the Baltic Coast and offering the shortest route to Berlin. The plan was soon abandoned and it would have been impossible to get a substantial fleet into the Baltic through the shallow waters of the Skagerrak and Kattegat against strong German resistance. In any case, even before the First World War had broken out, unrest was rife in Russia and the plan anticipated that most of the troops used would be Russian. *Furious* was converted to become the first aircraft carrier, being rebuilt several times between the two world wars, while her two sisters were converted later and incorporated more up-to-date ideas on aircraft carrier design. All three ships had not only the main flight deck, but also shorter take-off decks running from the forward end of the hangar deck, which became increasingly impractical as aircraft weights increased.

Compared to the loss of an aircraft carrier, the shooting down of a German aircraft by the Fleet Air Arm with fighters flying from *Ark Royal* on 26 September was small consolation. Nevertheless, it was interesting that the first German victim fell to naval aviation.

Worse was to follow. On 14 October *U-47* penetrated the sheltered anchorage at Scapa Flow in Orkney and torpedoed the battleship *Royal Oak*, which sank with the loss of 833 men. The submarine had fired two salvoes, each of three torpedoes. Two torpedoes of the first salvo missed and the one that did hit the ship failed to explode properly, with those on watch thinking that there had been an internal explosion.

Certainly, there was no alarm at first and no attempt to hunt the submarine. Forty-five minutes later, a second salvo exploded under the ship and her magazine blew up.

Then on 23 November the armed merchant cruiser *Rawalpindi*, a former P&O liner taken up from trade and armed, was sunk by the German battle-cruisers *Gneisenau* and *Scharnhorst* as she turned towards them in a desperate attempt to protect the convoy she was escorting. From the start, it was an unequal contest between two of the finest ships of the day and a vessel that could not match their firepower.

Meanwhile, on 16 October the Luftwaffe had mounted a raid on British warships moored in the Firth of Forth off Rosyth. At this early stage of the war, the *Athenia* incident notwithstanding, there was still concern over the possibility of civilian casualties. Nine Junkers Ju 88 bombers of *Kampfgeschwader* 30 were seeking the battle-cruiser *Hood*, but finding her in the dockyard at Rosyth turned instead to the two cruisers *Edinburgh* and *Southampton*, moored in the Forth. Both ships were bombed, although the damage to *Edinburgh* was slight. *Southampton* received a direct hit from a 1,100lb armour-piercing bomb that went through the port side and then travelled down through three decks before exiting through the starboard side; it then exploded, causing some slight damage to the ship. Had the bomb exploded during its journey through the ship, the damage would have been worse and had a magazine been caught in the explosion, she could have been lost.

What was the first good news of the war came on 13 December. The light cruisers *Ajax* and *Achilles*, the latter a Royal New Zealand Navy ship, were accompanying the heavy cruiser *Exeter* on the hunt for commerce raiders in the South Atlantic. One area that attracted commerce raiders was the estuary of the River Plate, between Argentina and Uruguay, frequented by British cargo ships carrying meat from these two countries to the UK. They encountered the powerful German *Panzerschiff Graf Spee*. Known in the British and American media as a 'pocket battleship', the Germans had three such vessels which they knew as 'armoured ships' and which had replaced three of the elderly coastal battleships that Germany was allowed to retain under the Treaty of Versailles. Fitted with 11in guns, the Germans believed that these ships could only be bested by a battleship. They were ideal for commerce raiding as their diesel engines gave them a long range.

Clearly, the British vessels with 6in guns for the light cruisers and 8in guns for the heavy cruiser were outgunned. The 11in-calibre guns of the *Panzerschiff* not only packed a heavier punch but also had a longer range. Superior tactics by the cruisers forced the *Graf Spee* to divide her fire while they damaged her so badly that she had to seek refuge in neutral Uruguay's capital and main port, Montevideo. The warships of belligerent navies were allowed just three days in a neutral port for temporary repairs. The ship's commanding officer put all but a skeleton crew ashore and sailed on 17 December, not to confront the British ships but to be scuttled.

Perhaps German confidence in their *Panzerschiffe* was misplaced, but in an unusual instance of foresight before the war one of the *Graf Spee*'s sister ships, *Deutschland*, was renamed *Lutzow* because someone had thought of the impact on morale if *Deutschland* was sunk.

Almost two months after the *Graf Spee* was scuttled, her supply ship the *Altmark* was intercepted by the British destroyer *Cossack* on 14 February 1940 in Jøssingfjord, in Norwegian territorial waters. Delayed by a Norwegian warship, *Cossack* eventually managed to put a boarding party aboard the *Altmark* and release 303 British merchant seamen who had been taken prisoner by the *Graf Spee* when their ships had been sunk. The *Altmark* was allowed to continue her voyage home afterwards. The Norwegian government protested to the British government, but neither ship should have been in Norwegian waters and the Norwegians had failed to board the German ship, yet despite this at first they insisted that there were no British prisoners aboard. *Cossack*'s commanding officer had taken a gamble that there were likely to be British prisoners aboard the ship and won.

At a Disadvantage
While the Royal Navy had been quick to instigate a convoy system, unlike in the First World War, in one sense it was worse off than in the previous conflict when it had bases in the south of Ireland. This disadvantage was probably even worse for the Royal Air Force as the ability to mount maritime-reconnaissance patrols from what had become the Republic of Ireland would have helped to reduce the size of the 'Atlantic Gap', that part of the route across the North Atlantic that was beyond the range of air patrols from Canada or Northern Ireland.

The treaty that had established what was at first known as the Irish Free State, which became the Republic of Ireland before the outbreak of the Second World War, had guaranteed the Royal Navy the use of the so-called 'treaty ports'. These included Berehaven in the south and Lough Swilly* in the north, but the latter was not such a loss as just over the border in Northern Ireland lay Londonderry with nearby Eglinton, which became an air base mainly for the Fleet Air Arm and is now Londonderry's airport.

There had in fact been no attempt to negotiate what might have called 'treaty airports', which was an unfortunate oversight on the part of the British negotiators, especially since maritime reconnaissance had already started to prove its value during the First World War. Perhaps they thought that flying boats could use the treaty ports, but by the outbreak of the Second World War landplanes were becoming an important element in maritime reconnaissance as the day of the flying boat drew to a close.

One reason why the Royal Navy was not able to use the treaty ports was that the British government did not insist on being able to use them. Many believe that this was because of the need to provide security for these bases from attacks by the Irish Republican Army, which had been very active in mainland Great Britain just before the war and which would doubtless have applied its energies against any attempt to station British service personnel in the Republic. At a time when the British army was under pressure in France and elsewhere, finding sufficient troops to defend bases in Ireland would have been an added burden.

If the British had lost some of their First World War naval bases, the Germans were to find that they had gained bases and were in a much stronger position than during the earlier conflict once their conquest of Norway and France was achieved in spring and early summer 1940. As we will see later, the German occupation of Norway made running the convoys to northern Russia so much more difficult. Just as useful, the occupation of France down to the Brittany peninsula gave the Germans the naval base of Brest and easy access to the open sea. No longer did their U-boats have to risk the voyage around the north of Scotland and down the west coast of Ireland and into the Western Approaches, except on the occasion when they first ventured forth after commissioning.

With German occupation of Europe extending from the far north of Norway down to the Bay of Biscay, the naval bases on the south coast

---

*Lough Swilly is in County Donegal, the most northerly county in the Irish Republic and in fact part of it is even further north than the most northerly point in Northern Ireland.

of England were subjected to heavy German aerial attack and attack by E-boats, fast-moving motor torpedo boats and gunboats. Western Approaches Command was moved from Devonport, the naval base at Plymouth, to Liverpool, which was in any case the destination for many of the eastbound convoys.

Chapter 6

The Norwegian Campaign and Dunkirk

In 1940, few could have realized the eventual significance of the occupation of Norway by the Germans. At the time it was simply the loss of another friendly country, but it did prompt the British government to send troops to occupy Iceland, which had seized independence from Denmark on that country also being overrun by German forces. The feared German occupation of Iceland would have been a disaster had it happened, giving the Germans control over a large area of the North Atlantic. Of course, the Germans might not have managed it, given the distance and the fact that their amphibious assault on Norway was not without its setbacks, but Norway had armed forces and Iceland did not.

The long period of inaction on the ground came to an abrupt end on 9 April 1940 when German troops invaded Denmark and Norway. The invasion of Denmark was over quickly, with Germany and Denmark sharing a land border while an invasion fleet sailed into the harbour at Copenhagen. There was no time for British or French intervention. Norway was different as the Germans had to invade by sea and the inhospitable terrain lent itself to resistance. Expecting the Second World War to follow the same pattern as the first, the leaders of both countries were taken by surprise.

The irony was that the British and French had planned to invade Norway earlier, during the winter of 1939-40, on the pretext of aiding Finland in her war with the Soviet Union – the so-called 'Winter War' – as the USSR tried to regain territory lost during the Bolshevik Revolution and the Russian Civil War that had followed.

German propaganda claimed that the reason for the invasion of Denmark and Norway was to forestall an Allied invasion, but the main reason was to ensure that supplies of Swedish iron ore continued to reach Germany as the use of Norwegian ports was vital to the Germans because the Gulf of Bothnia froze in winter, making the direct sea route from Sweden to German impassable.

After the *Altmark* incident already mentioned, there was no further action by the British in Norwegian waters until 8 April, when the Royal Navy began mining to prevent their use by German shipping. The Royal Navy had already begun laying mines in the approaches to the Kiel Canal and the Royal Air Force had dropped mines in this and other German waterways in operations known to the RAF as 'gardening'.

Even so, the Germans must have been preparing to invade both Denmark and Norway well before this as such a major operation could not be mounted overnight. The Germans had allocated substantial forces, with troops landed from the sea at the major ports of Oslo, Kristiansand, Bergen, Trondheim and Narvik, while air-landed troops arrived at the airports at Oslo and Stavanger. For the most part this operation went according to plan, but the loss of the cruiser *Blücher*, hit by two torpedoes fired from a coastal battery at the Drøbak Narrows, protecting the entrance to Oslo Fjord, with the main headquarters staff aboard, hindered the German landings and allowed the Norwegian government and the king to flee the city, giving time to organize resistance.

The Norwegian army had already started to mobilize and this encouraged the United Kingdom and France to send troops, assembling an initial expeditionary force of 13,000 supported by air and naval forces, including the despatch of aircraft carriers. The use of carrier-borne aircraft was necessary because of the limited number of airfields available ashore, and the nature of the terrain. Unfortunately at this time the Royal Navy had no high-performance aircraft embarked on its carriers that were capable of fending off German fighters.

The British and French agreed that the key to holding Norway would be the recapture of Trondheim, from which a counter-attack southwards could repel the invaders. Initially, however, Narvik was seen as being more easily taken and held at the outset. This was all very well in theory, but in practice the problem was that a substantial part of the available trained strength of both nations' armies and air forces were stationed in France in anticipation of a German attack, while it was estimated that an army of at least 50,000 troops, almost four times the number actually available, would be needed to liberate Norway.

At sea, the Royal Navy soon established control. A destroyer action in Narvik Fjord on 10 April saw two German destroyers and some merchantmen sunk, although later two British destroyers were also sunk. That same day, an air-raid by Fleet Air Arm aircraft operating from the shore station at Hatston on the mainland of Orkney sank the cruiser *Königsberg*, the first loss of a substantial operational warship to air power. Three days later, the veteran battleship HMS *Warspite* and nine destroyers sank another eight German destroyers in the Second Battle of Narvik. Such heavy losses affected the *Kriegsmarine* badly as it was very short of destroyers even before the outbreak of war.

Aided by these successes, British forces were landed at Narvik on 12 April. These troops, under Major General Mackesy, were expected to seize the town, using naval gunfire if necessary. It soon became clear that Mackesy had no intention of taking Narvik. At first, this was because he wished to wait for the snow to melt and for his force to be joined by a half brigade of French *Chasseurs Alpins* (mountain infantry), not appreciating that these troops were earmarked for other operations.

While the Germans were left to strengthen their defences at Narvik, British and French troops were being landed near Namsos, further south between Narvik and Trondheim. They were expected to move south to Trondheim, a distance of 100 miles, despite 4 feet of snow which hindered movement and with no protection from German air attack.

Advancing from the north, one British brigade managed to get to within 50 miles of Trondheim by 19 April before the Germans counter-attacked two days later, forcing them back. The northern advance on Trondheim was soon back where it started, at Namsos, from where it was evacuated on the night of 3 May.

Throughout this period, the British and French troops were subjected to heavy bombing by the Luftwaffe. Air cover was provided by fighters operating from British aircraft carriers and by RAF Gloster Gladiators operating from a frozen lake some 40 miles from Åndalsnes. The Gladiators, the RAF's last biplane fighters, were no match for the Luftwaffe's Messerschmitt Bf 109s; while at this time the Fleet Air Arm did not have any high-performance fighters. A squadron of Hawker Hurricanes based at an airfield ashore were too few and too late to make a difference.

Eventually, on 24 May it was decided to withdraw from Norway as the German invasion of France and the Low Countries was well advanced. Withdrawal started on 27 and 28 May, with more than 24,000 British, French, Polish and Norwegian troops having left by

8 June, shortly before the surrender of France. The need to reinforce the British and French units fighting in France was seen as a justification for withdrawal from Norway, but the battle for France was already lost.

Air cover was provided for the evacuation by aircraft from the carriers *Ark Royal* and *Glorious*, the sister of *Courageous*, and at first by RAF squadrons based ashore. It was then the turn of the RAF to be evacuated, and the order was given that the aircraft had to be destroyed as they did not have sufficient range to fly back to the UK. Realizing the need for every single aircraft and despite having no previous carrier landing experience, the Hurricane pilots decided to save their aircraft by flying them to the carriers. Despite her shorter landing deck, *Glorious* was chosen because her larger lifts meant that the aircraft, which did not have folding wings, could be struck down into the hangar without first having their wings removed. As the Hurricanes also lacked that other requirement for carrier operations, arrester hooks, sandbags were attached to their tail wheels to weigh them down and the aircraft were landed successfully aboard the ship.

By this time, *Glorious* was short of fuel and this was one reason why she left Norway steaming westwards to Scapa Flow in Orkney at a stately 17 knots, which her commanding officer considered fast enough to save the ship from submarine attack. Despite not being fitted with radar, her commanding officer did not order aerial reconnaissance patrols to be flown and did not order a lookout in the crow's nest. All of her aircraft were struck down into the hangar, while bombs and torpedoes were removed and returned to the magazines. This left the ship dependent on the protection of two destroyers. Her commanding officer, when once asked what he would do when faced with enemy warships, had replied by saying that he would steam towards them 'with all guns blazing'. Naval air power clearly didn't feature in his battle plans.

While most of her crew were below drinking tea and eating cake, at 1600 the two German battle-cruisers *Scharnhorst* and *Gneisenau* came into view. They would have spotted the carrier earlier as they were among the few German ships to be fitted with radar. At a range of 28,000 yards they both opened fire with their 11in guns; the limited armament of *Glorious*, with nothing heavier than 4.7in guns, had no chance of returning the fire. The carrier increased her speed and the order was given to launch her aircraft. Additional boilers were fired up and the five remaining Fairey Swordfish were brought up from the hangar and made ready to launch a torpedo attack.

At 1615 the first hit was scored on the carrier, destroying the aircraft that were on deck waiting for their crews. Once the range had been fixed, further shells struck the ship, penetrating the wooden flight deck and exploding among the precious Hurricanes in the hangar below. Fuel left in the Hurricanes ignited and their ammunition exploded, creating an inferno in the hangar deck. By the time a salvo destroyed the bridge at 1700, the ship was already a pillar of smoke, despite having increased her speed to 27 knots.

As this was happening, the destroyer escorts *Ardent* and *Acasta* were both lost in making a desperate torpedo attack on the *Scharnhorst*, which suffered damage from one of *Acasta*'s torpedoes.

An hour later, *Glorious* disappeared beneath the waves. It is thought that as many as 900 of her combined ship's company and embarked RAF personnel of 1,500 may have survived the attack, but just 39 men survived two days in cold water with no food or drink until they were rescued.

The first nine months of war had seen the Royal Navy lose two of its precious carriers, and in both cases the loss had been avoidable. The wasteful search for U-boats had been the downfall of *Courageous* and the lack of aerial reconnaissance had done the same for *Glorious*, while neither had been given adequate escorts.

Worse was to follow, for on 13 June fifteen Blackburn Skuas of No. 800 and 803 Naval Air Squadrons based on board *Ark Royal* were sent to attack the *Scharnhorst* and *Gneisenau* at Trondheim and ran into heavy anti-aircraft fire from the ships as well as a strong Luftwaffe fighter defence. The Skua, officially a fighter-dive-bomber, was described by one of its pilots as 'more dive-bomber than fighter' and didn't stand a chance. Eight of the fifteen were shot down. One survivor likened the attack to the Charge of the Light Brigade, but the reality was even worse as the one bomb that hit the *Scharnhorst* failed to explode, possibly because it was dropped too low to be primed.

The tragedy of the Royal Navy's first encounters with the two German battle-cruisers was all the more bitter because even while the troops were being withdrawn from Norway to reinforce the British and French armies in France, it was already too late to save Belgium and France. French surrender was still some time away, but the defenders were falling back in disarray towards the Channel ports.

Dunkirk

As Allied defeats continued to grow, the troops that had been moved to France in September 1939 had to be brought home or left to become prisoners of war. The move of the British Expeditionary Force (BEF) to France had been largely the work of the Merchant Navy using cross-Channel steamers, packet ships more used to carrying civilians – many of them day-trippers or holidaymakers – than troops, and mails rather than military equipment. Similar steamers from other routes around the British Isles were also called up for this service. The evacuation of troops from Dunkirk was to require not just the ferries but a wide variety of small craft including fishing vessels and pleasure-cruisers as well as small yachts and launches. Many of the smaller craft performed valuable work in taking men off the beaches and ferrying them to large ships for the return trip across the Channel.

The evacuation became known as Operation DYNAMO and was organized by Admiral Sir Bertram Ramsay at Dover. Ramsay had retired from the Royal Navy before the war and rejoined shortly before war broke out; he was in fact 'acting admiral' at the time.

Many rear-echelon or support troops were evacuated before the main evacuation began, with 28,000 having left France by 26 May when Operation DYNAMO officially started. In the days that followed, arrangements approached their climax. Early on 29 May, the Southern Railway packet ship *Brittany* was requisitioned by the government, joining the Channel Island ferry *Isle of Guernsey* and six cross-Channel packets that were working as hospital ships, while another eight were in service as military transports. At the time *Brittany* was requisitioned, warning was given that another two ships might be needed, but by noon that same day the situation was such that the Southern Railway was sent a signal that 'all available Southern Railway steamers of 1,000 tons gross with a range of 150 miles are required for immediate Government service.' Nine ships were quickly handed over with their crews, including four Isle of Wight ferries, of which two were car ferries with low open vehicle decks that were not well-suited to a squall in the English Channel.

All of the four large railway companies that operated the main-line railway network in Great Britain had already contributed ships, including those that operated on the Irish Sea and across the North Sea as well as the cross-Channel and Channel Island ships. The Southern Railway was the main operator across the English Channel and had lost two ships before Dunkirk. One of these was the *Maid of Kent*, clearly marked as a hospital ship and crowded with wounded soldiers when she was hit by five bombs and sunk in the harbour at Dieppe on 23 May. Later that day, *Brighton*, again marked as a hospital ship, was also bombed and sunk.

As the main evacuation got under way, more ships were sunk. On 30 May *Lorina* and *Normannia*, both acting as military transports, were sunk at Dunkirk, although the crew of the *Normannia* was saved and reached England. On 2 June another hospital ship, the *Paris*, was bombed and had to be abandoned.

In the confusion, as many men as possible were crowded aboard ships as they arrived with no attention given to the size of the ship, number of lifeboats or any other consideration. So it happened that the small Isle of Wight paddle-steamer *Whippingham* beat much larger ships to take the record for a single voyage by moving 2,700 men on 4 June.

The Great Western Railway (GWR) also pressed its Channel Island steamers into the evacuation, deploying the *St Helier* and the *St Julien*, while these were joined by the *St Andrew* and the *St David* from the company's Fishguard-Rosslare service. During several days on the evacuation, the *St Helier* carried 10,000 men.

Passenger ferries were the smart end of the operation, although it is doubtful that many of the evacuees appreciated this. Many had been without sleep, food or water for days before boarding the ships. Hitler had agreed to Göring's request that the Luftwaffe be allowed to destroy the BEF on the beaches, while Panzer divisions were held back. While the Luftwaffe failed in its task, its bombing accounted for many casualties on the beaches and on the ships. The less fortunate evacuees were taken off by smaller cargo ships, but these at least could get closer to the troops crowded on the beaches; two-thirds of those rescued were taken off the harbour's east mole straight onto ships. So desperate was the situation that the GWR sent the *Mew*, the Dartmouth-Kingswear ferry, but by the time she reached the Straits of Dover the evacuation was over.

As the evacuation at Dunkirk ended, many of the ships were sent further down the coast to St Valery but arrived after the port had fallen to the Germans and as they approached, the rescue fleet came under heavy shellfire with many of those on board killed.

Operation DYNAMO saw 338,226 troops moved from France to England, a far higher figure than had been expected, and while the bulk of these were British, there were also many French troops and smaller numbers from other countries that had been overrun by the Germans. Most of the 53,000 French personnel rescued left during the night of 3/4 June, by which time Ramsay had had to ban daylight passages.

Some of those evacuated were taken off by warships but a fighting ship is seldom the ideal vessel for an evacuation and the main role of the Royal Navy was to protect the evacuation fleet, keeping German warships, and especially the fast-moving E-boats that could have caused so much damage, away. The other role was to provide anti-aircraft cover for the evacuation fleet. While nothing larger than a destroyer could get close enough to help, shore-based Fleet Air Arm squadrons assisted RAF Coastal Command in reconnaissance and anti-shipping patrols.

Despite the best efforts of RAF Fighter Command, whose aircraft could only spend a limited amount of time over Dunkirk before running low on fuel, nine British and French destroyers were lost as well as eight troopships. Out of the officially recorded 848 civilian vessels, 72 were lost to enemy action and 163 lost in collisions with a further 45 damaged.

Britain's new wartime prime minister, Winston Churchill, was moved to remind the British people that 'wars are not won by evacuations', but there can be no doubt that the loss of more than a third of a million Allied troops would have been a shock to national morale so severe that the will to continue fighting might have been undermined at a time when there was still a substantial movement that wanted to negotiate a peace with Germany.

Chapter 7

At War with an Ally

The defeat of France and the armistice signed on 22 June 1940, with Italy having entered the war earlier on 10 June, completely changed the balance of power in the Mediterranean, at sea as much as on land and possibly even more. Overnight, the Royal Navy had lost the not inconsiderable power of the French fleet in the Mediterranean and simultaneously found itself facing the might of the Italian navy, the *Regina Marina*.

This was bad enough, but the big question that had to be tackled was what would be the fate of the French fleet? Would it be handed over to the Germans? Would the French change sides? This second scenario might seem unrealistic and even insulting to what had been only days previously an ally, but after French surrender with a large part of France left unoccupied and self-governing from Vichy, some members of the Vichy regime offered to ally themselves with Germany. It was German intransigence and their desire to leave the French in no doubt as to who was winning the war at that time that left this offer unused. There were also many in the Vichy regime and at senior level in the Vichy armed forces who had no liking for the British, while many other French people felt let down by the British withdrawal from France. The British for their part were angry that France had negotiated a separate armistice with Germany. Yet, as we will see, the truth was that the French *Marine Nationale* was to fulfil its pledge not to surrender its ships to the Germans, even when Vichy France was occupied. However, that was not known at the time.

As it was, with Italy now in the war, Malta was within reach of Axis air bases in Sicily and the south of Italy where the Italians had a strong naval base at Taranto. The Royal Navy and the *Marine Nationale* were sharing a base at Alexandria in Egypt. The *Marine Nationale* had bases in North Africa at Oran and Mers-el-Kébir, along the main shipping route across the Mediterranean, as well as at Dakar in West Africa, along the shipping lanes from Europe to the Cape. The main French naval base in the Mediterranean was at Toulon in the south of France, Vichy-held territory. There were also French ships that had escaped to Portsmouth and Plymouth, two of the Royal Navy's main home bases.

The Royal Navy had bases at Gibraltar, Malta and Alexandria. Gibraltar was safe as long as Spain remained neutral and was the key to the Mediterranean. Malta, the main base for the British Mediterranean Fleet, was to become barely tenable and would not have been defended had not the Admiralty insisted that it remain as a base for submarines and anti-shipping air operations, but most of the Mediterranean Fleet was moved to Alexandria before Italy entered the Second World War in June 1940.

Plans had been laid in case Gibraltar was invaded by Spanish and German forces. A team of six men was to be incarcerated in the famous Rock, supplied with food and drink for a considerable time and measures were taken to ensure that they could spy and report back on Axis shipping movements. In the end this wasn't necessary, but German agents in southern Spain and in the Spanish North African enclaves of Ceuta and Melilla kept a close eye on Allied shipping movements. The Mediterranean was closed to British shipping unless in convoy.

Tackling the French fleet was an unwelcome task for the Royal Navy which had been fighting alongside the French and both navies had co-operated during the Norwegian campaign. Yet, the overwhelming feeling was that something had to be done. The *Kriegsmarine* was far from its planned wartime strength and the ships of the *Marine Nationale* could help to fill the gap.

Mers-El-Kébir

North Africa was heavily influenced by France, which was one of the colonial powers in Morocco, while Algeria had been settled by more than a million people of French descent who lived alongside the indigenous Arab population. Naturally enough, the French had armed forces based in Algeria with a major naval base at Mers-el-Kébir, just outside Oran, which was also the base for a number of ships. These bases included some of the *Marine Nationale's* training facilities.

After the fall of France, ships stationed at Mers-el-Kébir included two elderly battleships plus the modern battle-cruisers *Dunkerque* and *Strasbourg* as well as six large destroyers of the *contre-torpilleur* type, sometimes described as super-destroyers and intended as a counter to Italy's light cruisers. Seven smaller destroyers and four submarines were based at Oran. *Dunkerque* had only recently returned to Mers-el-Kébir after a visit to Gibraltar.

This fleet had been busy since the outbreak of war escorting convoys between France and Algeria, fearful of an attack by the Italian fleet. The ships based at Mers-el-Kébir would have been valuable both to Germany and to Italy as both navies were short of destroyers, while the Italians had neglected the battle-cruiser; they did have six battleships, but only two of these could be described as modern.

The Royal Navy acted quickly to fill the gap in Allied capability in the Mediterranean following French surrender. On 28 June 1940, Force H was formed, based on Gibraltar. Officially a powerful naval squadron, it was a small fleet with an aircraft carrier – the Royal Navy's newest, HMS *Ark Royal* – and capital ships, as well as supporting cruisers and destroyers, capable of ranging far out into the North Atlantic or across the Mediterranean as far east as Malta or the coast of Italy.

One duty that fell to Force H was the escort of convoys to Malta. Mediterranean convoys needed fleet carriers with their larger complement of aircraft, whereas on the Arctic convoys escort carriers were supposed to be sufficient, although with fleet carriers often in a distant escort. On the North Atlantic, MAC ships – merchant aircraft carriers with a primitive flight deck above the cargo holds and cargo of oil tankers and grain carriers – were effective.

Force H was commanded by Vice Admiral Sir James Somerville, brought out of retirement and who had taken a substantial demotion from his previous rank of admiral of the fleet, equivalent to a fleet admiral in the USN, or a drop from five-star rank to three-star rank, to serve his country. Despite his age, Somerville was one of the most daring and competent British naval commanders of the Second World War with a temperament ideally suited to a flexible and independent command such as Force H would become. Earlier, he had assisted Ramsay in organizing Operation DYNAMO.

The British government was unaware that Darlan had ordered that French warships should be scuttled rather than fall into German or Italian hands. Darlan's anti-British attitude was well-known and in any case, the crew of a warship had to have time to scuttle it and if scuttled in harbour ships could be refloated and recommissioned.

On 3 July those French warships that had fled to British ports were seized. Force H was then ordered to Mers-el-Kébir and Somerville attempted to open negotiations with the French naval commander, Admiral Marcel-Bruno Gensoul. Gensoul was in a difficult position as he did not know what the policies of the new Vichy government would be, and whether his government would expect him to continue fighting or accept surrender and perhaps neutrality. Somerville's emissary was refused a meeting and so negotiations had to begin in writing. This was the main difference between the situation in Mers-el-Kébir and at Alexandria, as at the latter Cunningham already had not just contact with the French naval commander but a good working relationship.

Somerville wrote offering Gensoul the choice of four options. The first of these was that he should take his fleet to sea and join the Royal Navy in continuing the war, although this could mean that he would be branded a traitor by the Vichy regime. Alternatively, he could take his ships with a reduced crew to Gibraltar, closer than Malta which was not an option because of its proximity to Italy, and once at 'Gib' the crews would be repatriated. A variation on this option was to take the ships to the French West Indies, where they would be immobilized. Finally, there was the option of scuttling the ships at both Mers-el-Kébir and Oran within six hours. In fact the government had a fifth option in mind, which was that the ships could be immobilized in their Algerian ports but Somerville did not offer this in his letter, realizing that the facilities at Mers-el-Kébir were more than sufficient to return the ships to full fighting condition quickly.

It was made clear to Gensoul that if he did not accept one of these options, his ships would be sunk by the Royal Navy. Gensoul did not pass on the full list of options to his superiors, but simply told them that he had been given six hours to scuttle his ships or they would be attacked by the Royal Navy. Given such a stark choice, he was ordered to resist using all the force available to him.

In common with the rest of the members of the Royal Navy, Somerville was very unhappy with having to use force against a navy that had, only weeks before, been an ally, especially during the Norwegian campaign. In a desperate bid to avoid the use of force, Somerville sent one of his most senior officers, Captain Holland, commanding officer of the aircraft carrier *Ark Royal*, to see Gensoul with an ultimatum. Holland was flown in a Fairey Swordfish seaplane from Somerville's flagship, the battle-cruiser *Hood*, but while he was aboard Gensoul's flagship, the battle-cruiser *Dunkerque*, the French Admiralty signalled *en clair* for all French warships in the Mediterranean to converge on Oran and put themselves under Gensoul's command. This was picked up by the Admiralty in London who immediately ordered Somerville to take action while he only had the French warships already at Mers-el-Kébir and Oran to deal with rather than face the might of the entire French fleet in the Mediterranean.

Captain Holland left the *Dunkerque* at 1725 on 3 July, and after informing Somerville that Gensoul was refusing to accept any of the options presented to him, needed to regain command of his warship. Aboard *Ark Royal*, the arrester wires were removed from her flight deck and the Swordfish floatplane flew safely onto her paper-thin flight deck* without damage to the aircraft or the ship, thanks to the very low stalling speed of the Swordfish, an aircraft known affectionately to the Fleet Air Arm as the 'Stringbag'.

At 1754 Somerville opened fire, joined by aircraft from the *Ark Royal*. The elderly battleship *Bretagne* blew up and several other ships were badly damaged, including *Dunkerque* which although only slightly damaged in the initial salvoes of gunfire was then crippled in an attack by Swordfish torpedo-bombers from the British carrier on 6 July. A single broadside from one British ship blew an army barracks off the top of a hill.

The French warships returned the fire. Aboard HMS *Hood*, leading seaman Joseph Rockley remembered the French shells passing over the ship:

> It was my first experience of naval gunfire. Some shells passed overhead like an express train, but others wobbled, and I learned later that this was due to the rifling in their barrels being worn. They sounded like someone blowing hard into a glass in short, sharp breaths.
>
> It was impossible to tell at the time how much damage we had caused, but we later learnt that it had been considerable.

Aboard the French ships, opinions had been divided. Arsène le Poitevin was one of those who was pressing his superiors to continue the war alongside the British, but that was before the gunnery exchange at Mers-el-Kébir:

> It was terrible for us. Lots of sailors dead, and ships sunk or damaged. It was impossible to say anything nice about the British

---

*To keep within the British government's self-imposed displacement limit for an aircraft carrier, armour was sacrificed on *Ark Royal*. On one occasion, a plane catching the arrester wires dropped her remaining 6lb practice bombs and even these dropped through the flight deck to explode in the hangar deck below, killing several men working on aircraft.

for a long time. Later, people began to say that perhaps they had no choice.

At the same time, rather than simply rejecting the British ultimatum, had the commanding officers had the courage of their convictions, they should have gone to sea and fought, rather than just staying in harbour.

Many British sailors were upset by what had happened, but many maintained that their government had no choice. Everyone assumed that the Germans would take the French warships and use them in the war against the British, who by this time were fighting with the Empire mobilized but with no European allies.

The French lost 1,297 men in this action.

Alexandria

The decision to move the British Mediterranean Fleet from Malta to Alexandria was not taken lightly. Malta was not only a popular posting; it had the full depth of repair facilities and a skilled workforce, while Alexandria had little of this. From Malta, British warships and aircraft could range over the central Mediterranean with the island almost halfway between Gibraltar and Alexandria. This was why, as already mentioned, the new British naval command, Force H, had to be created and based on Gibraltar, but this was to be a highly successful unit able to operate in the Atlantic as in the hunt for the German battleship *Bismarck*, or in the Western Mediterranean with raids on Italian targets in the north of the country including the port and naval base of Genoa.

Egypt was very important to a maritime nation such as the United Kingdom, especially with a large empire, for one reason and that was the Suez Canal, the great short cut to the East that had opened in 1869 and in which the British and French were equal shareholders. The Anglo-Egyptian Treaty of August 1936 gave the British the right to defend the Suez Canal. This was in fact nothing new as Egypt was run almost as if it were a colony, despite having its own king, and had been a British protectorate between 1914 and 1922. The Royal Egyptian Navy was headed by an admiral on secondment from the Royal Navy. It could be said to be more under British control than the navies of any of the dominions.

The 1936 treaty had also given the British very extensive rights in the event of war to make full use of Egyptian 'ports, airports and means of communication' and ensured that the monarch, King Farouk, would give 'all the facilities and assistance in his power'.

The French did not have the same rights, but as shareholders in the Suez Canal they had a vested interest in its security. Basing French warships alongside their British counterparts at Alexandria made sense and ensured good communication, so long as the two navies were on the same side!

In Egypt and many other parts of the Middle East, the British position was under threat from increasingly strident Arab nationalism, which the Germans sought to exploit and indeed did so by supporting an uprising in Mesopotamia, present-day Iraq. The government in Egypt included many who held anti-British views. Nevertheless, on the outbreak of war martial law was imposed by the Egyptian government and reluctantly they started to arrest German nationals while diplomatic relations were cut off.

As the balance of power in the Mediterranean changed with the fall of France and Italy's belated entry into the war, there were also fears that Turkey, an ally of Germany during the First World War, would once again fight on the Axis side.

The British Mediterranean Fleet at Alexandria was under the command of Admiral Sir Andrew 'ABC' Cunningham, while the French Mediterranean Squadron was under the command of Vice Admiral Godfroy. Godfroy was under orders from his Admiralty to sail, but given the difficult political situation in France was attempting to confirm that the order was authentic. The head of the *Marine Nationale*, Admiral Jean Darlan, had given orders that ships were to be scuttled rather than handed over to the Germans, but he was also clear that the British were not to have them either. The men aboard the ships wanted to return to France to be with their families.

This put Cunningham in great difficulty as he could not put to sea and leave the French behind in case they either sailed for France, with the risk of the ships being seized by the Germans, or perhaps to Beirut. He later recalled:

During the last days of June we became aware that an operation was being planned against the French ships at Oran. An ultimatum was to be given to the French admiral in command, giving him four options. He might sail his ships to British ports and continue the fight with us, or sail his ships with British crews to a British port from which the crews would be repatriated whenever desired;

or sail his ships to a French port in the West Indies where they would be demilitarised to our satisfaction, or, if preferred, entrusted to the United States for the duration of the war, the crews being repatriated in either case, or, finally, to sink his ships.

The Admiralty was impatient and put considerable pressure on Cunningham to act quickly, but despite this Cunningham refused to be hurried into taking action that could further harm Anglo-French relations. He knew that Darlan would be fully aware of the action taken at Oran, and that his options in reality would be to either intern the ships or risk a bloody battle in sinking them. Godfroy initially offered to accept internment with the warheads taken off torpedoes and the ships relieved of their fuel while the ships' companies would be repatriated. He changed his mind on 4 July when the Vichy government ordered him to sail and ordered his ships to raise steam, which would take eight hours. Cunningham was alerted and went on deck, seeing that the French ships were raising steam and their guns were uncovered, ready for action. The British ships immediately did the same, removing the tompions – the muzzle covers made from steel or brass and usually decorated with the ship's crest – from their guns.

Aboard each French warship was a British liaison officer and the commanding officers had to maintain good contact with their French counterparts. Cunningham ordered his commanding officers to visit their French counterparts, while he sent a signal to each French warship individually advising them of the offer of repatriation if the warships were put out of use. The visitors to the French warships were not made unwelcome. On boarding a French cruiser, Captain Rory O'Connor of the battle-cruiser *Neptune* was greeted by the commanding officer with: 'When I saw the tompions being removed from your guns, I immediately ordered the tompions to be placed in mine.'

Aboard other ships, French ratings held meetings on deck while their commanding officers visited Godfroy aboard his flagship *Duquesne*.

The measures had the desired effect. An hour later Godfroy visited Cunningham and the two admirals agreed that all fuel oil was to be discharged from the French ships, their guns were to be disabled and 70 per cent of their crew members were to be landed for eventual repatriation. The British on their part were not to attempt to use the French ships. The French fleet no longer presented a threat by 7 July, enabling the Mediterranean Fleet to put to sea without any fear of French action to seize the port or the Suez Canal.

While Cunningham had shown considerable tact and diplomacy, avoiding bloodshed and any worsening of relations between the two countries, incorporating the French ships into the Royal Navy would not have been easy. Gun calibres varied, especially on the smaller warships, with the French using 5.1in instead of the British 6in, and 3.5in instead of 4in or the increasingly common 4.5in.

After Oran, the Vichy government broke off all diplomatic relations with the United Kingdom, although how long these could have been maintained is open to question. Vichy was not an ally of Germany and Italy, but senior members of the government and the armed forces had volunteered to support the Germans. As mentioned earlier, many disliked the British even before Oran and Alexandria and, of course, there were still the French warships based on Dakar in French West Africa to consider.

Dakar

A major naval base and commercial port, Dakar in West Africa had been in French hands since 1659, although France did not extend its possession to include the interior of the country until 1865 and French West Africa did not become a colonial entity until 1895. In contrast to the situation in the Mediterranean, the British did not simply want to secure the surrender of French warships at Dakar or have them immobilized, they also wanted to ensure that the port itself was not taken over by the Germans or the Italians as that would provide a convenient base from which to attack British convoys on their way to the Cape. The Cape route was important, but became even more so as the war continued after the Mediterranean became all but impassable for convoys from early 1941. Dakar also had the only dockyard between Gibraltar and the Cape.

After their experiences in North Africa, an attack was made on Dakar on 8 July. As at Oran and Mers-el-Kébir, the attack was by aircraft flying from the elderly and diminutive carrier *Hermes* accompanied by two heavy cruisers providing gunfire. The battleship *Richelieu* was hit, but was not put out of action.

An attempt to take Dakar was made in September. On 31 August 1940, 2,700 Free French troops and 4,200 British troops sailed from Liverpool under the command of Major General N. Irwin with Vice Admiral John Cunningham in command of the naval force. Accompanying the force was the leader of the Free French, General Charles de Gaulle, even though it was known that he would not be welcomed by the Vichy forces holding Dakar who would regard him as a *franc-tireur*, essentially an outlaw and outside the protection of the Geneva Conventions if taken prisoner.

Perhaps there were some grounds for optimism. The former German colony of Cameroon had been mandated to France under the Treaty of Versailles, and had tried to repudiate the armistice between France and Germany. Vichy forces had intervened, but a bloodless *coup d'état* in August had seen the French Cameroons aligned with the Free French.

Surprisingly, de Gaulle was not the main instigator of these moves to gather the French colonies around the Free French cause. Instead it was the work of a Major (later Lieutenant General) Philippe Leclerc, the *nom de guerre* of Captain Viscount Philippe de Hauteclocque, who had been among the first to rally to de Gaulle's side in London. De Gaulle had promoted Leclerc to major and sent him to rally support for the Free French in West Africa and Equatorial Africa. Leclerc had organized the successful coup in the Cameroons and then in the French Congo.

At this stage in the war, with the Vichy regime still largely an unknown quantity and the Free French still establishing themselves, British intelligence about the new Vichy regime in France was very poor, and far worse almost to the extent of being non-existent about the situation in the French African territories.

The Vichy regime was not content to accept the loss of its African colonies. Unknown to the British, as the Anglo-French force was leaving Liverpool a Vichy French cruiser squadron managed to leave its home port of Toulon in the south of France and slip out of the Mediterranean on its way to the Cameroons. The cruiser squadron was intended to return the Cameroons to Vichy control and support the Vichy authorities in Gabon, but it also put into Dakar. When the British discovered this, Churchill, realizing the dangers, wanted to recall the Dakar force.

Confusion between the naval commander in Gibraltar, Admiral Sir Dudley North, and the Admiralty in London as well as Somerville in command of Force H, had enabled the Vichy cruisers to leave the Mediterranean without being challenged. North had earned a sharp reprimand after he had protested about the action at Mers-el-Kébir, and had then been ordered to avoid incidents with the Vichy French. He allowed the French cruisers to slip through the Straits of Gibraltar believing that had the Admiralty wanted them stopped, it would have ordered Force H to intercept them. The Admiralty, on the other hand, did not know that the French ships were at sea.

By contrast, lax security on the part of the Free French in London meant that the Vichy regime soon knew that a combined Free French and British force had left Liverpool, although they did not know the destination. Before the force arrived off Dakar, on 19 September six Vichy cruisers attempted to escape from Dakar but were confronted by British warships. Two returned to Dakar, another two surrendered and were escorted to Casablanca, while the other two escaped.

Churchill had thought that the arrival of the Anglo-Free French force off Dakar would persuade those ashore to join the Free French, but the element of surprise was lost completely when de Gaulle broadcast just before the arrival, alerting the governor and the military commanders. Worse still, when the force finally arrived on 23 September, instead of finding Dakar basking in tropical sunshine, it was shrouded in fog. When Free French officers went ashore to negotiate the surrender of the garrison they were made unwelcome, with the battleship *Richelieu* opening fire as did the port's own artillery batteries, badly damaging an elderly British battleship and a cruiser.

Chapter 8

Night of Judgement

The Italian port and naval base closest to the island of Malta was at Taranto, in the instep of the heel of Italy. During the late 1930s, when Italy invaded Abyssinia, the League of Nations had considered intervention. It would have been easy to cut off Italian forces in Abyssinia by simply closing the Suez Canal to Italian shipping, which would have resulted in war in the Mediterranean with Italy fighting the United Kingdom and France. At the time, HMS *Glorious* was the British Mediterranean Fleet's aircraft carrier and one of her officers came up with the idea of an attack on the Italian fleet at Taranto. This would have been a daring raid, especially since the ship carried nothing more potent than the Fairey Seal biplane, and it was thought that the RAF flying from Malta would carry out the raid. If the carrier's aircraft, then largely manned by the RAF, had to do it, it would be one daring blow before she was withdrawn from the Mediterranean before she could be sunk by the Italians.

Intervention did not happen, largely because the French were reluctant. The United States was not a member of the League of Nations, even though it was the idea of an American president, and in any case at the time was extremely reluctant to intervene in any crisis outside of the Americas.

The plan to attack Taranto was revived after Italy entered the Second World War on the side of Germany, shortly before France surrendered.

The original plan was amended to include aircraft from two aircraft carriers: the *Eagle* which was the Mediterranean Fleet's carrier and the newly-commissioned *Illustrious* which had joined *Eagle*. A converted battleship, *Eagle* would have been withdrawn and possibly scrapped had war not intervened, but the plan to withdraw the four oldest carriers and replace them with four new fast, armoured carriers was changed, with the four elderly carriers retained in service and the order for new ships increased to six armoured carriers plus a maintenance carrier, *Ocean*. Meanwhile, a date was set for the attack on Taranto: 21 October 1940, the anniversary of Nelson's last great victory at Trafalgar in 1805.

Illustrious had worked up in the Caribbean and on her return home was almost immediately sent to reinforce the Mediterranean Fleet. Not only was an additional carrier welcome, especially since she was a fast armoured carrier of the latest design, but in addition to her Fairey Swordfish torpedo and dive-bombers, she also carried Fairey Fulmar fighters, giving the fleet modern monoplane fighter cover for the first time. Even so, the Fulmar, despite having a Rolls-Royce Merlin engine, was no Spitfire as its two-man crew made it too heavy to provide a sparkling performance. It was an improvement over the Gloster Sea Gladiator biplanes aboard *Eagle* but no match for the enemy's modern fighters. At the time, however, the Luftwaffe had still to put in an appearance over the Mediterranean and the Fulmar did not compare quite so badly with the Italian *Regia Aeronautica*'s fighters, many of which were still biplanes.

The commanding officer of *Illustrious*, Captain Denis Boyd, was summoned to the Admiralty in London to meet the First Sea Lord, Admiral of the Fleet Sir Dudley Pound. 'I want you,' Pound told him, 'in view of the desperate situation, to take *Illustrious*, through the Straits of Gibraltar and join Andrew. He needs you badly out there.' Andrew was, of course, none other than Admiral Sir Andrew Cunningham, RN, commander-in-chief of the Mediterranean Fleet.

Boyd took *Illustrious* from Scapa Flow on 23 August and after passing down the western side of the British Isles, passed through the Straits of Gibraltar on 30 August. While steaming eastwards across the Western Mediterranean, *Illustrious* had the support of Force H, while off Malta the British Mediterranean Fleet was waiting.

Code-named Operation JUDGEMENT, the plan was for a two-carrier attack on Taranto with the British Mediterranean Fleet operating with two aircraft carriers, but fate intervened; not once but on a number of occasions. A serious hangar fire aboard *Illustrious* meant that she could not be ready for the planned date of 21 October. Although the ship had lost just two of her aircraft in the fire, the rest had been thoroughly doused with water and had to be stripped down and rebuilt before any operational flying. Even more serious, *Eagle* had been attacked by Italian aircraft, which had damaged her aviation fuel system when near misses had exploded in the sea close to the ship and forced her to remain in Alexandria for repairs. Keeping *Eagle* in Alexandria was a wise precaution as both the USN and the Imperial Japanese Navy lost aircraft carriers after damage to their aviation fuel systems caused fuel vapour to spread through the ship and explode.

As a result, the date for the operation had to be put back to the next full moon, the night of 11/12 November, using just *Illustrious*. The original plan had called for thirty aircraft flying from both ships but this had to be cut to twenty-four, otherwise *Illustrious* would have had to forsake her Fulmar fighters to make room for additional Swordfish. Most of the aircraft came from the carrier's No. 815 and 819 Naval Air Squadrons, but these were complemented by aircraft from *Eagle*'s 813 and 824 NAS. For the attack the aircraft had to be modified, with the observer's cockpit, the middle one of three open cockpits on the Fairey Swordfish, taken over by a large fuel tank on the aircraft designated to act as torpedo-bombers. This meant that the observers were displaced into the rear cockpit, normally occupied by the aircraft's telegraphist/air-gunner – 'TAG' in naval jargon – which was much smaller. This was difficult as the observer had to have his bulky 'Bigsworth' board on which charts and maps were displayed during flight in a much smaller open cockpit. Although the observers in the aircraft allocated to dive-bombing could remain in their more spacious cockpit, the extra weight of the additional fuel tank meant that these aircraft also had to fly without a TAG to protect them.

Operation Judgement
The British army was still fighting a desperate battle in Greece at the time, so *Illustrious* slipped out of Alexandria using a convoy of reinforcements for Greece as cover. The ship had an escort of cruisers and destroyers. The decision to retain her fighters was fully justified when the Fulmars of No. 806 NAS shot down a number of Italian reconnaissance aircraft while on her way to Taranto, ensuring that secrecy was maintained while contributing to the squadron's impressive tally of twenty enemy aircraft while embarked aboard *Illustrious*.

Nevertheless, fate hadn't finished with Operation JUDGEMENT. On the day before the attack, a Swordfish had to ditch in the sea due to engine failure. The following day, another aircraft suffered from what appeared to be the same problem. It was discovered that one of the ship's aviation fuel tanks had become contaminated by sea water, so the entire fuel system had to be drained and then refuelled. Yet another aircraft suffered a failure shortly before the operation started, reducing the number available to twenty-one.

The raid was led by Lieutenant Commander Kenneth Williamson with Lieutenant Norman 'Blood' Scarlett-Streatfield as his observer, and consisted of two waves: the first with twelve aircraft and the second with nine. Finding their way from the flying-off point to Taranto was made much easier, despite thick cloud, when the port's anti-aircraft defences opened up, shooting at an RAF Short Sunderland flying boat on patrol from its base in Malta. The first two aircraft in the first wave were flare-droppers, followed closely by Swordfish carrying torpedoes so that they could strike at the Italian warships while these were silhouetted against the light of the flares. The second wave carried bombs and was to concentrate on shore installations, including a seaplane base and fuel storage tanks.

Everything at last seemed to be going smoothly as the aircraft prepared to take off but as the last aircraft moved out, its wing tip caught that of another, tearing the fabric and, even worse, breaking several of the ribs inside the wing. Without delay, the aircraft was taken out of service and struck down into the hangar for repairs. Given the damage, it was not ten minutes later but thirty minutes that the aircraft, L5F, could rumble down the flight deck. Few aircraft could have been repaired so quickly. A Swordfish could fly with almost all of its fabric gone, but it would have been foolhardy to have taken off with damaged ribs.

The second-wave aircraft also seemed to be fated. One lost its external fuel tank twenty minutes after taking off, and then the engine cut out and the aircraft began to lose height. While the pilot managed to restart the engine, he had no choice but to return to the ship, nursing a sickly engine, while there was still enough fuel left in the main tanks.

Ahead, the first wave had found thick cloud, an unwelcome hazard as aircraft could collide when flying in such conditions, unable to see the purple tail-light of the aircraft in front, so it was probably fortunate that most of the formation broke up at this point. For the pilots and observers in their open cockpits, it was also very cold at this time.

After so many setbacks, unknown to the attackers there had been a stroke of good fortune that morning. The Italian fleet had prepared to go to sea for a gunnery exercise, which meant that their crews had spent the morning in the tedious but essential chore of removing the torpedo nets that surrounded the ships. Before the vessels could leave port, the admiral had called off the gunnery exercise but no one had remembered to order that the nets be re-rigged. Provided the attackers could get close enough to drop their torpedoes, the Italian warships had no protection from such weapons.

At Taranto, the evening had passed with a succession of alerts followed by all-clears; this was not unusual in a wartime target area, but it had kept the anti-aircraft gunners on their toes. Around 1955 a report had been received of aircraft engines off the coast, but this was assumed to be just a reconnaissance flight, perhaps the RAF checking to see whether or not the Italian warships were at sea. Soon afterwards, just past 2000, there were more reports of aircraft engines from listening stations and alarms sounded, with anti-aircraft gun crews rushing to their posts while ashore civilians headed for the air-raid shelters. This was not the end of the alerts as more aircraft noise was picked up later, at least some of which was from a Short Sunderland patrolling the Gulf of Taranto. Later, a further alarm was sounded, but no action was taken until another twenty-five minutes had passed and it was clear that aircraft were approaching as the noises grew steadily louder.

Over Taranto
One of those charged with flare-dropping was Richard Janvin, and for him there was no need to dive down towards the harbour as the flares needed to be dropped from altitude:

> We had a grandstand view so we didn't go down to sea level. We dropped our flares at about 8,000 feet. And in fact we were fired at considerably. We had a fair amount of ack-ack fire and most extraordinary things that looked like flaming onions...one just sort of went through it and it made no great impression. One just didn't think that they would ever hit you.
>
> ...there was always fear but I think that in the same way one always had butterflies in the tummy beforehand, but when things were actually happening you didn't seem to notice the butterflies much.
>
> ...the torpedo aircraft went down and they attacked in two sub flights. The leader took his sub flight of three and attacked. And he...attacked a *Cavour*-class battleship, launched his torpedo, which hit and was shot immediately afterwards...
>
> ...we had bombs as well, and we dive-bombed some more fuel tanks, and then we returned to the carrier.

Meanwhile, leading the first wave, Williamson had swept through the barrage balloon cables, later maintaining that neither he nor Scarlett-Streatfield had noticed them even though these could easily tear the wings off an aircraft, and headed for the destroyers *Lampo* and *Fulmine*, which greeted the Swordfish with a barrage of machine-gun fire. They then turned towards the massive outline of a battleship and dropped to just 30 feet before releasing their torpedo, low enough to feel the splash as the torpedo hit the water so they may have been even lower. Torpedoes had to be dropped low; otherwise they broke upon impact with the water. There was no time to wait and watch their torpedo run towards the ship as they had to escape from the maelstrom of heavy anti-aircraft fire, but the night was soon shattered by a massive explosion. Their torpedo had found its mark and sunk the battleship *Conte di Cavour* in shallow water. As they struggled to get away, turning just above the water to escape, their Swordfish crashed, although later even Williamson and Scarlett-Streatfield were not sure whether they had been shot down or a wing had touched the water.

Many compared the scene over Taranto with the eruption of a volcano because the intense AA fire included many tracer shells, known to the British air-crew as 'flaming onions'. Italian AA gunnery seems to have been very inaccurate, but at least one benefit of so many tracer shells was that the pilots could see it coming and take evasive action.

Charles Lamb was another flare-dropper. He recalled seeing aircraft

flying into the harbour only a few feet above sea level – so low that one or two of them actually touched the water with their wheels as they sped through the harbour entrance. Nine other spidery biplanes dropped out of the night sky, appearing in a crescendo of noise in vertical dives from the slow moving glitter of the parachute flares.

The dive-bombers had the task of striking at the lightly-armoured cruisers and the destroyers, many of which were in the inner harbour (or Mar Piccolo) in which space was far tighter, while the AA fire continued to be intense. Dive-bombing has been credited with almost miraculous accuracy over the years as a result of the German blitzkrieg, although the need to pull out of the dive in time to allow the aircraft to climb away safely over the target meant that the pilot could not see his bomb hit it. Even so, while there was no doubt that it could be accurate, against well-drilled and experienced AA gunners with the nerve to withstand the attack, dive-bombing could be a very hazardous occupation. It was also not unknown for a Swordfish to have its wings ripped off in a dive, although some attribute this failing to the rudimentary wing-folding mechanism.

By contrast, the torpedo-bombers could keep low and presented a very difficult target for the AA gunners, especially if they could not depress their guns sufficiently to hit the aircraft. One advantage of a torpedo, as an American admiral put it, compared to bombs, was that 'it is much easier to get water into a ship from the bottom than from the top.' Bombs could, and often did, bounce off the heavy armour-plating on a battleship's deck or gun turrets. A bomb also had to be dropped from an altitude that was high enough for the bomb to arm itself before hitting the target.

As the second wave got into formation, the cloud cover that had been such a nuisance for the first wave had gone. While still 60 miles away from Taranto, the second-wave air-crew could see the fires started by the first wave's bombs.

An Anxious Wait

For those aboard *Illustrious*, the Flag Officer Carriers, Rear Admiral Lumley Lyster, a former commanding officer of *Glorious* at the time of the Abyssinian crisis, and the ship's commanding officer, Captain Denis Boyd, along with the rest of the ship's company had an anxious wait for news of the attack and to see how many of the lumbering Swordfish would return. Tension rose as the time for the first strike to have been completed came and then passed. There was no signal from Williamson: his aircraft had crashed and he and Scarlett-Streatfield were in the harbour waters, sheltering behind a buoy from gunfire and shrapnel. With hope fading, they waited for the return of the aircraft from the first strike, but while they waited, the signal came from the second strike: 'Attack completed'.

The fate of the first wave was unknown until the ship's radar officer, Lieutenant Schierbeck of the Royal Canadian Navy Volunteer Reserve, noticed the returning aircraft on his set. Shortly afterwards two aircraft arrived, their navigation lights switched on, glowing dimly in the dark but reassuring those waiting below. One after another, the aircraft hooked on the arrester wires, jerked abruptly in the air a few feet above the flight deck before dropping onto the deck. Unhooked, they then taxied forward to await their turn to have their wings folded before being struck down into the hangar, but almost before they stopped, excited observers jumped down from the aircraft and ran to the ready room for debriefing. Their obvious excitement told those waiting all they needed to know. The pilots, staying with their aircraft until they were struck down, were surprised to find that the

Swordfish were riddled with holes with torn fabric flapping around the fuselage and wings. One of the pilots was later able to count no fewer than seventeen shell-holes in his aircraft.

Operation JUDGEMENT had been a complete success. The RAF was suffering unsustainable losses on its bombing raids over enemy territory, but the Fleet Air Arm had done well to have lost just two aircraft, and even the crew of one of those, Williamson and Scarlett-Streatfield, had survived.

A second strike was considered, prompting one of the pilots to remark that 'even the Light Brigade was only asked to charge once!' Tired and exhausted, this thrilling news was passed to the aircrew at 0300, while their maintainers were told to 'do a major' on the aircraft. To everyone's relief, the idea was dropped. The Italians would be prepared for a further attack and, in any case, preparations were being made to move the major fleet units away from Taranto.

As *Illustrious* and her escorts re-joined the fleet in the morning, Cunningham, known for taking remarkable acts of bravery for granted as he considered it was only to be expected of naval officers, showed remarkable understatement even for him, with *Warspite* raising a hoist of flags simply signalling: '*Illustrious* manoeuvre well executed'.

Descending to the wardroom, the aircrew found that the stewards had painted a large 'Welcome Home' sign that was hanging from the deckhead; all their own idea.

One of the most spectacular aerial operations of all time, the raid never received the recognition it deserved as at the time senior officers failed to recognize just how successful it had been. When the first awards were announced, there was uproar aboard the ship and members of the ship's company tore down the notices announcing the awards as just six medals were granted, the highest being a DSC (Distinguished Service Cross) for Scarlett-Streatfield. The ship's company could be excused for believing that something better was deserved, such as a DSO or even a VC. There was no excuse for this. The morning of 12 November saw an RAF aircraft fly a reconnaissance sortie over Taranto, so the full success of the operation was soon known. Perhaps the relative lack of casualties convinced the senior officers that it had all been very easy? Cunningham was later to confess that he had not realized what a 'magnificent stroke it had been'.

Nevertheless, on the other side of the world, senior naval officers did take notice. The Imperial Japanese Navy had already war-gamed the attack on Pearl Harbor, but Taranto confirmed that their plan to destroy the United States Pacific Fleet and ensure that the large naval base of Pearl Harbor was out of action for at least six months was viable.

The Germans also noticed. They were outraged and incredulous that so much damage could have been inflicted on the *Regia Marina* while in harbour. Such damage and loss was only acceptable in a major naval battle but the Italians had three of their six battleships put out of action, although two were later to be repaired.

Taranto was what would today be described as a major 'game-changer'. The battleship was no longer the dominant ship in any large navy; that role had passed to the aircraft carrier. No one ship had ever caused so much damage as had *Illustrious* on that fateful night. Casualties at Taranto were remarkably light, with just 100 Italian deaths. This was simply because none of the warships had a magazine explode, although one Italian cruiser had a very close shave. Within eighteen months of this operation, carrier-to-carrier battles would become the accepted naval engagement with the opposing ships out of sight of one another.

Germany Takes Revenge

German shock soon passed and was replaced by anger and a desire for revenge, as well as ensuring that *Illustrious* would not remain a threat in the Mediterranean. Those who had predicted that after such a successful action the carrier would have to be removed from the Mediterranean for her own safety, and even survival, were soon proved right.

At the beginning of 1941, the Luftwaffe moved General Geissler's X Air Corps (*Fliegerkorps* X) from Poland to Sicily. Numerically much smaller than the 2,000 or more aircraft in the Italian *Regia Aeronautica*, this was an experienced and battle-hardened corps with considerable anti-shipping experience gained in the Norwegian campaign. The Luftwaffe's leaders knew about the importance of concentrating air power. X Air Corps was based in Sicily, just 60 miles from Malta, and was more powerful than the total of all Royal Air Force and Fleet Air Arm strength in the entire Mediterranean, which was far from concentrated but scattered over more than 2,000 miles from Gibraltar to Alexandria. Nevertheless, the priority was not to be Malta, which could wait until the Luftwaffe had dealt with British shipping, starting with *Illustrious*, and next would come the British Mediterranean Fleet and its base at Alexandria. There would also be mine-laying in the approaches to the Suez Canal and in the Grand Harbour at Malta.

Geissler had 150 Heinkel He 111 and Junkers Ju 88 twin-engined medium bombers as well as 150 Junkers Ju 87 Stuka dive-bombers and 50 Messerschmitt Bf 109 fighters. This force was waiting for *Illustrious* when she was sent back to the middle of the Mediterranean as part of a force to take over the convoy code-named Operation EXCESS early in 1941.

The convoy left the UK in December 1940 for Gibraltar, and as was common practice crossed the Bay of Biscay in company with a far larger convoy destined for the Cape. The two convoys divided at Gibraltar. Operation EXCESS was a small convoy of just five fast cargo ships, of which one was intended for Malta and the other four for Alexandria. On Christmas Day, the heavy cruiser *Hipper* was sighted and the convoy scattered in the Bay of Biscay. Force H left Gibraltar to provide support. In heavy seas one of the escorts, the elderly battleship *Renown*, was badly damaged and was delayed at Gibraltar for repairs. The bad weather also drove one of the cargo ships for Alexandria ashore and she had to be abandoned, but the rest of the ships reached Gibraltar safely. Nevertheless, these delays were to play a part in the events that followed in January.

On 6 January 1941, the convoy left Gibraltar for Malta and Alexandria. Force H escorted it as far as Sicily, where protection would be handed over to the British Mediterranean Fleet which had left Alexandria on 7 January. Malta-based RAF Vickers Wellington bombers also played a part in protecting the convoy, raiding Naples on 8 January, attacking the battleships *Giulio Cesare* and *Vittorio Veneto*, damaging the former and persuading the Italians to withdraw its heavy ships further north.

Handover was fixed for dawn on 10 January, which actually meant that most of Force H left the convoy at dusk the previous day, leaving the convoy protected by just the cruisers *Southampton* and *Gloucester* and two destroyers, which detached from the main force and passed with the convoy through the Sicilian Narrows in brilliant moonlight. Had the convoy been able to keep to its original schedule, it should have been passed between Force H and the Mediterranean Fleet in late December, before X Air Corps reached Sicily. The arrival of the Luftwaffe was known to the British due to the work of their signals monitoring station at Lascaris in Malta, but lacking any other information, the assumption was that the Luftwaffe was intended for attacks on Malta, while their primary target was *Illustrious*, a threat to Axis shipping in the Mediterranean.

That *Illustrious* might be vulnerable was not lost on the British, who were concerned about her safety when operating within range of enemy aircraft. Cunningham insisted that she be present with the main body of the fleet at all times because of the beneficial effect her presence had on morale aboard the other ships. He was also one of the first to realize that aircraft carriers were at their safest when surrounded by other ships that could provide protection against enemy aircraft and submarines, something that was to become apparent during the Pacific War. On the other hand, a fatal weakness of aircraft carriers at the time was the inability to receive and fly off aircraft at the same time, which meant that two carriers really needed to operate together.

The morning of 10 January passed uneventfully, but around 1230 two Italian torpedo-bombers made an unsuccessful attack on the carrier as Boyd successfully combed the torpedoes, manoeuvring his ship so that they raced past. The attack drew the patrolling Fulmar fighters down to a low level ready to fight off any other torpedo-bomber attacks. As relief Fulmars were being readied for take-off on the flight deck to relieve those already in the air, the carrier's radar spotted two large formations of aircraft approaching from the direction of Sicily. While the Fulmars were still struggling to get off the flight deck, forty-three Junkers Ju 87 Stuka dive-bombers attacked, screeching down from the sky towards *Illustrious*.

The first bomb narrowly missed the ship, the first of three near misses that day. Over the next ten minutes, no fewer than six 1,000lb bombs struck *Illustrious*. The carrier, and the others of her class, were the strongest of any operational during the Second World War, but their armoured decks were meant to resist 500lb bombs, not 1,000lb ones, while her lifts that moved the aircraft between the hangar and the flight deck were not armoured and bombs fell through these to explode on the hangar deck. The hangar deck was the ship's Achilles' heel, with aircraft parked, many fully-armed and all having at least some fuel left in their tanks. It was also the action station for all off-duty air-crew and many of them had already gathered there. The bombs exploded in this crowded space, with the effect enhanced by the armoured top, sides and bottom of the hangar deflecting their blast through the aircraft and the assembled naval airmen. Within seconds of the first bomb entering the hangar, it was a blazing inferno.

Boyd refused to order the magazines to be flooded while the bombing continued and her anti-aircraft armament was blazing away trying to protect the crippled carrier. This was the lesser evil as a bomb penetrating a magazine or rupturing a pipeline carrying aviation fuel to the aircraft or entering her aviation fuel tanks would have caused an explosion that would have torn the ship apart. By this time the carrier was a blazing, crippled wreck, unable to fly off aircraft or receive those already in the air.

It took three hours before damage control enabled the ship to head for Malta at just 17 knots, not much more than half her best speed. Those of her aircraft in the air either ditched if they were short of fuel or headed for Malta where they were welcome additions to those based ashore on the island. However, their arrival alerted those on Malta that something had gone badly wrong.

There were three air stations on Malta at the time. The aircraft from *Illustrious* headed for Hal Far, at the time an RAF base but one at which the Fleet Air Arm had what were known as 'lodging facilities', the base having been the Fleet Air Arm base on Malta while still part of the RAF. Post-war, it became RNAS Hal Far, HMS *Falcon*. There was also Luqa, another RAF station, and Ta Kali, used by the RAF but built after being selected as an airport by Imperial Airways looking ahead to the days when landplanes would relieve flying boats on the long-haul routes to the Empire.

Before *Illustrious* could reach Malta's Grand Harbour, Boyd's refusal to flood her magazines was vindicated as another twenty-five dive-bombers attacked. The ship's AA guns burst into life, and her Fulmar fighters that had reached Malta and refuelled at Hal Far returned to provide air cover.

At 2145 that evening, *Illustrious* limped into a darkened Grand Harbour, passing under the fortifications of the capital, Valletta, and on to the dockyard on the opposite side of the harbour.

The *Illustrious* Blitz

Illustrious was to spend two weeks in Malta. This was not enough time to repair her and return her to operational service. It was just enough time to make her seaworthy and habitable, so that she could escape to the United States for extensive repairs, being refitted at Norfolk, Virginia.

The first two days were overcast with low cloud that provided protection for the ships. The raids started on 13 January and became a daily occurrence with the Luftwaffe and the *Regia Aeronautica* operating jointly to give Malta what became known as 'the *Illustrious* Blitz'. At first, as the air-raid sirens sounded, the ship's company uncovered the guns and the dockyard workers and those of the crew not needed scrambled from their working places to the caves in nearby Senglea, used as air-raid shelters. Getting from far below decks in a large warship or from high up on the scaffolding surrounding her 'island' superstructure was no easy task.

On 16 January 1941 the air-raids reached a new peak for Malta, which many locals described as the first really heavy bombing raid. The Luftwaffe sent 44 Stukas, 17 Ju 88s and 10 Messerschmitt Me 110s, escorted by 10 *Regia Aeronautica* Fiat CR42 and some Macchi 200 fighters. The Stuka pilots dived through the intense anti-aircraft fire, with many diving below the high fortress walls of Valletta to deliver their bombs accurately. This first attack took just a few minutes, but was followed within fifteen minutes by another wave. *Illustrious* suffered yet another hit during the first attack, but near misses left the dockyard around her burning and cratered.

The blasts were such that aboard the carrier they swept away the ladders, scaffolding and tarpaulins shrouding the ship. The Luftwaffe had ensured that the bombs used this time were heavier as well, even though the Stuka dive-bombers struggled to lift 2,500lb bombs and took ninety minutes to reach 10,000 feet. Not only was *Illustrious* damaged by the bomb that hit her but three bombs that were near misses, falling into French Creek, flung her against the Parlatorio Wharf. All this was not without cost to the Luftwaffe which had ten aircraft shot down, with the AA fire and Malta's fighters taking an equal share of the victories and with no losses among the Malta-based Hurricanes and Fulmars. Had 2,500lb bombs been used on 10 January rather than 1,000lb bombs, the damage to the ship could have been so serious that she might not have survived.

Afterwards, all personnel not participating in the emergency repairs were taken off, even including the anti-aircraft gunners, and moved to temporary accommodation at RAF Hal Far. The removal of the AA gunners may seem strange, but ashore the army wanted to test a new box barrage system and found that the ship's AA fire got in the way.

Those sent ashore had no idea of how much progress was being made in getting the carrier ready, and it was not until they were recalled during the afternoon of 23 January that they realized she was ready to leave. After night fell, with the ship darkened and with some repair staging still hanging from her sides, she left the Grand Harbour quietly and in secret. Sir William Dobbie, the governor of Malta, was chairing a session of the Council of Malta, the island's governing body, when a servant entered and drew the blackout curtain before switching on the lights, but in the silence someone said: 'She's off – and safe.'

Illustrious reached Alexandria on 26 January, on the first stage of her passage to the United States who were still officially neutral but prepared to refit the crippled carrier at the major naval base at Norfolk, Virginia.

Many of the crew were taken off at Alexandria before she sailed through the Suez Canal on her long voyage to the United States and assigned to other ships and naval air squadrons. Those killed when she was attacked were buried at sea off Malta, between the coast at Dingli and the small uninhabited island of Fifla.

Chapter 9

Destroying Germany's Capital Ships

In marked contrast to the First World War, the *Kriegsmarine* had just two modern ocean-going battleships during the Second World War as well as two battle-cruisers. There were also the *Panzerschiffe* or 'armoured ships', otherwise known as 'pocket battleships', but these were primarily surface raiders and before long the Germans reclassified them as armoured cruisers.

Had the ambitious Plan Z been implemented in full, had there been the time, the money, the raw materials, the manpower and the fuel, Germany would have been able to send a much larger and more balanced fleet to sea. There was no prospect of a major naval engagement as at Jutland with such an imbalance between the Royal Navy and the *Kriegsmarine*, but even so, such powerful warships posed a threat. The German strategy was to wear the Royal Navy down, and even for such powerful ships commerce raiding was seen as the best strategy for it would be difficult to defend every convoy.

The loss of the *Graf Spee* after a battle with three British cruisers and her subsequent scuttling in the mouth of the River Plate has already been covered, but that left two battleships, *Bismarck* and *Tirpitz*, at large as well as the two battle-cruisers *Scharnhorst* and *Gneisenau* and the two surviving *Panzerschiffe*, *Lutzow* (previously *Deutschland*) and *Scheer*.

Even though they had lost the light cruiser *Konigsberg* to aerial attack, the Germans were still not too concerned about their major ships being attacked from the air, appreciating that a fast-moving ship on the open sea would present a difficult target for bombers, while torpedo-bombers were vulnerable to well-directed anti-aircraft fire.

One can ignore the two older battleships *Schlesien* and *Schleswig-Holstein*, both of which had been completed in 1906 and were officially classed as training ships. Neither took any real part in the Second World War.

Sink the *Bismarck*!
The first of the German battleships, *Bismarck*, would present a threat to British shipping, and this threat was renewed when her sister ship

Tirpitz entered service. *Bismarck*'s first operation, with her escorting heavy cruiser *Prinz Eugen*, was code-named Operation RHINE EXERCISE by the Germans. The two ships left Gotenhafen in Germany on 18 May 1941 under the command of Admiral Günther Lütjens. Anxious to avoid any encounters with the British Home Fleet with its wartime northern base at Scapa Flow in Orkney, Lütjens planned a route north of Iceland, but called first at Korsfjord to the south of Bergen in German-occupied Norway. This should have been an opportunity for the ship to fill her fuel tanks that had not been completely topped up before leaving Germany as a hose had given way, interrupting fuelling. Surprisingly the opportunity was not taken, which subsequently proved to be an incredible blunder.

Once at sea, the two ships were shadowed by the heavy cruisers HMS *Suffolk* and *Norfolk*, both equipped with radar that was put to good use in heavy weather. Vice Admiral Holland took the battle-cruiser *Hood*, for much of the interwar period the world's largest warship, and the new but not fully worked-up battleship *Prince of Wales* to confront the Germans. On 24 May the British intercepted the Germans and a classic naval gun battle broke out, during the course of which the *Hood*, with Holland on board, exploded with the loss of some 1,500 men, leaving just three survivors. After receiving several heavy hits from the two German ships, *Prince of Wales* was forced to break off the action. Despite these appalling setbacks, the British had managed to damage the *Bismarck*, hitting her three times and causing a serious fuel leak that forced Lütjens to attempt to head for St Nazaire in France, with Brest as an alternative. These problems were compounded by battle damage having severed the connections with the ship's forward fuel tanks.

Despite her damage, the *Prince of Wales* joined *Suffolk* and *Norfolk* in shadowing the *Bismarck* throughout 24 May. That evening, at 2230, nine Fairey Swordfish of No. 825 Naval Air Squadron from the new aircraft carrier *Victorious* found the *Bismarck* and launched a torpedo attack. As the ship increased her speed to 27 knots and zigzagged, the Swordfish launched their torpedoes so that these were heading for the battleship from different directions; at least one struck the ship, killing a warrant officer and wounding six ratings. This was followed by a brief gunnery exchange with the *Prince of Wales* before this was broken off in the fading light.

The following day Vice Admiral Somerville left Gibraltar with Force H, which included the aircraft carrier *Ark Royal* with Nos 800, 808,

818 and 820 Naval Air Squadrons embarked; the first two squadrons operated Fairey Fulmar fighters, and the last two operated Fairey Swordfish.

Contact with the *Bismarck* was lost early on 26 May, but a Royal Air Force Catalina flying boat discovered her later that day. In heavy seas, fifteen Swordfish took off from *Ark Royal* in the early afternoon, while the cruiser *Sheffield* shadowed the German ship. Unfortunately, the Swordfish crews had been briefed that the only ship they would find would be the *Bismarck*, and dropping out of the low clouds initially attacked *Sheffield* before realizing their mistake. A combination of prompt evasive action by the cruiser and problems with the magnetic detonators on their torpedoes meant that no damage was done.

Again, in low cloud and poor visibility, a further strike by fifteen Swordfish was launched from *Ark Royal* at 1915. This time the aircraft carried torpedoes with contact detonators. Directed to the target by *Sheffield*, the aircraft had to return for further directions in the poor visibility, but on the second occasion the sound of *Bismarck*'s AA fire told those aboard the British cruiser that the Swordfish had found their target. Aboard the battleship her flag captain, Captain Lindemann, attempted to zigzag once more, but two torpedoes struck the ship forward followed by one striking aft, jamming the twin rudders and forcing the ship into a continuous turn to port. All the Swordfish returned safely to the carrier.

That night, British destroyers carried out a torpedo attack, but failed to inflict any further serious damage to the stricken battleship in the dark and high seas. At daylight on 27 May, the battleships *Rodney* and *King George V* engaged the *Bismarck* and within ninety minutes she was burning fiercely. Two cruisers attacked with torpedoes, but a further strike by the Swordfish had to be abandoned because of the danger posed by heavy shellfire falling on the target from the two British battleships.

Eventually, the Germans were forced to abandon ship. Many of her crew got into the water, but the cruiser *Dorsetshire* was forced to cut short a rescue attempt when one of the survivors told his rescuers that U-boats were coming, with the result that just 115 of the 2,200 men aboard survived.

The Channel Dash

Following the loss of the *Bismarck*, not only was her erstwhile escort the heavy cruiser *Prinz Eugen* still a threat, but so too were the two battle-cruisers *Scharnhorst* and *Gneisenau*. These two ships had accounted for twenty-two merchantmen totalling 116,000 tons as they preyed upon the North Atlantic convoys in 1940. The Royal Navy had done well to force them to take refuge in Brest, along with *Prinz Eugen*. At Brest, all three ships were subjected to the attentions of RAF Bomber Command, but the size of bombs and the techniques used at that stage of the war meant that little real damage was inflicted and they were unlikely to be sunk. The *Kriegsmarine*'s natural instinct was to bring the two ships home in an exercise code-named Operation CERBERUS. Hitler intervened and ruled against taking the most obvious route around the west coast of Ireland, which would also have meant rounding the north of Scotland and passing close to the Home Fleet at Scapa Flow. Instead, Hitler ordered that the three ships were to take the shortest route, through the English Channel.

The British had expected the ships to be moved and had prepared contingency plans under the code-name Operation FULLER. These plans had recognized that the Germans might be impudent enough to take the direct route rather than head out into the Atlantic and around the British Isles.

Sadly, these plans fell apart due to obsessive secrecy, playing everything strictly according to orders, a lack of initiative, poor communication between the Admiralty and Air Ministry, poor weather and technical failures, much of which could be put down to sheer bad luck, as well as some bloody-mindedness, which could not.

A close watch was maintained on the three ships, and it was simply bad luck that the RAF failed to detect the break-out as the ships sailed from Brest on 11 February 1942 as technical failures hampered operations. When RAF fighter pilots discovered the ships by accident, one pair observed strict radio silence, obeying orders (which after all, are meant to be broken in certain cases), and wasting valuable time. The other pair radioed a warning, but they were not believed. The RAF took the view at one stage that they were not interested in reports about ships, while the Royal Navy, on hearing of a large number of German fighters circling over something in the Channel, stoutly maintained that they were not interested in reports of air activity! When someone with knowledge of the operation telephoned trying to contact another officer and bellowed 'Fuller' down the telephone, the switchboard operator simply replied: 'No one of that name here!' An officer with detailed plans had locked them away and gone on leave with the key!

Bad weather grounded RAF Coastal Command torpedo-bombers in Scotland until it was almost too late, and secrecy meant that they were armed with bombs, not torpedoes. Thick fog meant that the heavy coastal artillery batteries at Dover were unable to engage the German ships.

It fell to a detachment of six Swordfish from No. 825 NAS, based at HMS *Daedalus*, RNAS Lee-on-Solent, west of Portsmouth and not well-placed for intervention in the Straits of Dover, to face the three ships, which were escorted by a strong combat air patrol of thirty Luftwaffe fighters continuously refreshed from a force of 280 aircraft, and to tackle the Germans. Moved forward to Manston in Kent, they were put on standby on the afternoon of 12 February and were promised an escort of sixty Supermarine Spitfire fighters from RAF Fighter Command.

In the gloom of a late afternoon in winter, Lieutenant Commander Eugene Esmonde took his six aircraft into the air. A breakdown in communication meant that just ten Spitfires appeared. In poor light, they found the three ships with their escort of ten destroyers. The lumbering Swordfish were caught in a hail of fire from the fighters above and the warships below, but they pressed home their torpedo attack. Despite his aircraft being badly damaged as pieces were knocked off it in the heavy fire, Esmonde kept his aircraft in the air long enough to fire his torpedo before he crashed into the sea. His target, the *Prinz Eugen*, managed to avoid the torpedo. All six Swordfish were shot down with the loss of Esmonde and twelve others out of the eighteen naval airmen involved in the attack. Esmonde was awarded a posthumous Victoria Cross.

Instead of the planned 300 aircraft for Operation FULLER, the British then overreacted and 700 aircraft were put on standby. The only damage suffered by the German ships was when *Gneisenau* hit a mine as she approached Kiel.

Hidden Menace – The *Tirpitz*

Bismarck had one sister ship, the *Tirpitz*. If the definition of a truly successful deterrent is one that never has to be used, the *Tirpitz* can probably be counted among the most successful. This ship was never involved in a surface action and spent most of her short life sheltering in Norwegian fjords, but she was a constant thorn in the sides of the British and a very real threat to the Arctic convoys as they passed the coast of Norway on their way to Murmansk and Archangel. She suffered from the best that the Fleet Air Arm and the RAF could put into the air.

Tirpitz sailed from Wilhelmshaven for Norway on 16 January 1942. Her first operational sortie was on 9 March 1942 when Vice Admiral Ciliax took her to sea to destroy Convoy PQ12 bound for Russia. Having missed the convoy in bad weather, *Tirpitz* and her three escorting destroyers were discovered by the Royal Navy and attacked by Fairey Albacore torpedo-bombers of 817 and 832 squadrons flying from HMS *Victorious*. The ship escaped unscathed, but this attack and the earlier loss of the *Bismarck* led Hitler to order that she must stay in port if there was any risk of her encountering a British aircraft carrier.

On 4 July 1942 she moved her berth, leading the Norwegian Resistance to believe that she was being readied for sea. When the Allies received this news, it persuaded Admiral Sir Dudley Pound to order the Russia-bound convoy PQ17 to scatter, with disastrous results as merchantmen were left at the mercy of U-boats and the Luftwaffe. A more effective sortie by the ship was in late 1943, when she accompanied the battle-cruiser *Scharnhorst* and ten destroyers north to bombard shore installations at Spitzbergen on 6 September. Spitzbergen was Norwegian territory, but under a long-standing agreement that dated from Tsarist times, Russia had the rights to coal-mining and mineral extraction, something that endures to the present day.

After this she was moored in the Altenfjord where she was attacked by British midget submarines (or X-craft) on 22 September, putting her machinery and main armament out of action for six months.

In the far north of Norway, the Altenfjord was undoubtedly the safest natural harbour any ship has ever enjoyed. The steep sides of the high mountains on either side meant that attacking aircraft could not see the ship until it was too late, by which time they were in full view of her heavy anti-aircraft armament. During an attack, aircraft had to dive steeply and at all times were in real danger of flying into the sides of the mountains that surrounded the fjord. Despite these difficulties and the very real danger, the Fleet Air Arm mounted nine attacks and the RAF seven, the latter mainly flying from airfields in the Soviet Union.

The heaviest attack by the Fleet Air Arm was on 3 April 1944 in Operation TUNGSTEN, when Fairey Barracudas of Nos 827, 829, 830 and 831 Naval Air Squadrons flew from the aircraft carriers *Victorious* and *Furious* and the auxiliary or escort carriers *Fencer*, *Pursuer* and *Searcher*, to combat German fighter defences with a strong fighter cover provided by a mixed force of Supermarine Seafires, Grumman Hellcats and Wildcats* and Vought Corsairs from Nos 800, 801, 804, 880, 881, 882, 896, 1834, 1836 and 1840 NAS. Other squadrons remained close to the carriers, providing anti-submarine cover. Fourteen bombs hit the ship causing more than 400 casualties, but failed to sink her due to the maximum weight of any bomb used being no more than 500lb. Nevertheless, *Tirpitz* was out of action for another three months.

With such a large ship, so well sheltered and protected, different tactics were needed. On 15 September 1944 Avro Lancaster heavy bombers of RAF Bomber Command's 617 Squadron, the famous 'Dambusters', damaged the battleship so badly using 12,000lb 'Tallboy' bombs that she could not be repaired locally and had to be moved south to Tromsø, where bombers operating from Britain were able to reach her. On 12 November 1944 617's Lancasters attacked again, once more using 'Tallboys'. This time three of the large bombs hit the ship, causing her to capsize and trapping 1,000 members of her crew below decks.

Ironically, post-war investigation showed that she had not been taken to Tromsø for repairs, which would have needed her to go back to Wilhelmshaven, but to act as a large and supposedly unsinkable fortress!

Hitler's Favourite Ship

The battle-cruiser *Scharnhorst* had the reputation of being Hitler's favourite ship. In late December 1943, the Admiralty heard from Ultra intelligence that the battle-cruiser was on short notice to raise steam. She was well-known to the Royal Navy as one of the ships that sank the aircraft carrier *Glorious* in her retreat from Norway, and again as one of the three ships that took part in the so-called Channel Dash through the Straits of Dover.

The news about *Scharnhorst* was passed to Admiral Sir Bruce Fraser, Commander-in-Chief Home Fleet, on 21 December 1943 when he was aboard his flagship the battleship *Duke of York* as she entered Akureyri Fjord in Iceland escorted by the cruiser *Jamaica* and four destroyers. Fraser was intending to refuel the ships. The following day he assembled his captains for a conference. He intended that his squadron, to be known as Force Two, should head north at 15 knots to conserve fuel

---

*Originally known to the Fleet Air Arm as the Martlet, but on America's entry into the war names had to be standardized and so the aircraft became the Wildcat.

and if they did encounter *Scharnhorst, Jamaica* was to remain with the flagship while the destroyers were to divide into two divisions and mount a torpedo attack. *Duke of York* would open fire at a range of 7 miles, initially using star shells.

Meanwhile, part of Convoy JW55A had just arrived in the White Sea *en passage* to Archangel, while coming from Kola bound for the UK was RA55A, escorted by eight destroyers, three corvettes and a minesweeper. The balancing convoy for RA55A was JW55B with a mixed Royal Navy and Royal Canadian Navy escort, and the two convoys were due to cross off Bear Island on Christmas Day. JW55B's escort included a cruiser squadron under Rear Admiral Robert Burnett, which Fraser code-named Force One, consisting of *Belfast, Norfolk* and *Sheffield*.

Having completed refuelling, Fraser took Force Two to sea at 2300 on 23 December. Ultra decrypts had warned him that U-boats were waiting to attack JW55B and the *Scharnhorst* was on three hours' notice to sail. The Germans had discovered JW55B by accident, as the aircraft that spotted the convoy was on weather reconnaissance. Two U-boats, *U-601* and *U-716*, made contact with the convoy on 24 December, but were driven off by the escorts. At this time, Fraser was having a dummy attack made on his flagship by one of the escorting destroyers, despite the bad weather, while earlier he had exercised his force during the passage to Iceland.

Aboard the *Scharnhorst, Vizeadmiral* Kummetz had been taken ill and replaced by *Konteradmiral* (Rear Admiral) 'Achmed' Bey. Bey was not a big ship man, but instead an accomplished destroyer commander who had been flying his flag in the *Tirpitz* but was ordered to transfer to the *Scharnhorst*. He objected to plans to send the battle-cruiser to sea, instead proposing the destroyers be used; his weapon of choice. He was, in fact, told not to hazard the *Scharnhorst*, and if conditions were right he could make maximum use of destroyers. Later he was told by the head of the *Kriegsmarine, Grossadmiral* (equivalent to Admiral of the Fleet or the US Fleet Admiral) Karl Dönitz, that he was to disengage if a superior enemy force was encountered. Dönitz was, of course, not a battleship man but a successful submarine commander who had been leading Germany's U-boat fleet on the outbreak of war.

As this was happening, the two convoys passed, but both had their courses altered by Fraser, away from the Norwegian coast and towards the ice. Four of RA55A's destroyers were ordered to reinforce the escort for JW55B. RA55A later ran into extremely bad weather but reached

Loch Ewe in the west of Scotland on 1 January without trouble. The ships in JW55B were losing their formation in the bad weather, and on Christmas Day had difficulty in complying with an order to turn west, so instead the convoy reduced speed to allow the stragglers to regain the convoy.

U-601 continued to track the progress of the convoy, but the Germans remained unaware of the presence of Force Two. Although signals between Fraser and the two convoys had been intercepted, they had been misunderstood and the Germans expected the force to remain well to the west of the convoy.

Just before 1900 on Christmas Day, Bey ordered his flag captain, *Kapitän zur See* Hintze, to prepare to sail and the order was also passed to the German 4th Destroyer Flotilla. The five destroyers were ahead of the *Scharnhorst* as the force left the Altenfjord and sailed west at 25 knots. Bey was assured that no significant surface vessel was within 50 miles of JW55B, but this intelligence was out of date. Bey in turn warned naval headquarters at Kiel that the bad weather would affect the effectiveness of his destroyers, which were pitching and rolling badly in the severe weather and heavy seas.

The weather was so bad that even aboard the *Duke of York*, slightly larger than the *Scharnhorst* at 35,000 tons to 31,800 tons, the motion of the ship was uncomfortable. Despite having the heaviest armour-plating of any battleship of the day, the ship was vulnerable to bad weather because of her low hull lines that were designed to allow her 'A' turret to fire forwards. Oerlikon anti-aircraft cannon were swept off the foredeck by the waves crashing over the bows, despite steaming at a low speed, and icy sea water poured through the rivet holes from the displaced AA weapons into the mess deck below. 'A' turret, the most forward of her main armament, also suffered water ingression, with some of it even finding its way into the shell room below. Here, too, the ships that suffered most were the destroyers and, as with the Germans, they would find high speed impossible unless the sea conditions eased.

Both ships were a compromise. The *Duke of York* had been limited to 35,000 tons by the Washington Naval Treaty of 1922. She had been meant to have 16in guns, but a further treaty limited the maximum calibre to 14in. The *Scharnhorst* was originally intended to have 15in guns, but had been forced to make do with 11in as the larger calibre was not available when she was completed, and although it had always been the intention to upgrade her armament at a refit, this never happened.

Very early on 26 December, at 0130, a signal from the Admiralty based on an Ultra decrypt warned Fraser that a code-word had been flashed to the commanding officer of a battle group, suggesting that an operation was about to begin. This intelligence was ten hours old. Confirmation was not long in coming, for at 0217 the signal came: 'Emergency SCHARNHORST probably sailed 1800/25 December'. A further signal followed almost immediately, advising that a German patrol vessel had been warned at 1715 that the battle-cruiser would soon pass outward bound. Then at 0400, Fraser was told that the 'Admiralty appreciate that SCHARNHORST is now at sea'.

Unlike many of his contemporaries, Fraser was far less inclined to keep radio silence, believing that knowledge of the disposition of other fleet units and warning of impending events was far more important. The risk was that signals traffic betrayed both position and intention. Yet, on balance, he was almost certainly right, bearing in mind the number of occasions when the absence of communication had resulted in failure. Unaware that the convoy had been unable to turn west, he was concerned that he was too far away from them to help. He ordered speed to be increased to 24 knots and he then signalled Force One and the convoy to report their positions, even though this meant revealing his own. There was, in fact, no risk as the Germans either did not intercept the signals or they ignored them.

Fraser's belief in good communication was justified. He discovered that the convoy was 50 miles south of Bear Island, with Force One 150 miles from the convoy but planning to be within 30 miles of it by 0817. Force Two was 350 miles from the convoy and too far away to save it, but it would be able to stop the Germans from returning to their base. Realizing that the convoy had not turned west, Fraser ordered it to turn north. The order was received but it took time to re-transmit this to all the ships in the convoy, so the change of course was not made until 0600. Bey, meanwhile, was heading due north 100 miles from the convoy but just 90 miles from Force One. His plan was to attack the convoy as it cleared the North Cape.

The relatively narrow stretch of water between the edge of the Arctic ice cap and the enemy-held Norwegian coastline forced another compromise. At 0628 Fraser ordered JW55B to take a revised course, heading north-east to avoid being caught between the ice and the Germans.

Bey, meanwhile, who had informed Dönitz of the difficulties being suffered by his destroyers, was surprised to receive a signal telling him to leave them behind if they could not keep station and attack the convoy with his battle-cruiser alone. This was contrary to Bey's own instincts and experience.

U-boats *U-601* and *U-716* were still tailing the convoy, but had failed to notice the turn to the north. What happened as a result was that as the *Scharnhorst* approached the expected position of the convoy and her commanding officer, before sending the men to action stations, broadcast the message from Dönitz that a successful attack would relieve the situation on the Eastern Front, there was a massive anti-climax as nothing was found. Frustrated, Bey turned his force south-west and spread his destroyers at 5-mile intervals. At 0940, the northernmost destroyer passed the southernmost escort of the convoy at a distance of 15 miles, both unaware of the other's presence in the poor visibility. The weather continued to worsen and the destroyers suffered as ice built up on their decks and superstructure with frost and snow covering the optical gunnery control instruments, forcing Bey to reduce speed first to 12 knots and then to 10. The reduction in speed put the battle-cruiser at risk of attack by Allied submarines, so he ordered a zigzag course.

Force One had gone to action stations shortly before dawn, at around 0830, and shortly afterwards *Norfolk* picked up the radar echoes of a single ship 17 miles to the west-north-west. *Belfast*, Burnett's flagship, then picked up the same echoes. At 0921 the lookouts on the third cruiser, *Sheffield*, spotted a large ship on the horizon 7 miles to port. Immediately *Belfast* opened fire with star shells, but these fell short. At 0929, Burnett ordered the three ships to open fire with their main armament; 6in for *Belfast* and *Sheffield*, 8in for *Norfolk*. Force One turned to port to close the range, but this created difficulties as all three cruisers could not bring all their guns to bear on the German ship. Using radar control, *Norfolk* nevertheless succeeded in sending six broadsides towards *Scharnhorst* with three 8in shells exploding on the battle-cruiser, destroying her main radar scanner and her port high-angle gunnery director, while a fourth shell went through the upper deck without exploding.

As the shells exploded aboard *Scharnhorst*, Bey had her turn south-east and make smoke while her speed increased to 30 knots. At 0940, Force One ceased fire and gave chase, but the gap between the hunters and the pursued increased so that Burnett realized he had no chance of catching the German ship in such bad weather. Her greater size meant that she could cope more easily with the weather conditions. Burnett turned Force One back towards the convoy.

Bey was not running away but playing for time, planning to attack the convoy from the north while his destroyers attacked from the south. The destroyers' 5.9in guns were almost a match for the 6in guns of two of the British cruisers, while the destroyers could also use torpedoes against the cruisers.

Fraser ordered another change of course, ordering the convoy onto a northerly route, and used the four destroyers diverted from RA55A to reinforce the screen around Force One's cruisers. McCoy, senior officer of the convoy escort, was already offering assistance to Burnett. Shortly afterwards, Fraser ordered the convoy back onto a north-easterly course, again concerned about it becoming trapped between the ice and the Germans. Later he left the entire matter to Captain McCoy, who decided at noon to turn the convoy to the south-east. At the same time, *Belfast* found *Scharnhorst* on her radar again. Burnett's concern for the convoy was well-founded as the battle-cruiser had steamed in an arc and reappeared 40 miles to the north. At 1220, *Scharnhorst* came into sight and Burnett ordered his cruisers to open fire and his destroyers to mount a torpedo attack.

Fearing a torpedo attack, Hintze opened fire and started to take evasive action to avoid the destroyers. The range shortened to 4.5 miles while his gunnery direction officers concentrated their fire on *Norfolk*, which was not using flashless cordite so her range could be established easily. The heavy cruiser was soon taking fire, with an 11in shell knocking out her 'X' turret aft, and her radio sets were also disabled. *Sheffield* was showered with shell splinters. In return, just one British shell landed on the battle-cruiser's quarterdeck but failed to explode. Then disappearing at 2141, *Scharnhorst* raced off to the south-east. The high seas meant that the destroyers had been unable to get into position for a torpedo attack before the battle-cruiser disappeared from sight. This time the cruisers gave chase at 28 knots, using radar to maintain contact, while the destroyers did their best to keep up. By 1400 the battle-cruiser, instead of homing in on the convoy, was some 30 miles ahead of it, desperately seeking to return to the Altenfjord. Force One was now in the happy position of driving the German ship towards the 14in guns of the *Duke of York*.

Those leading Force Two were convinced that their prey had escaped and their concern deepened when they were discovered by a Blohm und Voss Bv 138 reconnaissance flying boat. They were not to know that the aircraft simply reported 'one big and several smaller ships', which raised no concerns at all. Fraser thought that if Force One could re-establish contact with *Scharnhorst*, he had no chance of finding the German ship. His real worry was that the German ship was not interested in the convoy to Russia but instead was interested in making a break-out into the Atlantic where it could menace the convoys from the United States and the fast troopships bringing men for the planned invasion of Europe. He turned Force Two to west-south-west, causing a ripple of disappointment to run through the ships as it appeared that their hopes for a decisive engagement with the German ships were about to be dashed, but almost immediately Force Two was ordered back onto its previous course as news of a fresh contact came.

At 1418, after his destroyers had failed to find the convoy, Bey ordered them to return to their base.

At 1530, aboard the ships of Force Two everyone went to action stations and they closed up for combat, closing all armoured hatches and watertight doors. They had not too long to wait. At 1618, the trace of *Scharnhorst* appeared on the *Duke of York*'s radar, and shortly after a series of smaller traces showed Force One, still in hot pursuit. At 1632 the battle-cruiser appeared on the fire-control radar at a distance of 11 miles, but Fraser decided to hold fire until the distance closed further. He ordered his destroyers to prepare for a torpedo attack, but to await the go-ahead.

At 1650, when Force Two and *Scharnhorst* were less than 7 miles apart, Fraser changed course so that all his guns and those of the escorting cruiser *Jamaica* could be brought to bear on the German ship. The 5.25in secondary armament of *Duke of York* fired four star shells that exploded above and behind *Scharnhorst*, illuminating her against the dark night sky and showing that she was completely unprepared for action, with her guns aligned fore and aft. Fraser ordered a full broadside with all ten 14in guns firing at once, with the 6in guns of *Jamaica* following. The radar-controlled guns were spot on target and the green glows of shell hits could be seen, having taken just fifteen seconds to travel the 6.8 miles separating the opposing ships. *Scharnhorst*'s 'A' turret was wrecked and Hintze swung his ship away to the north only to find himself facing the pursuing cruisers of Force One, and although *Sheffield* was dropping back with a technical problem, the other two cruisers opened fire, forcing Bey to turn eastwards.

Once again *Scharnhorst* began to outpace Force One, although her progress was reduced as Hintze swung her from side to side at intervals to allow his 'B' turret to return fire. At 1700 Force Two's destroyers were still trying to get into position for a torpedo attack. Two shells from the battle-cruiser passed harmlessly through the battleship's tripod main mast. At 1713 the destroyers were ordered to launch their torpedoes, but could not do so as they rolled and pitched in the heavy seas. *Jamaica* was also falling behind, and it looked as if the German ship would outpace the slightly slower British battleship. The only chance was a gunnery duel between the two ships but although the 14in guns of *Duke of York* could hit a target at 18 miles, the massive broadsides had damaged her gunnery radar and visual gunnery was being made difficult because of smoke coming from *Scharnhorst*.

Unknown to the British, one of *Duke of York*'s 14in shells had penetrated *Scharnhorst*'s starboard boiler room and her speed fell to 10 knots. Working quickly in appalling conditions amid escaping hot steam, her engine-room personnel reconnected the steam supply and her speed increased to 22 knots while the range opened up to 11 miles. Meanwhile, the four destroyers had closed on the battle-cruiser, and while the two on the port quarter attracted the fire of her secondary armament, the star shells from the destroyers also hid the approach of the two on her starboard side until they were 2 miles away. *Scharnhorst* turned abruptly to comb the torpedoes, but at 1852 *Scorpion* and *Stord* fired sixteen torpedoes and one of them struck the target. The change of course gave *Saumarez* and *Savage* their chance, and a dozen torpedoes were fired at the battle-cruiser with one of them wrecking a second boiler room and another distorting a propeller shaft. The speed of the wounded ship fell again to 10 knots.

The four destroyers withdrew, having taken battle damage and suffered casualties. The *Duke of York*'s gunnery radar had by this time been repaired and *Jamaica* was fast catching up. Force Two now opened fire with both ships quickly finding the range and, steaming past the battle-cruiser, repeatedly hit her with armour-piercing shells before *Jamaica* fell out of line to mount a torpedo attack as *Scharnhorst* slowed and her guns fell silent. As this happened, Force One emerged onto the scene with both *Belfast* and *Norfolk* prepared for a torpedo attack which came at 1918, while their destroyers also attacked, sending two torpedoes into the port side of the German ship where the bilges were already exposed.

Scharnhorst was by this time listing heavily to port, with her crew mustered on deck ready to abandon ship. Hintze ordered them to slide into the water on the port side and remember to inflate their life-jackets.

No one on the British ships saw the end of *Scharnhorst* as smoke obscured the view. When a radar operator reported that the blip was fading, he was told to retune his set. More than half an hour passed before *Belfast* confirmed that *Scharnhorst* had indeed been sunk. A single raft contained a few frozen survivors. One destroyer picked up 30 and another picked up 6 but 1,767 officers and men lost their lives, including the rear admiral and his flag captain. The loss of so many suggests that there must have been a sudden capsizing that trapped many on the port side, while others would have perished in the icy cold seas, especially those men from the engine and boiler rooms who would have been lightly clad, wearing just boiler suits.

Meanwhile, Convoy JW55B continued unmolested and reached Murmansk on 27 December and the Archangel portion reached that port safely on 29 December. The U-boats that had been shadowing were sent on a fruitless quest for survivors from *Scharnhorst*.

Famous for reputedly being Hitler's favourite ship, *Scharnhorst* had a sister ship, *Gneisenau*. She had been damaged during an air-raid on Kiel during the night of 26/27 February 1942 and in April she was moved to Gotenhafen for decommissioning. She was scuttled there shortly before the end of the war.

The Pocket Battleships

Re-classed as heavy cruisers in February 1940, the pocket battleships were officially *Panzerchiffe*, armoured ships. These had diesel engines and were intended to have a long range and operate as surface raiders, even though officially they were replacements for the elderly coastal battleships that the Germans were allowed to keep after the Treaty of Versailles.

The fate of the *Graf Spee* has already been covered.

Deutschland was renamed *Lutzow* in November 1939, for reasons already given. She was sunk in shallow water by an air-raid while lying at anchor near Swinemünde on 16 April 1945 but remained in action using her guns against advancing land forces until 28 April, after which a serious fire caused severe damage and put her out of action.

Admiral Scheer capsized on 10 April 1945 during an air-raid on Kiel.

Chapter 10

Battle of the Atlantic

Most naval engagements are over in a few hours and just a few might be spread over two or even three days, but the longest-running naval battle of the Second World War lasted for several years: the Battle of the Atlantic. Had the battle been lost, the Second World War would have been lost. Officially, the Battle of the Atlantic lasted from July 1940 to May 1945, but the first casualty on the North Atlantic occurred on the day war was declared. As mentioned earlier, the 13,500-ton liner *Athenia* was torpedoed off the Hebrides (see Chapter 5), the U-boat commander having ignored the requirements of the Hague Convention to surface and give warning of his intentions. This was just the start of the U-boat campaign. On 5 and 6 September another three British merchantmen were sunk off the coast of Spain, two of them going down with all hands.

The reason for the start of the Battle of the Atlantic being given as July 1940 was that by this time France had surrendered and the *Kriegsmarine* had bases on the Atlantic coast of France, such as at Brest and St Nazaire. This avoided the long and hazardous passage of U-boats around the north of Scotland and the west of Ireland, which not only meant that they were under threat of detection but also took far more time and fuel. It was also the case that on the outbreak of war in 1939 the *Kriegsmarine* had just fifty-nine U-boats, of which only thirty-five were suitable for longer-range operations.

There was another problem that delayed the start of the full force of the German U-boat onslaught. At first the *Kriegsmarine* suffered problems with its torpedoes under combat conditions. This surprises many, given the German reputation for engineering excellence and thoroughness, but it may have been another example of the so-called 'Führer system' at work in which intrigue was fundamental and any admission of weakness, underachievement or failure was damning.

There was certainly no shortage of targets, with the British Merchant Marine still the world's largest with 21 million tons of shipping; this was about the same as in 1914 but as the ships were generally bigger, there were fewer of them. On the eve of war, some 3 million tons of shipping were taken up for use by the armed forces, mainly to supply the Royal Navy and British Army, but also including a number 'taken up from trade' for naval use. These varied between passenger liners being converted to armed merchant cruisers down through minesweeping and anti-submarine trawlers, as well as small motor fishing vessels being put on the more humble harbour duties. Further allocations had to be made to cover the needs of the countries of the British Empire, so in the end the Merchant Navy had just 15.5 million tons of shipping available for civilian uses, a reduction of about a quarter.

However, it wasn't all loss. As Norway, Denmark and The Netherlands were overrun, those ships from their sizeable merchant fleets away from home often opted to head for a British port rather than face putting into what had become occupied territory. These remained legally owned as before, but found they were working alongside the British Merchant Navy. German and Italian ships caught on the outbreak of war in British or French ports were seized, and those that fell into British hands were expropriated by the British government which passed them to British ship-owners to manage, crew and operate, with names prefixed with 'Empire'. The same system was used for merchant ships built at the cost of the British government or provided from the United States under Lend-Lease, again with names prefixed by 'Empire'.

The Battle of the Atlantic can be divided into four distinct phases. The first ran from the fall of France in June 1940 to the entry of the United States into the war after the Japanese attack on the United States Pacific Fleet at Pearl Harbor. The second phase was the period from December 1941 to March 1943 when German U-boats seemed to dominate the North Atlantic, with their numbers increasing more quickly than the Allies could destroy them. In April and May 1943 came the MAC ships and the escort carriers, which combined to inflict losses on the U-boats that were so heavy as to prove unsustainable and led to their temporary withdrawal. Shortly afterwards came the fourth phase from June 1943 to May 1945 with the closure of the 'Atlantic Gap' using escort carriers and ever longer-range maritime-reconnaissance aircraft and continued losses by the U-boats. By this time too, the Allies had sufficient intelligence to be able to send small groups of warships, usually including an escort carrier, to hunt down the U-boat 'wolf packs'.

Overall, the war saw 785 U-boats sunk, while in the North Atlantic alone, no fewer than 2,232 ships totalling 11,899,732 tons were lost.

The Battle of the Atlantic was largely fought by German U-boats rather than surface raiders. Surface raiders, usually armed merchant ships with their guns concealed, were more likely to be found in the South Atlantic, the Indian Ocean and the Pacific, far from Germany and often far from British bases. These ships were often able to make use of neutral ports to refuel and obtain food.

At the outset the Germans had been planning to use surface raiders and, aware that a major confrontation with the Royal Navy could not be won, planned to use their battleships, battle-cruisers, *Panzerschiffe* and heavy cruisers against British merchant shipping, even when in convoy. The new battleship *Bismarck* and her heavy cruiser escort *Prinz Eugen* were intended to mount just such an offensive in the mission code-named Operation RHINE EXERCISE, but the early despatch of *Bismarck* by the Royal Navy ended this prematurely. Later, the two battle-cruisers *Scharnhorst* and *Gneisenau* together with *Prinz Eugen* presented a constant threat while they remained in harbour at Brest, with a considerable effort by RAF Bomber Command to try to sink these ships, with little success, until finally Hitler ordered them home in the Channel Dash of February 1942 that saw them removed from the scene. The other major German battleship, *Tirpitz*, posed a similar threat to the Arctic convoys to Russia while moored in a Norwegian fjord.

The fall of France and the German occupation of Denmark and Norway meant that the Germans did not have to depend on sea power alone to attack Allied shipping. Long-range Junkers and Focke-Wulf maritime-reconnaissance aircraft operated from bases along the Bay of Biscay coast and from bases in Norway. Others flew from Norway to France, or vice versa, along the west of Ireland, posing a threat to convoys as they approached Ireland or entered the Western Approaches.

Land-based maritime-reconnaissance aircraft were among the most effective anti-submarine measures during the Second World War, but the aircraft of the day had limited endurance. Despite successful experiments by the British with air-to-air or in-flight refuelling in the late 1930s, this had been for commercial flying boats and was not available for military operations. The result was that there was a significant stretch of the North Atlantic over which land-based air cover could not be provided until late in the war. This was the celebrated Atlantic Gap, also sometimes referred to as the 'Black Gap'. The best aircraft for longer-range maritime reconnaissance was the Consolidated B-24 Liberator, but this aircraft was also needed by the United States

Army Air Force for operations from India over Burma and beyond to attack Japanese forces in China, so inter-service demand and rivalry for deliveries of this aircraft were intense.

Even before the United States entered the war, the Royal Navy was not entirely on its own. While the United States was officially neutral from the outbreak of war in Europe, from September 1941 American warships began to escort convoys to the mid-ocean handover point, officially to ensure that neutral shipping was not engaged by German submarines. Inevitably a U-boat eventually attacked an American warship when the destroyer USS *Greer* found a German torpedo heading for it on 4 September while *en passage* from the United States to Iceland carrying mail and passengers. In response the destroyer attacked with depth-charges, but although a second torpedo was fired, neither the destroyer nor the U-boat suffered damage.

Once the United States entered the war, the Royal Navy made facilities available to the United States Navy at Londonderry in Northern Ireland. The new commander of the USN in the North Atlantic, Admiral Ernest King, had remarked on taking up his post that it was like being given a big slice of bread with 'damn little butter', referring to the shortage of ships. After the battleships USS *Idaho*, *Mississippi* and *New Mexico* had been transferred from the Pacific with the aircraft carrier *Yorktown* to the Atlantic, US President Franklin Roosevelt asked King how he liked the butter he was getting. Back came the reply: 'The butter's fine, but you keep giving me more bread.'

By July 1940, when the Battle of the Atlantic really began in earnest, the Royal Navy had already lost two of its aircraft carriers, the sisters *Courageous* and *Glorious*. Two ships of dated design, these were nevertheless among the most modern of the British carriers with only the new *Ark Royal* and even newer *Illustrious*, which was still being worked up in the Caribbean, being more up-to-date. The loss of *Courageous* to torpedoes from *U-29* on 17 September 1939 while she was 'trailing her cloak' hunting for submarines was especially wasteful. *Glorious* was sunk by gunfire from the German battle-cruisers *Scharnhorst* and *Gneisenau* during the withdrawal from Norway. Both ships would have been more usefully employed escorting convoys.

The First Phase
In 1940 from the end of August to the end of September, U-boats sank twenty-two ships from four convoys, a loss of 113,000 tons of shipping. At the beginning of this period, between 29 August and 2 September,

six U-boats sank ten ships totalling 40,000 tons from three convoys, HX66, OA204 and OB205. Later in September, five U-boats sank twelve ships totalling 73,000 tons from Convoy HX72 that had set sail from the Canadian port of Halifax, Nova Scotia. This was just the start.

There were two main hunting grounds of the U-boats. The first was the Atlantic Gap, that part of the mid-Atlantic out of reach of shore-based maritime-reconnaissance aircraft. The main targets in this vast area were not only the convoys running from the United States and Canada to the British Isles, but also those to and from the Caribbean, some of which would have used the Panama Canal to get to and from the Pacific and the West Coast of the United States and Canada. The other was the Bay of Biscay and the Atlantic off the coast of Portugal. This was the route for convoys to and from Gibraltar, which was the dividing point for convoys that would either head east across the Mediterranean or continue south to the Cape of Good Hope. Usually the convoys would sail as one as far as Gibraltar and then actually divide rather than sending separate convoys. As the situation in the Mediterranean grew worse, virtually cutting off Malta, even British forces in Egypt would be supplied via the Cape and the Suez Canal, which was no longer the short-cut to India, what was then always described as the Persian Gulf, and to Australia but the end of a roundabout and very much extended route to the Eastern Mediterranean and North Africa.

The situation grew worse as 1940 drew to a close. In October in the North Channel between Great Britain and Ireland, during the four days from 17 to 20 October nine U-boats found the convoys SC7 and HX79 with a total of seventy-nine ships. Between them, the U-boats sank no fewer than thirty-two of the vessels with a combined tonnage of 155,000 tons, and would no doubt have sunk many more but for the fact that they ran out of torpedoes. Just a few days later on 23 October two U-boats accounted for twelve ships, totalling 48,000 tons, from convoys SC11 and OB244. A further nine ships with a total tonnage of 53,000 tons were sunk from Convoy HX90 in December. This was in a year when the average number of U-boats at sea each day actually in operational zones was around a dozen. It was some time before the *Kriegsmarine* could have up to 100 U-boats patrolling daily.

The U-boats were not the only predators. Armed and camouflaged merchantmen were deployed as auxiliary cruisers as early as April 1940, with *Atlantis, Orion, Pingiun, Thor* and *Widder* patrolling around Britain's trade routes. In August, the *Komet* managed to reach the Pacific by sailing north of Siberia. As mentioned earlier, these were not auxiliary cruisers in the sense used by the British, who used fast merchantmen armed to act as convoy escorts. Instead the German ships were disguised to appear as true merchantmen, often wearing the flags of neutral countries, and only displayed their true colours and their intent at the last minute, making their operations more akin to piracy. As the second winter of the Second World War drew on, the battle-cruisers *Scharnhorst* and *Gneisenau* and the heavy cruiser *Hipper* operated in the Atlantic, while the heavy cruiser *Admiral Scheer*, earlier classified as a *Panzerschiff*, operated in the Atlantic and Indian oceans, and together they accounted for forty-nine ships totalling 271,000 tons between October and March.

British and French losses amounted to 509,320 tons during the last four months of 1939, all of which were in the Atlantic or the North Sea. In 1940, the total rose to 2,451,663 tons in the Atlantic and the North Sea, with a further 13,170 tons in the Mediterranean and 12,223 tons in the Indian Ocean. Most of the North Sea was to be closed to convoys as a result of Germany holding the entire coastline of mainland Europe from the North Cape to the Bay of Biscay. The two worst months of 1940 were June, with 356,937 tons lost in the Atlantic, 8,029 tons in the Mediterranean and 8,215 tons in the Indian Ocean, and October, when 361,459 tons were lost in the Atlantic. This meant that the total losses for the year were almost a sixth of the available tonnage of British merchant shipping, although this figure would have been boosted by new construction and by ships that had fled from the occupied territories or had diverted to British ports on their homeward voyages. Fortunately, among the occupied nations, both Norway and The Netherlands had considerable tonnages of merchant shipping. Losses reached a new monthly peak in May 1941 when 363,073 tons were lost in the Atlantic, but the overall total in the Atlantic fell to 2,214,408 tons. Unfortunately, the losses in the Mediterranean that year rose to 54,200 tons, while 40,666 tons were lost in the Pacific at the end of the year when Japan entered the war. The figure for the Indian Ocean fell to 9,161 tons.

The escort carrier, known to the Royal Navy as the auxiliary carrier, first appeared with Convoy HG76 which sailed from Gibraltar to the UK on 14 December 1941 with thirty-two ships including the CAM-ship* *Darwin*, the auxiliary carrier *Audacity*, two destroyers, four sloops

---

*Catapult-armed merchant ship, with a single Sea Hurricane fighter, which of course could only be used once.

and nine corvettes. Together these comprised the 36th Escort Group, commanded by the then Commander (later Captain) F.J. 'Johnny' Walker, RN, who was later awarded the VC. Walker became the Royal Navy's leading anti-submarine commander and on this occasion he was in the sloop *Stork*. Facing the convoy were the seven U-boats of the *Seerauder* Group, guided to the convoy by the Focke-Wulf Fw 200 Condors of *IKG40* based on Bordeaux.

At dusk on 15 December, the most southerly of the U-boats discovered the convoy and was soon joined by a second boat. The following morning *U-131* was attacked by Grumman Wildcats flying from *Audacity*, before being attacked and sunk by destroyers. On 17 December the destroyer *Stanley* was torpedoed and blown up by *U-434*, but in the frantic counter-attack led by Walker, the submarine was depth-charged and forced to the surface before being rammed and then sunk by further depth-charges. In the meantime other escorts found and sunk *U-567* commanded by Endrass, one of Germany's most experienced U-boat commanders. Despite this, the escorts themselves suffered a bitter blow on 20 December when *U-751* torpedoed and sank *Audacity*. A merchantman was also sunk. Nevertheless, four out of the seven U-boats were sunk.

That the British still had much to learn about the use of aircraft with convoys was conveyed by the fact that *Audacity* had no anti-submarine aircraft aboard. Her limited aircraft complement consisted solely of fighters although, of course, this could be for fear of ships being attacked by the Fw 200 or other shore-based German aircraft.

The Second Phase
The entry of the United States into the Second World War was the most dramatic move of the entire conflict, completely changing the strategic position. Oddly, while the Japanese attacked the US Pacific Fleet at Pearl Harbor without any declaration of war, forcing the United States to declare war on Japan, it was Germany that then declared war on the United States. How much longer the USA would have remained neutral in the European war had Germany not done so is difficult to say, but these moves formalized the unofficial alliance between the United Kingdom and the United States. The vital Lend-Lease supplies of military equipment including ships and aircraft continued, but it also included what some have described as 'reverse lend-lease' with corvettes fitted with ASDIC transferred from the Royal Navy and Royal

Canadian Navy to the United States Navy. The Americans also had the right to use British bases in the Caribbean.

The Germans were anxious to strike while the United States Navy was still relatively weak, with its available resources divided between the Atlantic and the Pacific. On 13 January 1942 the *Kriegsmarine* launched Operation *PAUKENSCHLAG* (Operation KETTLEDRUM BEAT) against American shipping. Between January and March, they accounted for 1.2 million tons of Allied shipping in the Atlantic, with losses reaching a monthly total of 628,074 tons in June. The total for the year was to be 5,366,973 tons for the Atlantic alone. This was in addition to losses in the Barents Sea of 234,158 tons, while losses in the Mediterranean almost quadrupled to 193,644 tons as the people of Malta and the British garrison on the island began to starve. There were also 666,003 tons lost in the Indian Ocean, but the losses in the Pacific were relatively modest at 85,494 tons, largely because so much of the land in that ocean was occupied by the Japanese. For the German submariners, this was their 'happy time'. The losses were made worse by the slowness in introducing coastal convoys off the East Coast of the United States for ships heading for the transatlantic convoy assembly points and the lack of a blackout in American East Coast cities; until the latter was done, ships were silhouetted against the bright background.

Nevertheless, the United States Navy was to bounce back quickly, especially in the Pacific where the Imperial Japanese Navy was put on the defensive within six months of the start of the war in the Pacific.

Another factor that drove the huge losses was the decision taken during the winter of 1941–42 that the Allies should send convoys to the Soviet Union. There were three routes to the USSR, of which the most famous was the Arctic convoy route that ran off the coast of Norway and round the North Cape to Archangel and Murmansk, mainly carrying supplies from the UK but also including war matériel from the United States, so many of these convoys were routed via Iceland. The other two routes included the main one from the United States via the South Atlantic and the Indian Ocean to the Gulf with consignments offloaded in Iran for onward transport to the USSR, while there was also the direct route from the West Coast of the USA and Canada to Vladivostok. However, the latter was the least important because of the severe limitations on the Trans-Siberian Railway, with many bottlenecks and much single-line working as well as disruption during the winter weather.

From September 1942 until the following March, the U-boats were at their most prolific in the North Atlantic with more than 100 in the area at any one time. Hitler had by this time decided that the German surface fleet was a waste of time and available resources, so the U-boats had the task of fulfilling Germany's maritime strategy on their own. It was even planned that the U-boats should undertake major battles against the convoys. Even before Hitler had become disappointed with his surface fleet, many in the *Kriegsmarine* had already come to the conclusion that with the available resources of manpower, fuel and raw materials, a massive programme of U-boat construction was the only element of Plan Z that could be fulfilled.

However, even as the U-boat force reached its peak, its decline was in sight. The appearance of the MAC-ships and the escort carriers lay behind the complete reversal in the fortunes of the submariners. As Allied successes against the U-boats started to rise, the Germans did not simply lose the submarines, they lost the U-boat commanders as well, bringing about a shortage of experienced personnel that was even more serious than the loss of the U-boats.

On 5 March 1943 Convoy SC122 left New York comprising more than fifty merchantmen, followed by a faster convoy, HX229, which left New York with forty ships on 8 March and was scheduled to overtake SC122 on 20 March. The faster-moving HX229 was first attacked on 16 March by up to forty U-boats and over two days lost ten ships. On 17 March the slower convoy, SC122, was also attacked. Over the next few days, the two convoys lost twenty-one ships totalling 141,000 tons for the loss of one U-boat.

Some trace the start of the demise of the U-boats to this great convoy battle of 16–20 March 1943 when a massive fleet of more than 100 submarines was deployed. Most of these U-boats had been at sea for some time without finding and sinking a single Allied merchantman. The entire U-boat campaign, despite its undoubted successes, suffered from exactly the same kind of missed opportunities that had bedevilled the surface fleet from the start of the war. Poor air-sea co-ordination and co-operation was one reason for this, but poor strategy and bad tactics were also to blame. One authority on the wartime German navy, Jak Mallman Showell, maintains that two-thirds of the U-boat fleet, some 800 craft, never got within reach of the enemy and that half of those that did only attacked four or fewer Allied ships. Most of the Allied losses were down to just 131 U-boats or, to be more accurate, their commanders.

On 23 March, just a few days after the heavy losses suffered by convoys SC122 and HX229, another convoy left Canada for the UK but despite repeated attacks by U-boats, crossed safely to arrive on 8 April without a single ship being lost. This was despite the Atlantic Gap still being some 500 miles wide.

The Third Phase
While the change in the fortunes of the convoys and the U-boats occurred over a fairly short period of time, it did not happen overnight. In fact what is generally regarded as the third phase in the Battle of the Atlantic started with two successes for the U-boats. Between 4 and 7 April, fifteen U-boats sank six ships from convoy HX231, but at the cost of two U-boats lost. Then there was the outstanding success of Henke in *U-515*, who showed that there were still opportunities for the most skilful and daring U-boat commanders. On 30 April and 1 May *U-515* sank seven ships totalling 43,000 tons off Freetown in West Africa using just seven torpedoes, but increasingly this type of success was to become much less common. This was borne out by the fact that in 1940, each U-boat on patrol sank an average of six merchantmen per month, but by 1942–43 on average it took more than two U-boats to sink a single merchantman.

From May 1943 onwards, the U-boats were on the defensive fighting for their survival. As early as May, forty U-boats were lost, many of them to aerial attack, with others the result of collaboration between aircraft and surface ships. Technical innovation was not sufficient to keep the U-boats ahead of the Allies and their anti-submarine measures. Snorkels were introduced to enable U-boats to recharge their batteries without surfacing and even to run under water using their diesel engines. Yet, radar fitted to aircraft could detect a snorkel or a periscope. U-boats began to appear with heavier anti-aircraft armament and while this could often be very effective in dealing with anti-submarine aircraft, it often reduced the speed of the U-boat when submerged. It did take some nerve on the part of the pilot of an anti-submarine aircraft to attack a U-boat on the surface fitted with powerful anti-aircraft guns. Some U-boat commanders opted to stay surfaced and engage an attacking aircraft, but for many it was a question of how quickly they could dive, known to them as the 'Battle of the Seconds'. There were cases of a U-boat inflicting fatal damage on a maritime-reconnaissance aircraft, but the odds tended to be on the side of the aircraft as the U-boat anti-aircraft armament was still too light and the firing platform was too unstable in a heavy North Atlantic swell.

The Atlantic Gap was also being closed with the appearance of the MAC-ships and the escort carriers, forcing the U-boats to abandon their pack tactics. The use of the pack or wolf pack was in fact a weakness as it required U-boat commanders to keep in touch with their headquarters and it became possible not just to trace the radio signals, but with the German Enigma codes broken, their intentions could also be understood. In August 1942 fifty Allied merchantmen were lost in the North Atlantic, but between September 1943 and May 1944 just sixteen were lost, and from May 1944 to VE-Day a year later, only another five.

Life aboard the escort carriers and the MAC-ships was hard and often uncomfortable. Aircrew spent hours in the ready room aboard the ships, which had just a single screw and were therefore more likely to roll, plodding at convoy speed across the North Atlantic. They found ways of occupying their time. One visitor, coming across aircrew squatting on the deck in the ready room playing dice or poker, recalls that they looked 'like a lot of thugs out of *The Rake's Progress* gambling in a graveyard'.

Mac-Ships and the Birth of Dutch Naval Aviation

Intended as an interim measure while the escort carriers made their appearance, the CAM-ships and MAC-ships were both merchant vessels rather than warships. While the escort carriers were at first conversions from cargo ships and later built on merchant hulls so that they could be converted to merchant ships after the war ended, they were always warships and commissioned into the United States Navy or Royal Navy.

The CAM-ships were catapult-armed merchant ships, with a single Hawker Sea Hurricane fighter that could be catapulted off when necessary. Most were manned by RAF pilots as deck-landing experience was not needed, although there were some Fleet Air Arm pilots as well. The fighter could only be used once as it had to be ditched and the pilot parachuted into the sea, hoping to be picked up by one of the convoy escorts. The big weakness was that, with an aircraft that could only be used once, convoy commodores were always reluctant to order the aircraft into the air in case a greater need for it might occur later.

The MAC-ships were merchant aircraft carriers. These were either oil tankers or grain carriers with a wooden flight deck laid over their cargo accommodation and the bridge offset to starboard to provide an island. As with the CAM-ships, they were owned and operated by merchant shipping companies and manned by merchant seamen, while the maintainers and aircrew were naval personnel. The reason why these ships were chosen was that neither had deck hatches to open to load or discharge their cargo.

No fighters were carried as the ships were too small and the flight decks too short for such high-performance aircraft; even tankers were very much smaller at the time than is the case today. The tankers could carry three Fairey Swordfish for anti-submarine patrols, while the grain carriers could carry four as the aft hold was used as a makeshift hangar, with the aircraft craned down, so that maintenance could take place in shelter. The grain ships also had a shorter flight deck at 413 to 424 feet compared with the 460 feet of the tankers, but the flight deck was always 62 feet wide.

The first MAC-ships did not appear until early 1943, by which time escort carriers were arriving in some numbers from the United States and the British had even converted a few captured enemy ships before this. Such improvised ships could have been available from the early days of the war but too few people in the Admiralty believed the concept would work, with aircraft expected to take off and land aboard ships with a 12-knot maximum speed. The Director of Naval Construction didn't help either, expecting design and development to take a year. Both the Admiralty and the Ministry of War Transport also thought that operations over a flight deck above several thousand gallons of highly flammable fuel would be too risky.

It was Sir James Lithgow, Director of Merchant Shipbuilding, who broke the impasse. Instead of taking a year to design the ships, he sketched out a rough design on the back of an envelope. 'I have two ships about to be built which can be converted without undue delay,' he claimed, adding with some perception: 'I am prepared to do this provided I am not interfered with by the Admiralty.'

The work on converting the first two MAC-ships started in June 1942 and by October a further ten were being converted. The first two were the *Empire MacAlpine** and *Empire MacAndrew,* but the plan to have a full thirty-two ships converted was scaled back to nineteen as the more capable escort carriers began to arrive.

---

*The 'Empire' prefix indicates that the ships were in government ownership, but managed by commercial ship-owners with a Merchant Navy crew.

Two naval air squadrons were assigned to the MAC-ships, Nos 836 and 860, based at RNAS Maydown, HMS *Shrike*, near Londonderry in Northern Ireland. Each MAC-ship flight was assigned a lettered suffix, so that those of No. 836 NAS were 836A, 836B and so on. At one time, No. 836 had ninety-two aircraft, a record for a naval air squadron and beating even the sixty-three operated by No. 700 NAS which covered the seaplanes flown off battleships and cruisers. Unlike 700, which was an administrative convenience without a commanding officer, 836 had a commanding officer, Ransford Slater, but he still only held the rank of lieutenant commander, equivalent to a squadron leader in the RAF or a major in the army. In the RAF he would almost certainly have been at least a wing commander, given the number of aircraft and the fact that each had a three-man crew. The smaller squadron, No. 860, was manned by members of the Royal Netherlands Navy who operated from two Dutch MAC-ships, MV *Acavus* and *Gadila*.

From March 1943 until VE-Day, MAC-ships made 323 crossings of the North Atlantic escorting 217 convoys, of which just one was successfully attacked by U-boats. The Swordfish made 4,177 patrols, an average of thirteen per crossing. There is no record of a successful attack on a U-boat by a Swordfish operating from a MAC-ship, but no ship was lost while in a convoy with a MAC-ship present and no MAC-ship was sunk.

With its experience of operating from the MAC-ships, the Royal Netherlands Navy introduced its own naval aviation, with the Royal Navy donating the escort carrier HMS *Nairana*, which the Dutch renamed *Karel Doorman* after the admiral who commanded the ABDA (American, British, Dutch, Australian) fleet cobbled together to face the Japanese in the Battle of the Java Sea in 1942. *Nairana* was one of the rare British escort carrier conversions and slightly larger than average.

The Birth Of Canadian Naval Aviation

The convoy war proved that air power at sea was essential. Plans for a Royal Canadian Naval Air Service dated from 1918 but as one Canadian historian aptly put it, were 'stillborn'. After the First World War, Admiral of the Fleet Lord Jellicoe had drawn up plans for a Canadian fleet that would have included aircraft carriers, but the Royal Canadian Navy struggled to survive in the immediate post-war years and even the Royal Canadian Air Force had a prolonged and difficult birth.

Nevertheless, war concentrates minds wonderfully and by 1942 it had become obvious that any navy that wished to engage the enemy on the high seas or in distant waters had to have its own aviation. Many Canadians had joined the Royal Navy's Fleet Air Arm and the numbers increased in December 1942 when the British Admiralty called for more Canadians to train as naval aviators while remaining in the Royal Canadian Navy. This seems like a cheeky means of a hard-pressed Imperial power asking the Canadian taxpayer to pay for those of their fellow countrymen assigned to the Fleet Air Arm, but it was also a result of none of the dominions taking defence seriously between the two world wars, leaving much to the United Kingdom, and the Canadians were if anything by far the worst offenders.

This is not to say that the Royal Canadian Navy was unco-operative and failed to appreciate the need for naval aviation. Captain Nelson Lay, RCN, Director of Operations, and Captain Harry de Wolf, Director of Naval Plans, pressed Vice Admiral (later Admiral) P.W. Nelles, Chief of the Canadian Naval Staff, to send senior officers to obtain up-to-date information on naval air operations, in particular regarding escort carriers. They also proposed that Canada should have four escort carriers, one for each of the four escort groups provided by Canadian ships in the Atlantic.

De Wolf was posted to command a warship shortly afterwards and it was not until spring 1943 that Lay was able to visit both the United States and the United Kingdom, spending two weeks with the USN and two months with the Royal Navy. The bias towards the Royal Navy was a reflection of the prevailing attitude at the time, when the 'British' model was usually the one adopted by the dominions rather than the 'American' one. Lay reported in August, advocating a Royal Canadian Naval Air Service modelled on the Fleet Air Arm. By this time, he was proposing two escort carriers be obtained to be manned by RCN personnel, while shore-based, long-range maritime reconnaissance remained the preserve of the Royal Canadian Air Force, again following British rather than American practice. One difference was that Lay suggested shore bases should be maintained and supported by the RCAF.

Two escort carriers were soon allocated, *Nabob* and *Puncher*, commissioned in September 1943 and February 1944 respectively. Built at Seattle, these were moved to Vancouver in British Columbia for the modifications that the Royal Navy regarded as so necessary but that so irritated the Americans,* including additional watertight subdivisions.

Surprisingly, there were differences even at this stage between the Royal Navy and the Royal Canadian Navy. The latter saw the ships as being employed on anti-submarine operations supporting convoy escort groups, but the former wanted the ships to be strike carriers, not least so that Canada did not appear to be receiving Lend-Lease aid from the United States. The ships were put on the Royal Navy's strength and were commissioned as 'HMS' rather than 'HMCS', being 'His Majesty's Ships' rather than his Canadian ones! Captain Lay nevertheless took command of *Nabob* while another Canadian officer, Captain Roger Bidwell, took command of *Puncher*.

If the Canadians were unhappy that *Nabob* was to operate in the strike role rather than hunting submarines and protecting the convoys, there was some consolation in that she was involved in one of the more notable operations of the war, attacking the German battleship *Tirpitz* cowering in a Norwegian fjord. For *Puncher*, the war was at first dull and boring, for after first going to sea in April 1944, she was initially used as an aircraft ferry and occasionally as a troopship. It was not until the following February that she had an operational role when fourteen Grumman Wildcats of the Fleet Air Arm's No. 881 NAS were flown aboard with four Fairey Barracudas from No. 821 NAS. From this time on to the end of the war in Europe, *Puncher* had a more exciting time, again off the coast of Norway but in her case her aircraft were involved in action against German coastal convoys carrying Swedish iron ore to Germany. *Puncher* then joined another escort carrier, *Premier*, with her Wildcats providing fighter escorts for *Premier*'s Grumman Avengers on mine-laying operations, something that the Royal Air Force described as 'gardening' operations, possibly because minefields are 'sown'. This was followed by other operations supporting mine-laying and also protecting British minesweepers.

In early April 1945, *Puncher* was intended to be part of a four-carrier group attacking a U-boat base at Kilbotn in Norway that had been used by U-boats attacking the Arctic convoys, but bad weather caused

---

*Irritated is an understatement. The USN could never understand, still less accept, the long delay between an escort carrier being supplied and it entering service with the Royal Navy. Nevertheless, these ships were even more dangerous than ordinary aircraft carriers. Designated 'CVE' by the USN – 'CV' for aircraft carrier and 'E' for escort – they were known by their crews as 'Combustible, Vulnerable, Expendable', so perhaps the RN had a point!

the operation to be cancelled. This was something of an anti-climax as there was no need for the ship in the Pacific and so, after just five operations, Captain Bidwell took her to Norfolk, Virginia, so that the Lend-Lease carrier could be handed back to the United States Navy in January 1946.

Post-war, the Royal Canadian Navy formed its own Fleet Air Arm with assistance from the Royal Navy. The *Colossus*-class aircraft carrier HMS *Warrior* was loaned until the first Canadian ship, the slightly larger *Majestic*-class carrier HMCS *Magnificent*, arrived.

The Fourth Phase
The fourth phase of the Battle of the Atlantic was marked by growing Allied aerial superiority pitched against German technical innovation.

The Allies were sufficiently strong and their intelligence so advanced that the 'hunter-killer' groups, discredited by the loss of HMS *Courageous*, returned. At first these were operated by the United States Navy, mainly in the mid and South Atlantic, but British and British-Canadian groups were formed later. The formation of the hunter-killer groups was necessary because with the Atlantic Gap finally closed, the *Kriegsmarine* ordered its U-boats away from the North Atlantic to the mid and South Atlantic.

Given the extended ranges this new strategy entailed, it was a further blow to the Germans that on 11 June 1944 *U-490*, the last of the supply boats that had acted as *milch* (milk) cows for the rest of the fleet, was sunk. By this time too, the Allies were ashore in France, although still stuck in Normandy.

German technical innovation for the U-boats was effectively a case of 'too little, too late'. On 12 June 1944, the first class III electro-submarine, *U-2321*, was commissioned. She was followed on 27 June by the first class XXI large electro-submarine, *U-2501*. These pennant numbers should not be taken at face value giving a false impression of the number of U-boats built as there were just under 1,200 built altogether and the '2XXX' series indicated a step-change in capability.

Known to the Germans as *Elektroboote* (electric boats), these were the first submarines designed to operate primarily submerged, while earlier types could be regarded as being primarily surface ships that could submerge as a means to escape detection or launch an attack. Major changes included greatly increased battery capacity, roughly triple that of the Type VIIC, which provided greater underwater range and dramatically reduced the time spent on or near the surface. Instead of surfacing to recharge their batteries every twenty-four hours, they could remain submerged at about 5 knots (5.8 mph; 9.3 km/h) for two or three days before recharging batteries, which took less than five hours submerged using the snorkel. The streamlined hulls also meant that they were quieter and more difficult to detect. The electro-submarines could also sacrifice range or endurance for a 'sprint' capability that enabled them to get into position for an attack. Combined with greater endurance, other facilities that enabled them to be superior for distant water operations were such amenities as a freezer for food.

The torpedo capacity was also increased and a hydraulic torpedo reloading system meant that all six bow tubes could be reloaded in less time than an earlier submarine could load a single tube and up to eighteen torpedoes could be fired within twenty minutes. There was also an increase in the number of torpedoes that could be carried by as much as 50 per cent, also extending the time the submarine could spend on patrol and reducing the need for support and supply submarines.

Hunter-Killer Groups

One of the few escort carriers actually converted in a British yard was HMS *Vindex*, originally laid down as the fast cargo liner *Port Sydney*. One reason for this ship being chosen was that the American escort carriers had welded hulls and the Admiralty was convinced that in Arctic conditions these were unsuitable (in fact, the Admiralty was wrong) and instead opted for ships with riveted hulls. Commissioned in late 1943, *Vindex* left the Clyde on 9 March 1944, not for Murmansk or Archangel but to form a U-boat hunter-killer group. Originally she had been intended to operate with a second auxiliary carrier, *Striker*, but escorts were still in short supply and *Striker* was sent to escort a convoy from West Africa to Gibraltar.

By this time, not only did the hunter-killer groups have a good idea of what they were looking for and where, but their escorts had been strengthened. *Vindex* was escorted by a destroyer, two frigates and two corvettes from the Royal Canadian Navy's 6th Escort Group. This was in complete contrast to the much larger *Courageous* 'trailing her cloak' in a desperate quest to find a U-boat but escorted by just two destroyers.

Vindex had a balanced air group consisting of six Sea Hurricanes and twelve Swordfish, although crews for only eight of the aircraft, allowing for breakdowns and accidents, usually survivable in the slow-moving

Swordfish. The latter were fitted with anti-surface vessel radar (ASV) and *Vindex* could launch her air patrols by day or by night, unlike some of the USN hunter-killer groups that operated in daylight only.

So late in the war, it may seem strange that the veteran Swordfish was the aircraft of choice for anti-submarine operations but there were good reasons for this. The Swordfish was a much younger design than appearances would suggest, but more importantly it could loiter on patrol in a way that a modern high-performance dive-bomber and torpedo-bomber such as the Grumman Avenger, excellent in so many ways, could not. What was a sad reflection on Fairey's design and development abilities was that the Albacore, another biplane that should have been a replacement, was unreliable and the monoplane Barracuda that followed was, in the words of one airframe fitter, 'a maintenance nightmare'. The Barracuda was hated by many in the Fleet Air Arm as it all too often failed to pull out of a dive.

The Sea Hurricane also tells us much about the priority given to the Fleet Air Arm. It still lacked the performance to tackle aircraft such as the Messerschmitt Bf 109 but at least it was an improvement on the Fulmar, which had a Rolls-Royce Merlin engine, as did the Hurricane and the Spitfire, but was burdened by having a two-man crew. The Sea Hurricane was a hastily-conceived compromise, fitted with an arrester hook for carrier landings and the fuselage fittings for an assisted take-off by what is now known as a catapult but was then described as an 'accelerator'. Unlike the Fulmar it did not have folding wings, so could only be allocated to carriers with large enough lifts to enable it to be struck down into the hangar deck. The naval aviators had to wait for the Supermarine Seafire for folding wings and high performance.

Most of the escort or auxiliary carriers did not have accelerators, which combined with their slow speed compared to other aircraft carriers meant that take-off could be difficult when winds were moderate or light. Aboard many British escort carriers, including *Vindex*, the Robinson Patent Disengaging Gear was fitted. This was positioned at the after end of the flight deck and aircraft would be attached to the gear by a strop while the pilot opened up the engine to maximum rpm when the strop would be released and the aircraft would thunder along the flight deck at maximum power, providing an extra knot or even a knot-and-a-half.

More effective still was rocket-assisted take-off gear, known as RATOG. Between one and four rockets would be placed under the lower wing on each side of a Swordfish. The pilots had to start the take-off run normally and almost reach flying speed before firing the rockets, as once these were fired lateral control became difficult and there was always the risk that the rockets could force the aircraft into the air before flying speed was reached. The rockets could be dropped once the aircraft was in the air. The technique enabled aircraft to take off safely with a full load of four depth-charges.

On other counts, the needs of naval aviators were also ignored. Despite naval aviation having existed since before the First World War, it was not until 1943 that an aviation medicine course was introduced at HMS *Daedalus*, RNAS Lee-on-Solent, situated on the Hampshire coast almost equidistant between Portsmouth and Southampton. The wardroom aboard *Vindex* expected to provide three meals a day: breakfast, lunch and dinner. Anti-submarine patrols that took off at midnight were expected to fly on an empty stomach in the cold of a North Atlantic winter. The weather was so cold that on one occasion when flying was suspended, many air-crews amused themselves by rolling a large snowball around the flight deck. The lack of a recent meal affected such matters as concentration and the chances of survival should they have to ditch the aircraft. This led to a near mutiny, with a senior observer telling the ship's Commander F (Commander Flying, now known as Commander Air), Lieutenant Commander Percy Gick that unless they were properly fed, they would refuse to fly. The commanding officer, Captain Bayliss, defused the situation by quietly stressing to the airmen their vital role in the war while at the same time also ensuring that arrangements were made for more flexible mealtimes for air-crew.

Chapter 11

War in the Mediterranean

The history of the Second World War in the Mediterranean tends to be dominated by the Fleet Air Arm's daring and highly successful attack on the Italian fleet at Taranto, and by the great siege of Malta. True, most accounts also give much consideration to the German invasion of Crete, but that always emerges as an airborne attack for the simple reason that the German parachute and glider-borne assault on the island, although extremely costly, won the day while the seaborne assault was tackled by the Royal Navy so effectively that it was an irrelevance.

All of this overlooks what happened in Greece and to a lesser extent Albania, as well as in North Africa, and although both of these were army matters with increasingly strong and effective support by the British Empire air forces in the latter, the Royal Navy was also involved in both, even with a secret base in Albania for the Fleet Air Arm. Then there was also the Battle of Matapan, a major naval engagement, and many minor actions at sea and off the North African coast, while Force H raided naval bases in northern Italy.

Taranto and Malta both deserve chapters of their own, as in Chapters 8 and 13 respectively. The fall of France also brought the Royal Navy into conflict with what had been its only ally outside the British Empire, and while conflict was avoided by common sense and diplomacy at Alexandria, the action at Mers-el-Kébir and Oran damaged Anglo-French relations for the rest of the war and many years beyond, while there was further action in the Atlantic off Dakar in West Africa as well.

As elsewhere, when looking at the naval aspects of the Second World War, the convoy battles loom large. Convoys across the Mediterranean have sometimes been overlooked by the layman as for the people at home in the British Isles, those across the North Atlantic and the Bay of Biscay, bringing food and fuel, were vital for the country's survival and so very important. Next were the Arctic convoys to Murmansk and Archangel in the far north of the Soviet Union, on which the weather was as much a threat to survival as action by the enemy. Yet, it was in the Mediterranean where it could be argued that convoys were most at risk. The shipping situation was so bad that Allied forces in North Africa could not be supplied by the direct route across the Mediterranean, but instead had to take the roundabout route via the Cape of Good Hope and then north up the coast of East Africa and through the Suez Canal. A more roundabout route would be hard to devise. The Suez Canal was no longer available as a short cut to India and Australia.

We will see in Chapter 13 how instead of using merchant shipping, at times Malta was only kept in the war by using fast minelayers and large minelaying submarines to carry essential supplies as convoys could not get through, whether running from Gibraltar in the west or Alexandria in the east.

For the Royal Navy, playing very much a secondary role in the war in the Pacific, only in the Mediterranean was a major sea battle possible, with the Italian *Regia Marina* having six battleships while the British Mediterranean Fleet had three. There were two major naval engagements between Italy entering the war on 10 June 1940 and Italian surrender in 1943 after the landings at Salerno, after which the bulk of the Italian fleet was escorted to Malta.

Bringing the Enemy to Battle

It would have been reasonable to expect the Italians to have sent their six battleships to bombard Malta as soon as Italy entered the war, but instead the opening rounds were by the Italian air force, the *Regia Aeronautica*, which initiated a bombing campaign starting early on 11 June.

On 8 July 1940 the British submarine *Phoenix* alerted Admiral Sir Andrew 'ABC' Cunningham, Commander-in-Chief of the British Mediterranean Fleet, that two Italian battleships were at sea 200 miles east of Malta and on a southerly course. Aerial reconnaissance found that the battleships were escorted by six cruisers and seven destroyers and this force was escorting a large convoy. Cunningham decided to put his ships between the Italians and their major naval base at Taranto.

The following morning, a Malta-based flying boat found the Italians 145 miles west of the Mediterranean Fleet at 0730. This was later confirmed by aircraft flown off the aircraft carrier *Eagle*. By noon the distance between the fleet and the convoy had closed to 80 miles and it was not until then that the Italian commander, Admiral Campioni, heading for Sicily and shore-based air cover, realized the proximity of the Mediterranean Fleet when it was discovered by a seaplane catapulted from his flagship, *Giulio Cesare*.

With the exception of *Warspite*, Cunningham's flagship, most of the British ships were outgunned by the Italians. To slow the Italians down, *Eagle* launched two strikes using Fairey Swordfish armed with torpedoes with the first before noon and the second wave at 1600, but neither scored any hits and failed to slow the larger ships or even sink a cruiser. Shortly before 1500, two British cruisers spotted four of the Italian cruisers who opened fire with their 8in guns, outranging their British opponents who only had 6in guns. Cunningham, ahead of his other two battleships, raced ahead to intervene and save his cruisers, opening fire at a range of just under 15 miles and forcing the Italians to withdraw under a smokescreen.

Eagle and the two older battleships, *Malaya* and *Royal Sovereign*, struggled to catch up with *Warspite* and were met by fire from two Italian heavy cruisers. As the two older ships caught up with *Warspite*, they opened fire. At 1600, both sides had their battleships within range and sight of one another and almost immediately after the second Swordfish strike at 1600, the Battle of Punto Stilo, also known as the Battle of Calabria, got under way. The Italians managed to straddle the British ships with ranging shots, but the *Giulio Cesare* was hit at the base of her funnels by a salvo of 15in shells and this led the Italians to break off the engagement under cover of a heavy smokescreen. Cunningham also turned, realizing that the bulk of his force could not catch the Italians and that there was a risk of Italian submarine or air attack. Shortly afterwards, Italian bombers arrived to attack the Mediterranean Fleet but bombed their own ships by mistake, witnessed with delight by the crew of *Warspite*'s Swordfish floatplane which had been in the air throughout the action helping with gunnery control.

This was the only naval engagement during the Second World War between two full battle fleets. The Imperial Japanese Navy attempted to force such an engagement in the Battle of Leyte Gulf, but again failed as carrier-borne aircraft took over. All other naval engagements either involved a single capital ship on one side or the other, or more usually were between carrier fleets with the opposing ships out of sight of one another.

More typical of the actions between the British and Italian navies in the Mediterranean was that off Cape Spada in Crete on 19 July 1940. Two Italian light cruisers, *Bartolomeo Colleoni* and *Giovanni dalle Bande Nere*, engaged the Australian light cruiser HMAS *Sydney*, accompanied by five destroyers. The Italians had the advantage at the start of this engagement as their ships outgunned the destroyers and they outnumbered the Australian cruiser. This changed when a direct hit by *Sydney* put the *Colleoni's* boilers out of action and she lost way before sinking. *Bande Nere* hit *Sydney* but the Australian ship struck back and damaged the Italian vessel, which then took refuge in Benghazi, Libya.

In mid-August 1940, expecting an Italian thrust towards the Suez Canal, Cunningham took his three battleships and the newly-arrived heavy cruiser *Kent* to bombard coastal positions around Bardia and Fort Capuzzo, near Sollum, now Salum. In addition to fighters from *Eagle*, RAF fighters also supported the operation flying from a base in Egypt. The fighters accounted for twelve of the Savoia-Marchetti SM.79 heavy bombers sent to attack the British ships. More typical of the war in the Mediterranean was the night of 22/23 August when destroyers were sent to bombard the seaplane base at Bomba, west of Tobruk, and three of *Eagle's* Swordfish attacked enemy shipping. The Swordfish were led by Captain Oliver 'Olly' Patch of the Royal Marines. At Bomba, they found a large Italian depot ship with a destroyer on one side and a submarine lying on the other, while a second larger submarine lay astern. Patch torpedoed and sank the larger submarine, while the other two aircraft dealt with the other submarine and the destroyer alongside the depot ship, which also sank. Cunningham noted that it was 'a most daring and gallant effort on the part of our young men from the *Eagle*'.

The light cruiser *Ajax* had a busy war, especially during the early years as she was also present at the Battle of the River Plate. On the night of 11/12 October, she encountered four Italian destroyers and three motor torpedo boats off the coast of Tunisia. In the action that ensued, she sank one of the destroyers and two of the MTBs.

The next big event in the Mediterranean was the attack on the Italian fleet at Taranto, covered earlier (see Chapter 8).

On 27 November Force H, based on Gibraltar and under the command of Vice Admiral (later Admiral of the Fleet) Sir James Somerville with the battleship *Ramillies*, battle-cruiser *Renown* and the aircraft carrier *Ark Royal*, was escorting three fast freighters from Gibraltar to Alexandria when Admiral Campioni was sent with two battleships, *Vittorio Veneto* and *Giulio Cesare*, to intercept them. The Italians were spotted by British reconnaissance aircraft off Cape Teulada in Sardinia and Somerville turned Force H towards them. Both sides were supported by cruisers, five British against six Italian, and these were the first to engage. The elderly *Ramillies* soon fell behind but *Renown* followed closely on the British cruisers and when she joined the action the Italian cruisers withdrew behind their battleships, which then opened fire. *Ark Royal* sent her Swordfish to attack the Italians and although no torpedo strikes were made, this encouraged Campioni to break off the battle, having no aircraft of his own. The outcome was that one Italian destroyer was badly damaged, as was the British cruiser *Berwick*. The convoy, Somerville's priority, was untouched.

Towards the end of the year on 18 December the Mediterranean Fleet sent two battleships, *Warspite* and *Valiant* – the latter a new arrival in the Mediterranean – to bombard the port of Valona in Albania which was being used by the Italians for their invasion of Greece. This was followed on 20 December by a rare visit to Malta by Cunningham aboard *Warspite*, where he received a warm welcome. At the time, no one ashore in Malta or aboard the ship could have realized that it was to be the last visit to Malta for a very long time and that after a promising start, the situation in the Mediterranean was to change for the worse.

On the Defensive

The year 1941 had started badly and was to get worse. *Illustrious* was badly disabled by the attack on 10 January, covered in Chapter 8. The following day, the Luftwaffe found the two cruisers *Gloucester* and *Southampton* escorting four merchantmen towards Alexandria and in the subsequent attack *Southampton* had to be abandoned. The four cargo ships survived and reached their destination safely.

This was an interesting tactic as the Luftwaffe was more concerned about sinking British warships than sinking cargo ships at the time, when in fact sinking the cargo ships would have had a greater and more immediate impact on the war in the desert and even on the Royal Navy as supplies would have run short. One criticism of the Imperial Japanese Navy in the Pacific War was that it concentrated more on warships than troopships and by the time it turned its attention to the troopships, it was too late as the troops aboard had already landed ashore. The lesson was always that warships could wait for another day.

Force H continued to do all it could to maintain pressure on the Axis forces in the Mediterranean. On 9 February Somerville took the battleship *Malaya*, battle-cruiser *Renown* and the aircraft carrier *Ark Royal*, with a cruiser and ten destroyers as escorts, into the Gulf of Genoa, steaming into a relatively confined area close to the mainland of Italy. *Ark Royal's* aircraft dropped bombs on the port of Leghorn and dropped mines in the approaches to the naval base of La Spezia, while the two capital ships bombarded Genoa itself. In response, the Italian battleships *Vittorio Veneto, Giulio Cesare* and *Andrea Doria*, with three cruisers and ten destroyers, were sent to intercept Force H which they outgunned and outnumbered but failed to make contact, otherwise Somerville would have had the decisive naval engagement that Cunningham had been seeking.

This was a rare bright spot. On 25 March Italian torpedo boats sank a tanker in the anchorage of Suda Bay, Crete, and the next day they inflicted such serious damage on the heavy cruiser *York* that her commanding officer had to run her aground to avoid sinking but, as she lay stranded, Luftwaffe bombers appeared and destroyed her.

Nevertheless, a major naval engagement was in the offing. The Germans were willing to help their Italian allies in the invasion of Yugoslavia and Greece, even though this played a part in the delayed start of the planned invasion of the Soviet Union, Operation BARBAROSSA. In return, they expected the *Regia Marina* to cut British sea communications between Alexandria and Athens. Italian ships were sent into the waters south of Greece to attack British convoys, but were soon spotted by British aerial reconnaissance.

Considerable effort was devoted to convincing the many Axis spies in Alexandria that the Mediterranean Fleet was staying in port, even down to officers going ashore with suitcases and a formal reception planned for the evening. Later, the officers returned after dark, the reception was cancelled and late in the evening of 27 March 1941 the fleet slipped out of Alexandria, ready for what would become known as the Battle of Matapan.

The Battle of Matapan started on the morning of 28 March when the aircraft carrier *Formidable*, ordered to the Mediterranean to replace *Illustrious*, flew off aircraft for reconnaissance, fighter air patrols and anti-submarine patrols. Shortly afterwards reports were received of cruisers and destroyers. What was happening was that British light cruisers were being pursued by Italian heavy cruisers, joined by the Italian battleship *Vittorio Veneto*. *Formidable* flew off six Fairey Albacores escorted by Fulmar fighters.

As the Fulmars shot down a Junkers Ju 88 fighter that was attempting to attack the Albacores and drove another off, the six Albacores dived down through heavy anti-aircraft fire to torpedo the *Vittorio Veneto*. No strikes were made but the Italian battleship broke off its pursuit of the British cruisers.

Next, two Italian bombers attempted to attack *Formidable*, which flew off a strike of three Albacores and two Swordfish, escorted once again by Fulmar fighters. The Fulmars machine-gunned the *Veneto's* AA defences while the Albacores pressed home their torpedo attack, with the leading aircraft dropping its torpedo 1,000 yards ahead of the ship. The torpedo struck the ship almost immediately after the plane crashed, hitting her 15 feet below the waterline and allowing water to gush in just above the port outer screw so that within minutes the engines stopped. Damage-control parties laboured to get the ship under way again using her two starboard engines, but she could only manage 15 knots.

Formidable then sent a third air strike that arrived over the *Veneto* at dusk, with the battleship laying a dense smokescreen and using searchlights to dazzle the attackers as well as using AA fire. The attack was unsuccessful. Meanwhile, an aircraft flying from Maleme in Crete spotted the Italian heavy cruiser *Pola* and torpedoed it, causing such severe damage that she lost speed and drifted out of position. Two other heavy cruisers, *Zara* and *Fiume*, were sent to provide assistance to the crippled ship.

The Italians were unprepared for a night action, being weak in night gunnery, so Cunningham decided to press home his advantage. The opposing fleets were off Cape Matapan, usually described as Akra Tainaron in modern atlases. Cunningham at first thought the *Pola* was the *Vittorio Veneto*, but as his ships prepared to open fire the *Zara* and the *Fiume* raced across his path, illuminated by a searchlight aboard a destroyer. In the battle that followed, both these heavy cruisers and two destroyers were sunk by the 15in guns of Cunningham's three battleships, while a torpedo attack by three destroyers sank the *Pola*.

Next morning, the Mediterranean Fleet rescued 900 Italian survivors before the threat of an Italian air attack stopped the rescue. Cunningham relayed the position of the remaining survivors to Rome, saving many more lives. This was a noble and humanitarian gesture as it inevitably also gave the Italians the position of his fleet.

This proof of continued British dominance of the Eastern Mediterranean did not stop the Germans starting their assault on Yugoslavia and Greece on 6 April. In true blitzkrieg tradition, the attack began with air attacks by the Luftwaffe. On one raid a British ammunition ship was blown up in Piraeus, taking ten other ships with her and damaging the port's facilities so badly that it was put out of action, creating a major problem for the British expeditionary force ashore. By 23 April the Greek army had surrendered and the Mediterranean Fleet was busy evacuating British forces to Crete under heavy aerial attack. Had Crete been used simply as a convenient staging post for a planned withdrawal to Egypt, all might have been well, but the decision was taken to defend the island despite the shortage of aircraft and heavy weapons and, crucially as it happened, communications equipment.

Behind Enemy Lines

While the Greek campaign was in full swing, a most unusual and even irregular operation was being mounted by the Royal Air Force and the Fleet Air Arm. This started even before the German assault on Greece, while the fighting was still between Greece and Italy.

No. 815 Naval Air Squadron had been based on Crete, with its Fairey Swordfish being used mainly on patrols looking for and attacking German and Italian submarines. While Germany was not engaged in war with Greece, the possibility of German intervention to help the Italians was growing daily, especially when German forces invaded Bulgaria on 2 March 1941.

On 10 March, 815 was moved to Athens, using the then civil airport at Eleusis. There was an air of unreality about the place with German officers off duty on the streets in full uniform, 'attached to the German embassy', passing British soldiers, sailors and airmen, also in full uniform.

Two days later, while remaining based on Eleusis No. 815 NAS was allocated a forward base for a strike against enemy shipping using the harbour at Valona, now known as Vlorë, in neighbouring Albania. Despite the base being behind enemy lines, high up in the mountains, it had remained undiscovered by the Italians, even though it was being used by two RAF bomber squadrons, one with Bristol Blenheims and the other with Vickers Wellingtons. It soon became clear why the base had not been discovered. First 815's Swordfish had to fly to Corfu, and from that island's southernmost tip fly the 10 miles east to Albania, unless spotted by enemy aircraft, in which case they were ordered to turn back rather than lead the enemy to the secret base in the valley of Paramythia. An air vice marshal made it perfectly clear that it would be better to lose the entire Swordfish squadron than reveal the location, indeed the existence, of the base.

Flying from Corfu to Albania, the Swordfish crews would see a large range of mountains to starboard and select the highest mountain, just over 7,000 feet high, or as one officer put it, 'the third on the right', after which they would come across a wide dry river bed at the foot of the mountain. The river bed would then lead them north, albeit with many curves, and they were comforted by the knowledge that if a Blenheim could do it, so could a Swordfish!

Paramythia, or 'the Valley of Fairy Tales', was 10 miles long and 3,000 feet deep, with the surrounding mountains rising to 7,000 feet. A Swordfish, laden with a torpedo, had to climb 3,000 feet after take-off before it could set course for Valona. This meant that the airspeed would fall to just 70 knots and require the aircraft to circle as it climbed. These conditions were so demanding that even the faster and more powerful Blenheims and Wellingtons confined their sorties to daylight. Lieutenant Commander Jackie Jago, 815's commanding officer, pointed out to the air vice marshal that his unit was a night-flying squadron and that they would rather risk hitting a mountain at night than attack a well-defended port in their slow aircraft in broad daylight. In the end a compromise was reached: the aircraft would take off on a clear moonlit night to minimize the risk of hitting a mountain, while the return would be timed so that the Swordfish came across the river bed at dawn. Another precaution was that the squadron would visit Paramythia a day early to allow time for practice take-offs and landings without torpedoes.

There were other problems with the airfield. Apart from speed and high mountains, there was no means of pilots flying into Paramythia obtaining an accurate local barometric pressure reading because of the need to maintain radio silence. One pilot noted that on his first flight, his altimeter showed him to be flying at less than 2,000 feet, even though the airfield was at 3,000 feet. Fuel had to be flown in by Douglas Bostons carrying large fuel drums and as a result, so that the fuel could be saved for the two RAF squadrons, the Fleet Air Arm squadron would only be allowed to top up when landing at Paramythia after a sortie, with the crew having a quick meal before returning to Eleusis. On the outward flight, they would have to carry their torpedoes as otherwise not only would the weapons have to be stocked at Paramythia, there would also have to be trolleys and skilled ratings at the base for them to be loaded onto the Swordfish.

Valona was an important target because the port was closest to the frontier with Greece, giving the shortest overland supply line for Italian forces bogged down in fierce fighting with the Greeks. The only alternative port was Durazzo, 60 miles to the north by air or sea, but more than 100 miles further by road. If Valona could be made untenable, instead of an 80-mile journey over a mountain road so exposed that it could only be used at night, the Italian supply lorries would be faced with a journey of more than 180 miles.

With a large harbour and an anchorage some 10 miles long and 5 miles wide, Valona was surrounded by hills and mountains to seaward as well as to the south, with the peaks at between 1,000 and 3,000 feet. The Swordfish had to fly from Eleusis to Paramythia, refuel and then take off again and fly towards Corfu, climbing over the sea to an altitude of 10,000 feet, which was cold even in summer in an open cockpit, and would take half an hour with the aircraft carrying a 1,750lb torpedo slung under the fuselage. The aircraft would then turn towards Valona, descending on half throttle before entering the harbour through a gap, 1,250 feet high, between a hill and a small mountain village. This did allow altimeters to be adjusted because of the known height of the gap and by making an estimate of the aircraft's height above it. The plan was to arrive over the anchorage at an altitude of just 60 feet, at least in theory.

The first raid was on 13 March, with the aircraft taking off shortly before 0300 from Paramythia. An hour later, the first flight of Swordfish passed through the gap, with the pilots hastily resetting their altimeters to 1,300 feet while continuing to descend towards the harbour. It was known that at least six large merchant vessels would be in the harbour. The leading aircraft was flown by the squadron commander, Lieutenant Commander Jago, but its blue formation light suddenly disappeared, leaving the following aircraft's pilot unsure whether the first aircraft had been shot down by the heavy anti-aircraft fire that had just started or had suffered sudden mechanical failure. The second aircraft, flown by Lieutenant Charles Lamb, took the lead, as Lamb recalled later:

I thought that I had plenty of height to reach the shipping at anchor right ahead...when my wheels struck the water with a terrible lurch, and my throat constricted in the awful spasm which people have in mind when they say 'my heart leapt into my mouth'. Instinctively, I held the aircraft steady in case it somersaulted, and opened the throttle wide and pressed the release button because the water would have activated the Duplex pistol on the nose of the torpedo and started the pistol's propeller. The sudden deceleration only lasted for about two seconds...but they were the longest two seconds I have ever known. Fortunately, we were within fifteen hundred yards of a big ship, right ahead, her hulk a black shape against a searchlight wavering about from the town behind her, so my fish wasn't wasted. But after that experience I set my altimeter with very great care when coming through that gap, and insisted on the aircraft entering the harbour in very open formation, so that there was time to do so.

It says a great deal for the sturdy construction of the Swordfish undercarriage that it could be dipped into the sea at a speed of ninety knots or more, and held there for a few seconds without being torn off; and for the power of the Bristol engine and the stability of the aircraft as a whole that the ailerons and wings were sufficiently strong to keep it steady with such a sudden deceleration, and force through the water and into the air again without any damage whatsoever.

The instinctive reaction of most pilots would have been to yank back the control column as hard as possible, but it was important to hold the aircraft steady to avoid somersaulting or stalling. Lamb was sufficiently concerned to ask his telegraphist/air-gunner to lean over the side to see if the aircraft still had its undercarriage so that he would know whether or not he should prepare for a belly-landing.

At least three ships had been set on fire during the attack. The Italians claimed that no damage had been done and that three aircraft had been shot down and their crews taken prisoner. This at least indicated to the rest of 815's air-crew that their commander had survived.

Following this first attack, it was decided to divide the squadron in two, with half held at Paramythia ready to attack while the other half was rearming at Eleusis. Four nights of further attacks followed, resulting in the masters of the merchant vessels refusing to remain in harbour after dark and instead anchoring off the coast, which made finding the ships more difficult for 815. The squadron was divided yet again, with the half making the attack being split between those going into the harbour at Valona and the remainder ranging north along the coast towards Durazzo.

Meanwhile, the Italians had improved their air defences. They worked out the approach taken by the Swordfish on their way to the harbour and moored a flak ship to cover the approach and placed additional flak ships in the harbour itself. One pilot discovered these additional ships for the first time on a night when there was no worthwhile merchant shipping in the harbour, so he used his torpedo on one of the flak ships and literally blew the small vessel out of the water!

Far cleverer was the placing of a large illuminated buoy 'as big as the Albert Hall' in the middle of the harbour, so brightly lit that no matter from which direction the Swordfish approached, they would be highlighted against it for the benefit of the AA gunners. Unfortunately for the Italians, when the 'tail-end Charlie' Swordfish pilot saw all five aircraft ahead of him highlighted by the buoy, he dropped his torpedo in its direction, blowing it up and extinguishing all the lights at once. The Italians claimed that the Fleet Air Arm had sunk a hospital ship but the pilots did not see any red crosses.

Flying at night, encounters with enemy fighters were a rare event. Charles Lamb was flying from Eleusis to Paramythia after debriefing a senior RAF officer on a raid against Durazzo. He was giving a young sub-lieutenant observer a lift, not because he needed a navigator but because he needed someone to watch the skies behind his aircraft for fighters and to make sure that they were not tracked heading into Paramythia. This was fortunate because at 5,000 feet over Corfu, the observer suddenly shouted: 'Fighters astern – on both sides!' Looking over his shoulder, Lamb saw two Fiat CR.22 biplane fighters, each fitted with twin 12.7mm machine guns. These aircraft would have posed no threat at all to many aircraft of the day, but they were a very real hazard for a plodding Stringbag*, as the Swordfish was affectionately known to the Fleet Air Arm.

Lamb immediately jettisoned his torpedo and started the defensive manoeuvre he had been taught and that he had earlier rehearsed when his ship was working-up in Bermuda. He stood the Swordfish on its tail as the two Fiats opened fire, causing them to shoot past. He then dived vertically on full power, hoping that his observer was safely strapped in and that the wings wouldn't tear off as he reached almost 200 knots. He levelled out closer to the sea than he had ever done before, prior to climbing so steeply that his observer blacked out briefly. He saw the two Fiats approach again, still in formation rather than in line which he felt might have given them a greater chance of success, and repeated his stall, dive and climb manoeuvre again, glancing around just to see the two fighters crashing into the sea.

On checking with his observer that he was all right, all Lamb got in reply was a murmur. On landing, he looked into the rear cockpit to

---

*The Swordfish was known as the 'Stringbag' because of its spidery construction and the fact that it could carry such an assortment of munitions, akin to the variety one might find in a housewife's string bag.

see if the observer was in fact fine, only to find that the young man had been violently sick and was in tears; probably, Lamb thought, at being discovered in such a mess.

They had in fact been very lucky, as when Lamb pulled his parachute out of the aircraft, it fell apart. His aircraft had been hit and a machine-gun shell had lodged just inches away from what he described as his 'most sensitive anatomy'.

There were further operations from Paramythia, starting on 9 April and continuing for eight days. In these operations another four significant merchant vessels were sunk and, even more importantly, the Axis powers stopped using the port.

The slow and obsolescent Swordfish did well, for by the time operations ceased, all the Wellingtons had been lost in their daylight raids, except for one that could not be flown as there were no surviving pilots for the aircraft. There was an even bigger problem, not on the horizon but seen by those at Paramythia waiting to make their one last sortie on 17 April: a Junkers Ju 88 landed at the airfield! The aircraft was carrying King Peter of Yugoslavia into exile, but it was clear that the base was no longer secret and therefore no longer usable. The Ju 88 had been shadowed by a squadron of Heinkel He 111s that attacked but could inflict little damage in the failing light without flying into the sides of the mountains.

Crete

Despite the valiant efforts of those who flew out of Paramythia, it was clear that the battle for Greece had been lost. Even at Eleusis, the squadron was not safe and two Swordfish were lost in bombing raids. No. 815 NAS was moved to Crete and started flying anti-submarine patrols, but a series of engine failures soon saw them down to three aircraft, with the remaining five unserviceable. This was a squadron that at its peak had had twenty-two aircraft. The three aircraft were flown to Egypt with some difficulty with faltering engines, with one pilot considering ditching when he saw ships of the Mediterranean Fleet and only changed his mind when he realized that the approaching Fairey Fulmar fighters hadn't recognized his aircraft and were prepared to shoot him down. He sought refuge in a cloud. Another aircraft made a dead-stick landing after its engine finally failed.

Evacuating British forces to Crete was sensible and eased the evacuation of Greece, but attempting to establish Crete as a base was over-optimistic. It was fine as a staging post, but the British forces in Crete had had to abandon artillery, vehicles and communications equipment in their escape from Greece and were in no state to defend the island when, on 20 May, the German airborne invasion began.

Few could have foreseen that the German assault would come by air, despite earlier experience in Norway and the Low Countries. As they arrived, the Germans were helped by the fact that most of the British and Greek forces defending the island had been deployed to the coast, expecting a seaborne invasion. Göring had persuaded Hitler that the Luftwaffe's paratroops* should mount the invasion with the army and navy playing a supporting role. The army used barges for the invasion and suffered serious casualties, with the Royal Navy completely wiping out one convoy. Despite the British and Greek forces' lack of weaponry and communications equipment, the invasion proved so costly that for a time Hitler banned all further airborne assaults. Gliders lay burnt out on the landing-grounds while the bodies of paratroopers hung lifeless in the trees, and it was only the lack of good communications between the defending units that prevented the German assault being repelled.

At sea, during the night of 21/22 May the cruisers *Ajax*, *Dido* and *Orion* with four destroyers completely destroyed one convoy carrying troops and munitions. The Luftwaffe responded on 22 May with a crippling attack on the Mediterranean Fleet, sinking the cruisers *Fiji* and *Gloucester* and badly damaging *Warspite* and the cruisers *Carlisle* and *Naiad*. Cunningham sent the battleships *Queen Elizabeth* and *Barham* with nine destroyers to attack Axis airfields in the Dodecanese; these were aided by aircraft from *Formidable* but by this time the carrier's air power was extremely limited due to a shortage of aircraft and she could do little to defend herself when the Luftwaffe turned its attention on her, causing serious damage. Even so, the Mediterranean Fleet continued to evacuate the last of the 17,000 British, Empire and Greek troops from Crete long after the deadline set by the Admiralty.

Yet, the stark truth was that for the second time in five months during the war in the Mediterranean, an aircraft carrier was damaged beyond local repair and had to be sent away. This time, there was no replacement available.

---

*In contrast to the practice in most countries, German paratroops were part of the air force, the Luftwaffe, rather than the army.

Alexandria

Withdrawing the British Mediterranean Fleet from Malta to Alexandria in Egypt was not simply a good idea but also a necessity. The fleet would have been a sitting duck in Malta's Grand Harbour and too far away at Gibraltar for operations off Greece and for the later invasion of Syria, as well as support for the British Eighth Army in Egypt. However, Alexandria – 'Alex' to those stationed there – was not the ideal naval base for a large fleet. It lacked the repair facilities needed by capital ships, which by this time could fairly be said to include aircraft carriers as well as battleships and battle-cruisers. A floating dry dock was useful for anything up to and including a cruiser but not for major fleet units. There was also the question of skilled dockyard manpower.

While the Egyptian authorities had, if sometimes reluctantly, rounded up German and then Italian nationals and sent the diplomats home, there were still German and Italian spies in the country. Events were also to prove that Alexandria was far from secure in any sense.

The night of 18/19 December 1941 was a bad one for the British Mediterranean Fleet, leaving it at the nadir of its misfortunes. That night, the Malta-based Force K, a cruiser and destroyer raiding force, ran into an Italian minefield off Tripoli. The cruiser *Neptune* was sunk with a destroyer and two other cruisers, *Aurora* and *Penelope*, were badly damaged.

Almost 1,000 miles to the east, an Italian submarine surfaced in the darkness just over a mile from the entrance to the harbour at Alexandria and released three two-man human torpedoes into the water. The attackers were lucky, for as they arrived the harbour defences were opened for Rear Admiral Philip Vian's destroyers. The human torpedoes were intended for the British battleships. Acting with considerable bravery, one of the Italians who had arrived with the human torpedoes, Luigi de la Penne, fixed his warhead to the bottom of the battleship *Valiant* but he and his companion then lost their torpedo and had to swim to a buoy from which they were rescued and taken prisoner by the British. Another pair managed to blow the stern off the tanker *Sagona* and also damage the destroyer *Jervis* that was lying alongside. Unable to escape through the dock entrance through which they had entered the harbour, they went ashore but were soon spotted and arrested. The third two-man team fixed their charge to the bottom of the battleship *Queen Elizabeth* and also attempted to escape, hoping to be picked up by a submarine. They too were spotted and arrested after coming ashore, giving themselves away by trying to spend English £5 notes that were no longer legal tender in Egypt.

Despite being detained aboard *Valiant*, de la Penne kept quiet about his explosive charge until it exploded and the battleship's hull ripped open below the waterline and she settled in the harbour. The same happened to the *Queen Elizabeth*.

Fortunately for the Royal Navy, both these major ships were in shallow water and aerial reconnaissance showed them sitting in the harbour as if they were undamaged. The crews of the human torpedoes had failed to return, so there was no indication that they had been successful. Better still, the discovery of one of the torpedoes enabled the Royal Navy to embark on its own programme of human torpedoes, which became known to the service as 'chariots'; a far kinder name than that used by the Italians that translated simply and unglamorously as 'pigs'. Yet, at this time Cunningham was without an operational battleship or, more serious still, an aircraft carrier.

Somerville was not that much better off. On 13 November, off Gibraltar, *U-81* had torpedoed Force H's aircraft carrier, *Ark Royal*, knocking out her engine rooms and, of course, pumps, so that she sank the next day. The irony was that most naval officers had expected her to succumb to aerial attack, given the thin plating of her unarmoured flight deck.

As the winter drew on and fighting in Russia became virtually impossible, the Luftwaffe units deployed east returned to increase the pressure on the Mediterranean Fleet and Malta.

Chapter 12

Disaster and Revenge in the Far East

War with Japan had been seen as a serious possibility for some time. Japan had been a First World War ally but the country's territorial ambitions were increasingly clear and during the Russian Civil War, Japan's assistance to its allies was noticeably self-serving. Construction had gone ahead on a major naval base at Singapore, intended to be a Far East Gibraltar, and the dominions of Australia and New Zealand had both been promised that in the event of war with Japan, the United Kingdom would send a 'strong fleet' to the Far East. What no one had considered was that the country could be faced with a major war in Europe at the same time.

Japan had been working to create an empire in Asia since the beginning of the twentieth century. The initial objective was Korea, but mainland China was also seen as ripe for Japanese expansion. The territories granted to the European powers had also been eyed enviously by Japan, which ably demonstrated its ability to face a European power in war, and especially war at sea, when it soundly defeated the Imperial Russian Navy in the Battle of Tsushima in 1905, bringing an end to the Russo-Japanese War of 1904–05.

Conflict with Japan did not depend on a formal declaration of war. Japanese strategy was based on making a surprise first strike, catching their opponent off guard.

There was a major difference in Japan before the First World War and before the Second World War. Before the first, Japan was still an importer of Western technology, but by the second it had become an industrial power. This had not been done without Western help. In the years after the First World War, a British Naval Mission visited Japan and British combat aircraft were sold to the country as well as the rights to manufacture under licence. The mission eventually ended, with many misgivings among those involved about Japan's future intentions, but it was too late as the damage was already done.

The Imperial Japanese Navy

Japan made it clear that she was unhappy with the conditions of the Washington Naval Treaty of 1922, expecting parity with the United Kingdom and United States, each of which had a total allowance of 525,000 tons of warships against the 315,000 tons allocated to Japan. This issue was raised again at the London Naval Conference of 1930 when Japan demanded parity with the USA and UK.

In many ways, Japan's ultimate reason for territorial aggression was the same as Germany's, demanding *Lebensraum* ('living space'), as Japan also had a growing population and was unable to grow sufficient food to feed her people.

The League of Nations had allowed Japan to base troops, known as the Kwantung Army, to guard the Southern Manchurian Railway. On 18 September 1931, an explosion on the railway gave Japan the excuse to allow the Kwantung Army to occupy the Chinese province of Mukden, followed by Manchuria. The following year, the Kwantung Army created a new state, Manchukuo, but this was refused recognition by the League of Nations. By this time the Imperial Japanese Navy had become involved as unrest around the major Chinese city and port of Shanghai, known as the Shanghai disturbances, gave Japan an excuse to send troops to the area, ostensibly to protect Japanese interests and its own nationals resident in the city. The aircraft carrier *Kaga* was sent from Japan, arriving off Shanghai on 30 January 1932 with twenty-four Nakajima A1N Type 3 fighters and thirty-six Mitsubishi B1M Type 13 attack aircraft, sufficient to give Japan air control over the area. Another carrier, the *Hosho*, arrived shortly afterwards with reinforcements.

China was, at the time, backward and the authority of the central government in Peking was weak. Nevertheless, while Japanese ground forces initially enjoyed overwhelming superiority, Japan soon realized that it had underestimated the capabilities of the Chinese 19th Route Army. Japanese retaliation was severe, with aircraft from the *Kaga* destroying the Chinese areas of Shanghai but at this stage still avoiding the foreign concessions, those areas held by European powers. The Japanese maintained their overwhelming aerial superiority, even when Chinese aircraft were deployed in the area. The conflict lasted throughout February and until mid-March, by which time Shanghai was firmly under Japanese control and by May the Chinese were forced to accept a demilitarized zone.

Despite this, the Japanese Naval Air Force still seems to have found Japanese aircraft disappointing and continued to prefer those of European production, despite the country's policies damaging relations with the United Kingdom and France. Many Japanese aircraft were designed and developed but failed to enter production. To meet the need for a dive-bomber for carrier squadrons, the Heinkel He 50 was licence-produced as the Aichi D1A1 Type 94.

The year 1932 was the first in which the Japanese Navy Air Force (JNAF) and Japanese Army Air Force (JAAF) started annual air defence exercises. As the 1930s continued, the quality and performance of the aircraft produced by Japanese industry started to improve; by 1937 the latest designs showed much promise and these were to be the aircraft that would provide the mainstay of the JNAF during the Second World War.

In May 1933, the Imperial Japanese Navy received its first aircraft carrier to have been designed as such rather than converted from a battleship or battle-cruiser. This was the *Ryujo*, designed to have as low a displacement tonnage as possible but carry the maximum number of aircraft. Her tonnage on commissioning was 10,600 tons, small even for the day; it would have been even lower had not problems with stability and sea-keeping required enlarged torpedo bulges and modifications to her bows. Unlike Western aircraft carriers of the day, *Ryujo* did not have an island but instead had a bridge below the forward end of the flight deck overlooking the fo'c'sle, while two funnels on the starboard side ducted downwards; this was to be a feature of many Japanese aircraft carriers including some with islands. Originally designed with six twin 5in gun turrets, these had to be removed to improve stability.

Up to forty-eight aircraft could be carried when acting as an aircraft transport, but this dropped to thirty-six for operational flying. Apart from her size, another design deficiency was that of her two aircraft lifts: that forward was too small to handle most JNAF aircraft so that only that aft could be used, making efficient use of the hangar deck difficult. The flight deck was also too short to range an adequate number of aircraft ready to take off on operations.

Such were the shortcomings of the *Ryujo* that the next aircraft carriers to be supplied to the JNAF were built to a more substantial and practical size, but with three carriers already, two of which were converted capital ships, only one of the new design could be completed without infringing the limits imposed by the Washington Naval Treaty.

It could have been worse, as Japan's first carrier had been granted an exemption under the treaty as an experimental ship.

The first of the new carriers, *Soryu*, was laid down in 1934 and a second followed a year later. While a more substantial 15,900 tons, as with the *Ryujo*, adequate armour was not provided. This ship had a conventional island but still had the downward ducted funnels. Unusually, the *Soryu* had three lifts, and while the flight deck ran the entire length of the ship, the hangar did not and the fo'c'sle and quarterdeck were both open. Despite the problems with *Ryujo*, *Soryu* also had a narrow beam but this did at least give her the high speed of 34.5 knots. On entering service in December 1937, she was able to accommodate more than sixty aircraft.

The next carrier was heavier still at 17,300 tons but still with the same aircraft accommodation and turn of speed as *Soryu* when she entered service in July 1939. *Hiryu* had a broader beam and an improved range. Her big claim to fame, however, was that she was one of just two aircraft carriers ever to have the island on the port side, although the funnels were still to starboard.

Before this, in 1934, Japan had formally notified the other signatories to the Washington Naval Treaty that she now no longer regarded herself as being bound by the restrictions of the treaty. During the late 1930s, several more aircraft carriers were laid down while others were converted from other naval vessels. The Royal Navy and the French *Marine Nationale* had both operated aircraft-carrying submarines, although the British submarine, *M2*, had sunk, and Japan alone took a more thorough interest in this type of submarine. While the British and French submarines carried just one seaplane each, some of the Japanese submarines carried two, and towards the end of the war a new class of large submarines capable of carrying three aircraft each was completed but did not see active service. These were captured and scuttled by the USN to avoid having to share the secrets of these craft with the Soviet Union.

Tensions between China and Japan continued to grow as the decade passed. Full-scale war followed a major clash on 7 July 1937 with heavy fighting near the capital, then known as Peking. The main opposition to the Japanese was led by General Chiang Kai-shek, who was broadly supported by the West although he had also negotiated a non-aggression pact with the Soviet Union. Before the end of the month, on 28 July, Peking was occupied and the Chinese government moved to Nanking, which lasted until 13 December. There were also amphibious landings near Shanghai, which was completely occupied.

Preparing for War

War with the United States was seen by many Japanese as inevitable. Japanese naval officers had to learn a foreign language during their training and many, including Mitsuo Fuchida who was later to lead the attack on the US Pacific Fleet at Pearl Harbor, chose English.

The Japanese were jealous of European control over so much of the Far East. They saw France with Indo-China; The Netherlands with the East Indies with its extensive oil production; and worst of all, the United Kingdom with Malaya's tin and rubber, while the UK also had Singapore and Hong Kong, Burma with its timber output and, of course, India, then a single large country. There was also a strong American influence, with the Philippines run virtually as an American colony. This jealousy was also tainted with contempt for the colonial powers and the United States, with the USN viewed as a golf and bridge club for its officers in the eyes of one Japanese naval officer.

The Europeans and Americans were also suspicious of Japanese intentions. They had seen Japan seize Korea, and even before the intervention in Manchuria, concerns about Japanese intentions had been raised during the Allied operations in Siberia during the Russian Civil War. It was clear that Allied forces in Siberia were hampered by the Japanese, who had their own agenda. Many Americans involved in political life were reluctant to act, advocating a policy of isolationism, but public opinion in the United States began to change as news came through of Japanese atrocities in China, especially after the rape of the former Nationalist Chinese capital of Nanking following its fall to Japanese forces in December 1937. The United States was also unsympathetic to the European colonial powers; there was concern about the extent of the Japanese advance into China, militarily weak and divided. It was also clear that Japan had set its sights on French Indo-China, which would be a convenient source of food for Japan's large population. Alarm bells rang when Japan and the Soviet Union signed a non-aggression pact.

In December 1940, the United States imposed an embargo on the sale of war materials to Japan, including scrap metal. This was followed in July 1941 by the freezing of Japanese assets in the USA following the Japanese invasion of French Indo-China. Both the United Kingdom and the Netherlands East Indies government followed the American lead, denying Japan the currency with which to buy oil and raw materials as well as banning the sale of these commodities. This left Japan with a strategic reserve of just eighteen months of fuel oil, some 55 million barrels, unless she could find an alternative source by invading the Netherlands East Indies.

Many Japanese realized that their country could not win a war against the United States. Among those opposed to war was the Commander-in-Chief of the Combined Fleet, Admiral Yamamoto Isoroku, who had been sent to Washington in 1926 as Japan's naval attaché. He had earlier attended Harvard University between 1919 and 1921, and had also spent some time at the US Naval War College. Clearly Japan had derived the maximum advantage from her First World War alliances. Yamamoto was well-disposed towards the United States, although he also seems to have been cynical about the peacetime United States Navy which he viewed more as a club for bridge and golf. Yet, Yamamoto was also as aware as anyone in Japan about his country's weaknesses, especially compared to the United States. He knew that Japan could not match the USA industrially or militarily and that it lacked the natural resources and manpower of the USA. As war drew closer, he realized that it was a dangerous course and believed that Japan could achieve a major victory in the first year of war but during the second year the United States would be able to recover and move to the offensive. The problem was that while the Imperial Japanese Navy was far stronger than the United States Navy in the Pacific, it could not match the full strength of the combined Pacific and Atlantic fleets.

While war was an objective, especially for the army faction, planning did not begin in earnest until 1940, with Yamamoto and his staff giving priority to neutralizing the United States Navy. It was soon decided that Japan would need to inflict a knockout blow on the US Pacific and Asiatic fleets that would leave Japan with a minimum of six months and ideally even longer in which to establish an empire across the Pacific and South-East Asia, which with conscious irony it named the Great East Asia Co-Prosperity Sphere. The 'empire' was necessary to secure adequate supplies of fuel, food and raw materials. Yamamoto, unlike many senior Japanese naval officers, was no fan of the battleship and because of the distances involved, it was clear that the major role would be played by the aircraft carrier. Even so, many senior officers did their best to discourage promising young officers from specializing in naval aviation and often argued that only a battleship could sink a battleship, to which Yamamoto would respond by quoting an old

Japanese proverb: 'The fiercest serpent may be overcome by a swarm of ants.'

It was clear that what was needed was a devastating attack against the US Pacific Fleet at its main base at Pearl Harbor on the Hawaiian island of Oahu, using carrier-borne aircraft and seeking to inflict serious damage, not just on the ships but on the base itself as well. The operation was war-gamed but the British attack on the Italian fleet at Taranto proved to the Japanese that their strategy was the right one. The Royal Navy had used just one carrier and twenty-one obsolescent aircraft; the Imperial Japanese Navy would use many more ships and even more aircraft. It would take time for the United States Navy to repair or replace the ships and to get the naval base fully operational again.

Planning was delegated to two officers. One was Commander Minoru Genda, who favoured an aerial attack using torpedo-bombers, and his friend, Mitsuo Fuchida, whom Genda selected to lead the attack. Like Yamamoto, Fuchida was a fluent English-speaker. Fuchida did not agree with the plan for a torpedo attack as he expected the Americans to protect their ships with torpedo nets, while the water at Pearl Harbor would only be around 40 feet deep. In addition, if the entire US Pacific Fleet was in port, many ships would be double-berthed with some vessels protecting the one lying alongside. All this was true, but Genda in turn pointed out that bombs would only bounce off armour-plating.

Japanese planning was thorough. Six aircraft carriers were assigned to the attack with a total of 432 aircraft between them, of which 353 were to be used in the attack and to provide fighter cover. The remaining aircraft were a mixture of spares to allow for the inevitable losses, and for the air defence of the carriers. Another contrast with the British attack was that the Imperial Japanese Navy had far superior aircraft. Naturally enough, the aircraft used included the famous Mitsubishi A6M or 'Zero', a single-seat fighter. The main strike aircraft was the Nakajima B5N, to which the Allies were later to give the code-name 'Kate'. The B5N was a single-engined monoplane of all-metal construction with power-folding wings, retractable undercarriage and a top speed of 230 mph, more than twice that of the Swordfish. There would be forty of these carrying torpedoes, with more than 100 carrying bombs. The third aircraft assigned to the operation was the Aichi D3A1, later code-named 'Val' by the Allies. The D3A1 was a dive-bomber, the Japanese equivalent of the German Stuka, and like the Stuka it was a low-wing monoplane with a fixed spatted undercarriage.

If the aircraft were advanced enough to hold their own with Western designs, and indeed be ahead of those in the Royal Navy's Fleet Air Arm, the ships were a different story. These reflected Japan's growing isolation from the Western powers and the absence of the latest thinking in aircraft carrier design.

Six aircraft carriers were intended to take part in the attack on Pearl Harbor, with the fleet named the 'Combined Striking Force' and divided into three carrier divisions. The flagship was the First Carrier Division's *Akagi*, converted from a battle-cruiser and accompanied by the *Kaga*, converted from a battleship. The Second Carrier Division had the smaller aircraft carriers *Hiryu* and *Soryu*, which could have been described as sisters but for *Soryu* having a conventional starboard-side island and *Hiryu* having hers to port. The idea of this unusual arrangement, also used on *Akagi*, was that the two ships could operate together but their air groups would not get in each other's way after taking off. Some accounts suggest that ships with a port-side island had a far higher accident rate when aircraft were landing. The two newest ships were in the newly-formed Fifth Carrier Division, which had the large sisters *Shokaku* and *Zuikaku* that could be regarded as the Japanese equivalent of the British *Illustrious* class, but unlike the British ship they had little deck armour. They both had starboard-side islands, but still had the downward-curving funnels. Each had three lifts and could accommodate up to seventy aircraft.

This fleet was escorted by two battleships, *Hiei* and *Kirishima*, three cruisers and nine destroyers. This was a light escort for so many carriers that could have been vulnerable to heavy gunfire from the US Pacific Fleet's battleships or torpedo attack from its submarines.

Admiral Yamamoto, fully aware of the importance of the operation and the strength of the United States Navy, visited *Akagi* before the attack and addressed the aircrew:

Japan has faced many worthy opponents in her long history. Mongols, Chinese, Russians, but the United States is the most worthy of all. Admiral Kimmel, commander-in-chief of the Pacific Fleet, is known to be far-sighted and aggressive. You may have to fight your way to the target.

Yet, as with the British at Taranto, the Japanese were to have the element of surprise. The Americans were to ignore even those warning signs that did appear.

There was no declaration of war. The operation was scheduled for 8 December 1941, but as the two countries were on opposite sides of the International Date Line, for the United States it was 7 December, a Sunday. The Japanese chose this day because they believed, rightly, that they would find the defences at a low ebb with most, if not all, of the commanders away from their posts and their subordinates at rest. This was a shrewd assessment as both the army and navy commanders were spending the morning playing golf together. Yamamoto, with his experience of life in the United States Navy, was obviously aware that this could be the case.

Fate also played a part. The Japanese had to approach their flying-off positions sailing through a tropical storm and on the morning of 7 December, conditions were still so bad that had it been an exercise, it would have been postponed. Yet, over Pearl Harbor the weather was perfect.

Japan Attacks
US intelligence was sufficiently advanced and well-organized that they knew the Japanese fleet was at sea, but they had convinced themselves that the Japanese were headed for somewhere in South-East Asia. The course a future war with Japan might take had been considered at a naval staff conference in March 1941, called as war between the United States and Japan seemed increasingly probable. Few of the senior officers present thought an attack on Pearl Harbor was likely, with the consensus being that 'the Japs would never sail into us'. The stark truth was that, despite the United States having a large aircraft carrier fleet and high-performance naval aircraft, the strength of Japanese naval aviation being known, and the Royal Navy's success at Taranto also known, the possibility of an attack by carrier-borne aircraft was discounted. If the Imperial Japanese Navy was to attack Pearl Harbor, the USN still hung on to the notion that it would be by means of a heavy bombardment by a large battle fleet.

Later the chief of naval operations, Admiral Harold Stark, signalled Admiral Husband Kimmel in command of the US Pacific Fleet, and Admiral Thomas Hart in command of the US Asiatic Fleet based on Manila in the Philippines, to expect an enemy attack on 24 November. Yet, Stark had no further intelligence to hand, but only suggested that either the Philippines or Guam could be possibilities. A further warning was sent on 27 November after American Secretary of State Cornell Hull had rejected a plea from the Japanese ambassador in Washington that the US should accept the status quo in Asia the previous day. Hull had told the Japanese that normal economic relations would only be resumed if Japan withdrew from China and French Indo-China. Stark's message was clear: 'This dispatch is to be considered a war warning. Negotiations with Japan looking for stabilization of conditions in the Pacific have ceased. An aggressive move by Japan is expected within the next few days...Execute appropriate defensive deployment...'

Kimmel was sufficiently concerned to ensure that his aircraft carriers were not in Pearl Harbor, but incredibly he failed to send his main force of battleships to sea or liaise with the US army in Hawaii, produce a defensive plan or even order a state of alert. Clearly, he could not send every ship to sea indefinitely, but he could have reduced the numbers in port at any one time and put his commanders on the alert. No attempt was made to defend Guam or strengthen the US Asiatic Fleet. In what today would be described as a 'deteriorating international situation', little action was taken, even though all involved should have known, and indeed should have been reminded, that the Russo-Japanese War of 1904–05 had started without a declaration of war. Fighters were not on stand-by at their air stations; no ships were on reconnaissance or picket duty at sea. Ships in port did not have torpedo nets deployed, despite the lessons of Taranto and the growing tension between the United States and Japan.

The Philippines were especially vulnerable. The United States had just 19,000 troops garrisoned on the islands, supported by 160,000 locally-raised troops. This was a much larger area to cover than Hawaii – 115,707 square miles against 6,424 square miles – with many good landing areas. The US Asiatic Fleet was much weaker than the US Pacific Fleet and would have been unable to counter a strong Japanese attack on its own as it lacked both aircraft carriers and battleships.

The Japanese fleet was already at sea on 26 November. No doubt someone in Tokyo had anticipated the ambassador's pleadings in Washington being rejected.

Incredibly, when a radar operator at the northern tip of Oahu reported blips to his duty officer, Lieutenant Kermit Tyler, the latter simply replied: 'Well, don't worry about it.' The only thing that can be stated in Tyler's defence was that he had been told to expect a flight of Boeing B-17 Fortress bombers, but there was no attempt to check the number of blips or the direction of their approach. Shortly afterwards, the radar station closed for the day.

Just how much could have been done had Tyler sounded the alarm is open to question. As fighters were not on stand-by, few could have been got into the air in time to be effective against the first wave of Japanese bombers. On the other hand, those aboard the ships could have been alerted and gone to battle stations.

Even when a US destroyer discovered and sank a Japanese submarine that morning, no alert was sounded. It was to take until 2002 for the wreck to be discovered and identified, but in wartime that is a luxury and the mere fact that there had been an incident should have set alarm bells ringing across Hawaii.

Further west, a misunderstanding between Japanese commanders had seen the invasion of Malaya and Siam (present-day Thailand) begin at 01.15 hours, but as in Europe, communication between the wartime allies on the eve of war was poor.

Meanwhile, the aircrew for the first wave from *Akagi* had been awakened at 0500 as their ships ploughed through the tail of a tropical storm. As already mentioned, the raid was to be led by Mitsuo Fuchida, but while he was an experienced naval pilot, on this occasion he was being flown by Lieutenant Mutsuzaki so that he could direct the operation. On the flight deck, as he climbed into his aircraft a senior maintenance crewman approached Fuchida with a white scarf that he handed over, saying: 'All of the maintenance crew would like to go along to Pearl Harbor. Since we can't, we would like you to take this *hachimaki* ['helmet-scarf'] as a symbol that we are with you in spirit.' Fuchida tied the *hachimaki* around his flight helmet in the manner of a samurai.

Airborne at 0615, the 183 aircraft of the first wave flew in the direction of Pearl Harbor, 275 nautical miles away. As they approached the target, Fuchida pushed back the cockpit canopy and let the *hachimaki* stream out behind him and waved with both arms to the other airmen before closing the canopy again. At this stage he could see clouds below that he feared might obscure the target area, but he was encouraged as the sun rose and he saw its red disc, which reminded him of the Japanese naval ensign and struck him as a good omen. His fears about the weather over Pearl Harbor were soon dispelled as they tuned in to a weather forecast from a radio station in Hawaii, which assured him of a bright and cloudless day. His decision to learn English as a cadet was paying dividends.

At 0730 Fuchida's formation passed over the northern tip of Oahu at 10,000 feet, and he ordered the aircraft into their attack formations.

As they drew closer, at 0749 he then fired a rocket signal to start the attack but saw that the torpedo-bombers were already diving towards the ships in the harbour. He then fired a second rocket to alert the fighters, but this was mistaken for a warning of American fighters by the leader of the dive-bombers, who decided to press ahead with their attack. So many aircraft diving down towards the harbour could have led to collisions and chaos, but in fact they simply produced an attack in overwhelming numbers that added to the surprise and the chaos and confusion in and around the harbour and aboard the ships.

Below, in Pearl Harbor, sailors realized what was happening and the alert was sounded at 0758: 'Air raid, Pearl Harbor, this is no drill.' This was too late as no one was at their battle stations, with ships' companies racing from their accommodation or mess halls to man the guns.

Meanwhile, Fuchida was still at 10,000 feet, watching the action but disappointed to see that there were no aircraft carriers in the harbour. Nevertheless, the US Pacific Fleet's eight battleships were all present, including the USS *Pennsylvania* in dry dock, and there was also the target ship *Utah*, which Japanese naval intelligence wrongly believed to still be active.

Having expected to have to fight their way to the target area, the Japanese airmen were surprised that there was no fighter attack and no anti-aircraft fire from the ships and harbour installations below. The Japanese Zero fighters, with no American fighters to tackle, raced across the dockyards and the airbases at Ewa, Kaneohe Bay, Hickham and Wheeler Fields, strafing in what the Americans called 'fighter ramrod' attacks. As American fighters struggled to get into the air, they were shot down before they could gain height or speed. Almost 200 USAAF and USN aircraft were destroyed on the ground.

Another surprise for the Japanese was that the Americans had not deployed torpedo nets, leaving their ships exposed as the torpedo-bombers raced across the harbour so low that many thought they would never clear the towering superstructures of the larger ships. The first anti-aircraft fire did not start until the high-altitude bombers, sometimes known as 'level bombers', started their bombing runs, having of necessity to fly a straight and level course before releasing their bombs. Dive-bombers struck at shore installations on Ford Island, starting fires and sending debris into the air. Within minutes the clear blue skies of a fine morning were spoiled by clouds of thick black smoke rising high into the air.

Fuchida's aircraft was shaken by a direct hit and a near miss, but his pilot assured him that all was well. Fuchida's aircraft dropped its bombs and Fuchida then made three passes over his target, the battleship USS *California*. Making even a second pass was later to be discouraged as by that time, the AA gunners would have got a firm fix on the aircraft. On the second pass, his aircraft was rocked by the blast from the battleship *Arizona* as she blew up.

Fuchida was unknowingly taking on the role later defined by the Royal Air Force as the 'master bomber', directing his aircraft and waiting for the second wave of 170 aircraft to arrive. What was more important, however, was that he hung around long enough to be able to provide an accurate assessment of the bombing for the commander of the carrier force, Vice Admiral Chuichi Nagumo.

Despite the brilliance of the Japanese planning, many senior officers in the Imperial Japanese Navy still thought in terms of battleships and the success of the attack would be measured by the USN's losses of these capital ships. The 'big gun' navy was still alive and well in the IJN, as elsewhere. For these there was much to be pleased about. The *Arizona* was burning fiercely while the *Oklahoma* and *Utah* had both capsized, and the *California* and *West Virginia* were settling in the water. The light cruiser *Helena* was crippled.

The second wave consisted entirely of bombers as torpedo-bombers were regarded as vulnerable once the defences had been alerted. Their attack started exactly fifty minutes after the first-wave attack, and by this time the Americans had got a number of fighters into the air so most of the twenty-nine Japanese aircraft shot down were in the second wave.

One target for the second wave was the battleship *Nevada*, whose commanding officer had decided that his ship would be far safer at sea, moving at high speed rather than moored in harbour like a sitting duck. The aircraft of the second wave concentrated on the ship, realizing that if they could sink her in the harbour mouth, the entire base could be closed for several months. They attacked in overwhelming strength, inflicting serious damage on the ship, but her commanding officer was equal to the challenge, beaching his ship so that she could be saved and also avoid causing an obstruction for other ships. Other aircraft in the second wave attacked the battleship *Pennsylvania* and two destroyers which were also in dry dock.

The Fatal Decision

Genda was waiting to welcome Fuchida back aboard *Akagi*, with the news that twenty-nine aircraft had been lost in the attack and a further fifteen so badly damaged on return to their carriers that they had to be pushed over the sides of the flight decks and into the sea rather than delay other aircraft, running low on fuel, from landing. The rest were being hastily struck down into the hangar decks of the ships to be refuelled and re-armed as at least one and possibly two further strikes were planned for the afternoon.

This was a dangerous time, as the six ships were unable to fly off aircraft while others were still landing and the flight deck was congested. Had the US Pacific Fleet's three carriers been close and known of the position of the Japanese carriers, an effective strike could have been mounted. With six ships, it would have made sense to leave one or even two out of the operation, ready to provide air cover if necessary, but this was overlooked in the desire to send as many aircraft as possible to Pearl Harbor.

Fuchida had almost been shot down. The explosion that he had felt over the target area had damaged the aircraft, punching a large hole in the fuselage and as he stepped down from the aircraft, his attention was drawn to a control wire hanging by a thread and had it snapped, his aircraft would have spun out of control.

However, there was no time for Fuchida to ponder on his near escape; he had to report immediately to Nagumo with details of the damage done in the attack. He first consulted his flight commanders so that he could provide a comprehensive report, but soon Nagumo was impatiently demanding to see him.

When Fuchida reached Nagumo, he found him with *Akagi*'s commanding officer, Captain Kiichi Hasegawa. He reported that four battleships had been sunk and another three badly damaged. He then went on to report other ships that had been sunk, basing his report on a berthing chart provided by Japanese naval intelligence. Nagumo asked him if he thought that Pearl Harbor would be operational within six months, to which Fuchida replied that while the battleships would not be able to operate for six months, there were many smaller vessels that were still operational as well as the shore installations. He also suspected that there were still many airworthy aircraft, despite so many having been destroyed on the ground. In fact, he felt that an attack by a third wave of aircraft was needed, and that the port might need even a fourth attack.

While the three men conferred, aircraft were being refuelled and re-armed, with torpedoes being fitted to the dive-bombers as these would be more effective against ships at sea. The urgency with which this was done was driven not by the need for a third or fourth attack, but by concerns that the Japanese carriers were vulnerable to attack from the American carriers known to be at sea. There were also fears that land-based aircraft from Hawaii would attack. The meeting then broke up and Fuchida took a hasty lunch of bean paste and rice wafers.

There was no attempt to mount a reconnaissance to find the American carriers and no attempt at a post-attack photographic reconnaissance over Pearl Harbor, as the British had done at Taranto using RAF reconnaissance aircraft based on Malta.

Even before Fuchida had finished his meal, the decision was taken not to mount a further attack. Nagumo signalled to the other ships that they should withdraw north-west. Fuchida dashed to the bridge and did the unthinkable for a Japanese officer, demanding to know why further attacks had not been ordered. Nagumo ignored him and left it to his chief of staff, Kusaka, to tell Fuchida abruptly that the raid's objectives had been met!

Fuchida's fears were shared by Yamamoto when he received the signal telling him of the decision. His original scheme, of a year of decisive victories, was in ruins.

No one in the Allied camp was to realize this at the time. On the same day as the attack on Pearl Harbor, the Japanese had landed in Malaya and Siam, at the start of a long march south that would end with the capture of Singapore and a humiliating defeat for the British. On 10 December the first Japanese forces landed on Luzon, before which the US Asiatic Fleet had been crippled by attacks by aircraft based in Formosa.

Within weeks, Japan had acquired some of the most important items for a wartime economy, including Malaya's rubber. It was also enhancing its food supplies. Malaya, with its rubber and tin, has in recent years been viewed by economic historians as having been the most worthwhile of Britain's colonial possessions. However, Japan still needed a source of fuel, without which any chance of remaining in the war, let alone winning it, would be lost.

Fighting for the East Indies

The Netherlands East Indies (present-day Indonesia) were among the most prized of the colonial possessions of any of the European powers.

The most significant of the country's production was oil. This was an important asset for the Dutch as the colonial rulers, but even more so to the Japanese for whom it was vital. Japan could only gain territory by basing troops there, but first the seas had to be controlled and, importantly, the skies above them.

The Royal Navy had tried to stop Japan reinforcing its troops in Siam and Malaya by sending the new battleship *Prince of Wales* and the elderly battle-cruiser *Repulse*. These two ships had been meant to operate in conjunction with the new aircraft carrier *Indomitable*, a sister ship of *Illustrious*, but she had run aground and was not available, leaving them with just four destroyers for protection. Worse, the commander of this small squadron, Rear Admiral Tom Phillips, still believed that they could attack the invasion fleet and also believed that radio silence should be maintained, making it virtually impossible for the RAF to provide air cover. On 10 December, both ships were sunk by Japanese bombers and torpedo-bombers flying from airfields near Saigon in French Indo-China.

The speed of the Japanese advance and the heavy losses being suffered by the Allies made it difficult to regroup and move to the offensive, or even establish a strong defensive position. Japan had control of the sea and of the skies.

In an attempt to turn the tide, in January 1942 an Allied combat group was hastily assembled including British, Dutch, American and Australian ships under the command of Rear Admiral Karel Doorman. Unwittingly, this assembly was given the title of the 'Combined Striking Force', the same name given by the Japanese to their force that attacked Pearl Harbor. A command was assembled for the armed forces of these four countries as they attempted to secure the Netherlands East Indies; this was ABDA (American, British, Dutch and Australian Command), staffed according to the numbers supplied by each country.

This was no grand command possessing a balanced fleet and everything needed to fight and win, but instead a collection of assorted ships left over from the fighting in and around the Philippines, Malaya, Singapore and the East Indies. It had no aircraft carriers. There was little time to exercise or train together, or to establish any kind of cohesion or communication. The British and Australians had a degree of integration, and the British and Americans had co-operated during the closing stages of the First World War, but the Dutch had not worked with another navy since 1816 when a combined British, Dutch and American naval squadron had been assembled in the Mediterranean to

A fleet at peace. This is Taranto in the 1930s. The ships are moored stern to the quayside, an arrangement known as 'Mediterranean mooring'. However, at the time of the attack most ships were anchored in the harbour, making them easier targets. (*Source unknown*)

The year is 1933 and the new German *Panzerschiff* or 'armoured ship', *Deutschland*, known to the British and American media as a pocket battleship, passes through Kiel Bay. The smaller ship to starboard is a training vessel. The ship's name was changed to *Lutzow* as someone foresaw the potential effect on morale of *Deutschland* being sunk! (*German Federal Archives*)

A pre-war shot of the cruiser HMS *Cornwall* and the aircraft carrier HMS *Hermes* on the China Station. The Royal Navy was the most widely scattered of any of the navies of the belligerent powers in the Second World War. (*US Naval Historical Records Centre*)

British heavy cruiser *Dorsetshire* on a visit to Australia in 1938, with Sydney Harbour Bridge in the background. These ships were classed as heavy cruisers under the terms of the Washington Naval Treaty of 1922, which stipulated that heavy cruisers had 8in guns and light cruisers 6in; tonnage had nothing to do with their classification. (*Imperial War Museum*)

Another *Panzerschiff* was the *Admiral Graf Spee*, the first of the trio of ships to be lost when attacked by three British cruisers in December 1939. After putting most of her crew ashore in Montevideo, the capital of neutral Uruguay, her commanding officer scuttled her, believing that stronger British forces were waiting for his ship. (*German Federal Archives*)

Two of the three ships that accounted for the *Graf Spee*: HMS *Achilles* is seen from the deck of her sister ship, *Ajax*. HMS *Achilles* had earlier been transferred to the Royal New Zealand Navy. (*Source unknown*)

In an attempt to obtain the surrender of the French fleet at Mers-el-Kébir and Oran, repeated attempts were made to open communications but the French resolutely refused to surrender their ships or put them beyond use. Captain Holland, commanding officer of *Ark Royal*, was sent by seaplane to negotiate, and on his way back the problem was how to return to his own command quickly. The first of these three images shows the Swordfish seaplane approaching the carrier, with the arrester wires removed from the flight deck. (*Author's collection*)

Touchdown! To reduce her top weight and also ensure that she remained within her specified tonnage, *Ark Royal* had a very thin flight deck, so the danger of damage was very real. (*Author's collection*)

Safely down! Deck crew rush out with wheels in order to manoeuvre the Swordfish. (*Author's collection*)

Although a battle-cruiser, HMS *Hood* was the Royal Navy's largest warship for many years. She was meant to be one of a class of four ships, but design defects meant that the rest of the class was cancelled. She was due to be refitted and partially rebuilt in the early 1940s; however, she blew up in the famous encounter with the *Bismarck* and *Prinz Eugen* before that could be done. (*US National Archives*)

The sleek lines of the pride of the German Navy, the battleship *Bismarck*, possibly passing through the Kiel Canal as the water appears calm and tugs are in attendance. She was not to survive for much longer than the *Hood*. (*German Federal Archive*)

The Royal Navy tracked down and sank *Bismarck*, with the campaign aided considerably by the use of carrier-borne aircraft that crippled the ship. Here are Fairey Swordfish aboard HMS *Victorious* before taking off on a strike against the German battleship. (*Imperial War Museum*)

Survivors from the *Bismarck* desperately attempt to board the British cruiser *Dorsetshire*, but after one of them told the cruiser's crew that a submarine was coming the rescue had to be abandoned, meaning that most of the German sailors died. (*Imperial War Museum*)

n wartime many ships are, in naval terms, 'taken up from trade' for a variety of tasks. At the top end of the scale were the armed cruisers, although these were overwhelmed when facing major warships. Much further down the scale were the converted trawlers, used for minesweeping and convoy escorts: this is His Majesty's Trawler, HMT *Acacia*. (*Imperial War Museum*)

The Germans also used armed trawlers and this is the *Kapitan Stemmer*, armed and with much communications equipment that she would not have needed in her peacetime role. (*German Federal Archive*)

HMS *Exeter* was the third of the trio of cruisers that fought in the Battle of the River Plate with the *Graf Spee*. A heavy cruiser, she had the heaviest armament of any of the three vessels but her 8in guns should not have been a match for the 11in guns of the German ship. She is seen here off Sumatra in 1942, not long before her own demise. (*Australian War Memorial*)

A Japanese photograph showing HMS *Exeter* sinking in the Battle of the Java Sea. The odds were heavily stacked against her and the other ships due to the lack of carrier-borne aircraft to defend them. (*US National Archives*)

Another Japanese photograph showing heavy cruisers HMS *Dorsetshire* and *Cornwall* sinking off Malaya after being attacked by Japanese aircraft. The pattern left by the wake of the two ships as they tried to evade Japanese attack can be seen clearly. (*US National Archives*)

Undoubtedly the most successful of the many different conversions of merchant ships during the Second World War were the MAC ships, or merchant aircraft carriers, which were tankers and grain carriers fitted with a wooden flight deck. None of these were lost to enemy action, but they saved many merchant ships and seamen in the convoys they escorted. The puff of steam is from a valve that leaked steam to show the wind direction. (*Author's collection*)

It is difficult to say whether taking off or landing was more dangerous on the short and narrow flight deck, but the Fairey Swordfish and their pilots were always up to the challenge. The position of the other ships in the convoy shows that the *Adula* had to change course to head into the wind. These ships were still manned by the Merchant Navy and operated by ship-owners but of course the air-crew, the maintainers and the 'batsman' were all Royal Navy personnel. (*Author's collection*)

Supposedly intended as a replacement for the Swordfish, the Fairey Albacore brought the luxury of an enclosed cockpit but engine problems meant that it never really displaced the Swordfish. Towards the end of the war there were plans to build a batch of Swordfish with cockpit canopies for the Royal Canadian Navy.
(*Author's collection*)

Intended to do the same job as the Swordfish was the Fairey Albacore. One of the roles for this aircraft was supposed to be dive-bombing; however, it was notorious for not always pulling out of a dive. Dive-bombing was meant to ensure accuracy, but judging when to pull out was difficult as altimeters could not unwind fast enough to show the true height above the target. (*Author's collection*)

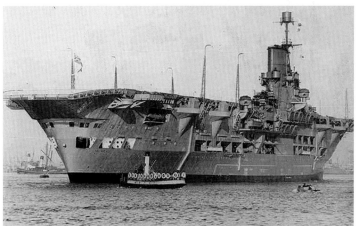

The last aircraft carrier to join the Royal Navy before the outbreak of war was HMS *Ark Royal*, only the second British carrier to have been laid down as such. Her high freeboard is due to a combination of two hangar decks and a full-length flight deck. (*Author's collection*)

Another image of *Ark Royal* showing her three aircraft lifts, which had to be relatively narrow to avoid weakening her thin flight deck even further. Everyone expected her to be at the mercy of aerial attack, but ironically she would be lost to a single torpedo fired by a U-boat off Gibraltar that disabled her machinery. (*Author's collection*)

The shortage of flight decks was eventually solved by the escort carrier, known to the Royal Navy as auxiliary carriers, which was a better term as they did more than just escort convoys: ferrying aircraft, acting as maintenance carriers, supporting aircraft providing air cover for ground forces during the Mediterranean invasions and also as US forces island-hopped across the Pacific towards Japan. This is HMS *Ameer* (an alternative spelling of 'Emir') refuelling a Canadian destroyer. (*Imperial War Museum*)

A broadside view of HMS *Achates*, a British destroyer commissioned in 1930 and one of a class of nine vessels. Despite severe economic depression for most of the period between the two world wars, the Royal Navy received around eight new destroyers almost every year. (*Imperial War Museum*)

The Arctic convoys saw those involved battling with the weather as much as with the Germans. This is the light cruiser HMS *Scylla*, with her crew attempting to clear the forecastle of ice, which even covered the armament. Ships could even become top-heavy with ice and roll over. (*IWM A15365*)

The Swordfish was invaluable as an anti-submarine aircraft and was also used for reconnaissance. However, despite being a single-engined biplane and frequently seen over and around convoys, they were often mistaken for German Junkers Ju 88s by anti-aircraft gunners aboard convoy ships, despite the Ju 88 being a sleek twin-engined monoplane. One Swordfish pilot devised this Valentine card in an attempt to stop a convoy's AA fire being aimed at his aircraft. (*Author's collection*)

SAINT VALENTINE'S DAY 1945.

The single-engined Stringbag
Has flown for quite a time.
Its prehistoric silhouette
Is known in every clime.
How different the 88,
With fuselage so slim —
A monoplane with motors two;
Don't make mistakes with him!

Yet what a metamorphosis
A bit of action brings,
When Junkers fly at 80 knots
And grow some second wings,
And Stringbags (clearly Nazified)
And Wildcat sixes too
Become the targets of all guns
Whilst 88's fly through.....

The leopard cannot change his spots,
Nor I (alas!) change mine:
Remember this, and I'll be pleased
To be your Valentine.

The *Illustrious*-class aircraft carriers were the most successful of the Second World War, having strong armoured protection and speed, with the latter attribute not only making flying operations easier but also making them a more difficult target for submarines. This is the third ship of the class, HMS *Victorious*, seen here in Icelandic waters. (*Author's collection*)

Contrast the clean lines of *Victorious* with those of HMS *Glorious*, a converted 'light' battle-cruiser. Her design incorporated a separate take-off deck as well as a main flight deck that could be used for both landing and taking off but which was, of course, far too short as aircraft sizes and weights increased. This is one of the last photographs to be taken of her, off Norway, and seen here with the RAF Hawker Hurricanes ranged aft on her flight deck. (*Source unknown*)

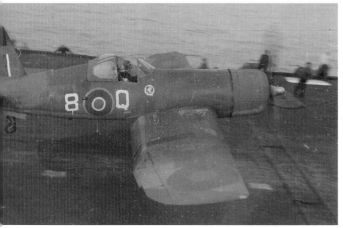

The new generation of more capable aircraft carriers allowed higher-performance aircraft to be operated, one of which was the Vought Corsair supplied from the United States after the USN initially believed that the aircraft was too large and heavy to be flown from carriers. Some believe that it was the best carrier fighter of the war. (*Author's collection*)

One of the most modern battleships was HMS *Prince of Wales*, but she was hampered by having 14in guns rather than 16in as originally planned in order to comply with new but short-lived international agreements. The low bows of this class were intended to allow her 'A' turret to fire forward but adversely affected sea-keeping. She was sunk by the Japanese on 10 December 1941. (*Imperial War Museum*)

Another casualty was HMS *Eagle*, torpedoed while escorting Operation PEDESTAL, the Malta convoy of August 1942. She was meant to be retired once the first of the new fast armoured carriers arrived but as war loomed, not only was she and the other three older carriers retained but an additional three carriers were ordered, one of which was a maintenance ship. (*Imperial War Museum*)

HMS *Safari*, one of the larger submarines used by the Royal Navy. These suffered heavy losses, especially in the Mediterranean where larger submarines were at a disadvantage, even though their size also meant that they were useful in helping to keep the island supplied. (*Imperial War Museum*)

An aerial view of HMS *Triumph*, famous for being the only British submarine to survive striking a mine. The crew were having lunch at the time, which was served around midnight on submarines, as she was on the surface in bad weather recharging her batteries. Eyewitness accounts tell of an explosive pulse travelling through the boat with some soup being spilled, but fortunately the torpedoes loaded in her forward tubes did not explode and she was able to limp into Chatham for repairs. (*Author's collection*)

Malta spent all of 1942 and much of the following year on the verge of collapse. Food supplies were very short and fuel was scarce, crucial for Malta's survival. Relief finally came with the convoy of August 1942, code-named Operation PEDESTAL. This is the crippled tanker *Ohio*, being helped into Grand Harbour with her vital cargo of fuel. She settled on the harbour bottom after unloading and, once refloated, broke her back.

Experience earlier in the war had shown that reconnaissance was essential for successful landings and that the landing fleet and bombardment ships needed guidance to the right positions. Off Normandy, this was done by X-craft, midget submarines with a four-man crew, which were skilfully navigated so that they could show lights to seaward. Other uses included an attack on the German battleship *Tirpitz* in a Norwegian fjord. This is a preserved X-craft, *X-24*, at the Submarine Museum in Gosport, Hampshire. (*RN Submarine Museum*)

The Germans expected attacks on *Tirpitz* from the air, and together the Royal Air Force and the Fleet Air Arm ensured that they weren't disappointed. The efforts made to hide the ship, or at least break up her outline, can be seen here. (*German Federal Archive*)

This is what the ship normally looked like: a sister of the ill-fated *Bismarck*, but in the end also to be sunk when the RAF used 12,000lb 'Tallboy' bombs that capsized her. (*German Federal Archive*)

Good images of *Tirpitz* were hard to come by, so the United States Navy prepared this drawing so that naval officers who encountered the ship would be quick to recognize her. The fact that the drawing shows her from above indicates that the main audience for the image would be the crew of reconnaissance or attacking aircraft. (*US National Archives*)

Convoy speeds were so low that destroyers were wasted as escorts and in any case were not sturdy enough for prolonged exposure to heavy seas, so the corvette was developed from a design for a commercial whaling ship. This is HMS *Dianthus*, with members of her crew reloading a depth-charge launcher. (*Imperial War Museum*)

The corvette was a highly successful development, so much so that under what was known unofficially as 'reverse lend-lease' a number of ships were transferred to the United States Navy, giving them access to British sonar technology. This is the former HMS *Milfoil* in her new role as USS *Intensity*. (*US National Archives*)

A convoy of landing craft crosses the English Channel bound for Normandy with barrage balloons to provide extra protection from attack by German aircraft. In fact, there was no German aerial intervention and the landings largely caught the Germans by surprise, partly because of doubts over the landing site and partly because of bad weather. (*Imperial War Museum*)

The battleship HMS *Nelson* on gunnery trials. She had nine 16in guns in three turrets, all of which were mounted forward. Not only could a 16in shell pack a heavier punch than a 15 or 14in shell, it also had longer range. After the landings, the Germans found moving troops and tanks difficult for more than 20 miles from the coast because of the naval bombardment. (*Imperial War Museum*)

Into the 'Jaws of Death' was the original caption for this official US photograph of troops aboard to charge ashore at what became known as 'Bloody Omaha'. The Germans were not only well-positioned and well-garrisoned at this point, but the pre-landing bombing and naval bombardment had largely left the defences unscathed. (*US Coast Guard Service*)

Two prefabricated harbours, known as Mulberry Harbours, had to be towed into position and assembled after the landings as landing ships were severely limited in the volume of cargo they could carry, and which had of necessity to be self-propelled. The harbours meant that supplies could be shipped directly from the United States. A severe storm damaged both harbours and rendered that in the US sector unusable. (*US National Archives*)

The vast thirst of the combined Allied aircraft, tanks and supply vehicles meant that an oil pipeline was needed, known as PLUTO for 'pipeline under the ocean'. PLUTO ran from Shanklin on the east coast of the Isle of Wight. (*Source unknown*)

Even as the Germans began to withdraw from Greece and the Balkans, harried by Allied air and naval forces, there was an attempted Communist coup in Greece. Here is Winston Churchill disembarking from the cruiser HMS *Ajax* for a meeting ashore in Athens. (*Imperial War Museum*)

attack the Barbary pirates. Doorman was given command because of his seniority, not because of his experience and certainly not because he had the strongest force or the most powerful ships.

The Japanese were by this time becoming thinly stretched, with their Combined Striking Force having covered landings across the Pacific and it was left to the Second Carrier Division under Rear Admiral Yamaguchi with *Soryu* and *Hiryu* to send off the first air strikes against Ambon for the invasion of the Netherlands East Indies.

The USN had started to fight back, with the carriers USS *Enterprise* and *Yorktown*, escorted by five cruisers and ten destroyers, attacking Japanese bases in the Marshall Islands on 1 February 1942. The damage was slight, but the Japanese were reminded in no uncertain terms that they had failed to destroy the American carrier force.

On 4 February, the Allies tried to attack a Japanese landing force in the Straits of Macassar, with Doorman taking four cruisers and eight destroyers. This force had to withdraw under heavy aerial attack by Japanese bombers, which severely damaged the USS *Marblehead* and also caused damage to another American cruiser, the *Houston*. On 13 February, even while they were taking Singapore, Japanese forces also landed at Palembang on Sumatra with just one carrier, *Ryujo*, covering the assault. Finally, Japan had its oil supply.

Doorman's Combined Striking Force bore no real resemblance to its Japanese counterpart and namesake. Instead of six aircraft carriers, it had none. What he did have were two heavy and three light cruisers, as well as nine destroyers. The heavy cruisers were the USS *Houston* and HMS *Exeter*, while the light cruisers were Doorman's flagship *De Ruyter*, another Dutch cruiser *Java* and HMAS *Perth*. He did not have reconnaissance aircraft and communications between his ships was difficult. There had been no exercises together, while the ships needed refitting and the crews resting. They had spent some time trying to intercept Japanese troop convoys but with little success.

At 1427 on 27 February 1942, while his ships were refuelling, Doorman heard that a Japanese invasion force had been detected in the Macassar Straits, escorted by two heavy cruisers, *Nachi* and *Haguro*, and two light cruisers, *Jintsu* and *Naka*, with fourteen destroyers, under the command of Vice Admiral Takagi.

The Battle of the Java Sea commenced at 1620 with a long-range gunnery duel between the opposing heavy cruisers. In an attempt to use his light cruisers, Doorman started to close the range and at 1630 his light cruisers joined the gunnery duel. Shortly afterwards, the

Japanese destroyers raced towards Doorman's force, led by the *Jintsu*, ready for a torpedo attack. At 1708, *Exeter* was torpedoed and badly damaged, dropping out of line, but not realizing what had happened, both *Houston* and *Perth* followed her, with the Allied line becoming confused. In the chaos, Doorman attempted to restore order and launch a counter-attack, but he then lost the destroyer *Kortenaer* and almost immediately afterwards she was followed by another destroyer. Doorman sent *Exeter* back to Surabaya with the destroyer *Witte de With* as an escort.

As darkness fell, Japanese aircraft marked the position of the Allied ships with flares, while Doorman tried to get his fleet around the Japanese warships to strike at the invasion force. He had to send the four American destroyers back to Surabaya to refuel and re-arm as they had used all their torpedoes. At 2300 a further attack was mounted by the Japanese against the Allied cruisers, with an attack using twelve torpedoes sinking the *Java* at 2332, followed within minutes by *De Ruyter*, with Doorman going down with his ship. Both *Perth* and *Houston* managed to escape to Java.

The Japanese troopships reached Java without loss and the landings began on 28 February.

The following day, 1 March, *Exeter*, by now escorted by two destroyers, was caught by four Japanese cruisers and aircraft from the carrier *Ryujo* and all three ships were sunk.

Allied forces on Java surrendered on 9 March, marking the end of the brief life of ABDA.

Ceylon

As the Japanese 'empire' spread steadily westwards and southwards, the strains began to tell. In a raid on Java, *Kaga* scraped a reef and had to return to Japan for repairs, but by this time the distances between its major bases and the front line was increasing. Singapore to Japan was a comparable distance to Southampton to New York, so ships had to be rotated out of operations for far longer than was desirable. There was also a tendency to disagree over priorities and a certain amount of what might be regarded as costly and unnecessary diversions, as when an attack was made on Darwin in Australia's Northern Territory.

Japan wanted to include Burma in its empire, seeing it as a route into India, while the country was also a valuable further resource of oil and timber. Before invading Burma, Japan needed to deal with the Royal Navy's Eastern Fleet. Yamamoto sent five aircraft carriers –

Akagi, Shokaku, Zuikaku, Hiryu and *Soryu* – into the Indian Ocean on 26 March 1942. The objective was to attack British bases in Ceylon, off the southern tip of India.

The British Eastern Fleet was a formidable force commanded by Vice Admiral Sir James Somerville, with three aircraft carriers including the two modern ships, *Indomitable* and *Formidable*, as well as the elderly and small *Hermes*, by this time more of a liability than an asset as she was unable to keep up with the fast modern armoured carriers and would have been better used in convoy protection. Somerville also had the battleships *Warspite, Resolution, Revenge, Ramillies* and *Royal Sovereign*, all veterans of the First World War, but *Warspite* at least had been modernized.

The advancing Japanese were first spotted on 4 April by a patrolling RAF Consolidated Catalina flying boat, which managed to transmit a warning before it was shot down by Zero fighters. The following day, Mitsuo Fuchida led a massed attack against Colombo, Ceylon's major port and capital, striking at 0800. He fully expected a repeat of his success at Pearl Harbor, but the Eastern Fleet was absent; however, the port was very busy with merchant shipping. The RAF put its small force of fighters into the air to fight off the Japanese attack, but their Hawker Hurricanes were no match for the agile, fast Zero and almost all were shot down. The Japanese inflicted serious damage on port installations and among the ships hit were an armed merchant cruiser and a destroyer. Nevertheless, effective anti-aircraft fire meant that the Japanese suffered their first serious losses of the war.

Having been alerted to the approach of the Japanese but not knowing where and when they would strike, Somerville had sensibly decided that his ships would be safer at sea rather than sitting ducks in harbour at Colombo or Trincomalee. The two large carriers had gone to Gan, the southernmost island of Addu Atoll, where a secret refuelling anchorage had been constructed.

On his return from the raid, Fuchida suggested to Nagumo that they send reconnaissance aircraft to locate the British warships, and on this occasion Nagumo agreed. Fuchida remained aboard his ship while a strong force of aircraft was assembled ready for a second attack on Colombo if one was ordered. At noon, a strong force of fifty aircraft from *Soryu* discovered the two heavy cruisers *Cornwall* and *Dorsetshire*, without air cover, and in just twenty minutes sank both ships.

Hermes had left Trincomalee and headed north, but returned to the port on 6 April. On 8 April, following an intelligence assessment that Trincomalee was likely to be the next target of the Japanese, she returned to sea but this time she headed south. Early on 9 April, *Hermes* was spotted by Japanese aircraft and ordered to return to Trincomalee where it was felt that the harbour's AA defences would be able to protect her. Shortly before 0730, Fuchida led a force of 100 aircraft to attack Trincomalee, but again was disappointed to find the British Eastern Fleet missing. The RAF sent eleven Hurricanes into the air, but nine were shot down. Again damage was done to the shore installations, although the first wave of the attack sank only one merchant vessel but more ships were sunk by the second wave.

After landing back aboard *Akagi*, Fuchida was told that a British aircraft carrier had been spotted. While his aircraft were hastily refuelled and re-armed, *Akagi* was attacked by nine Bristol Blenheim bombers, which failed to hit her. The Japanese planned to attack *Hermes* with dive-bombers escorted by Zero fighters in case the carrier put up fighters, while torpedo-bombers were also prepared in case the initial attack failed. They didn't realize that *Hermes* was unable to operate fighters because of her poor speed and small size, and that day she was without aircraft of any kind; her only defence was her own AA armament and that of her escort, the Australian destroyer HMAS *Vampire*. Fuchida was not ready in time to lead the attack, which was led by another officer, Egusa, but he arrived in time to find the carrier sinking and the destroyer dead in the water, crippled by explosions from her own magazines. Donald Farquharson-Roberts, a young officer in the Royal Marines aboard *Hermes*, recalled:

> The planes seemed to have no fear. They came in at masthead height and at least one was reported as being below the fighting top...Marine Youle...told me he was firing downwards...I saw a plane coming straight for my gun. I saw the bomb swing clear and come straight for ME. I was standing about 6 feet behind the gun and it hit the deck in front of me...and went straight through the deck.
>
> I never heard the command to abandon ship, although I was told it was given. I took leave of the old girl by stepping into the water on the port side...There was then only a drop of about 10 feet. I swam clear but the stern was swinging away from me as she had full helm on and the engines were still going full ahead...

Farquharson-Roberts' own gun had jammed during the attack. The first bomb had hit the carrier at 1055 and she sank in less than twenty minutes. Fortunately, the Japanese had failed to spot an Australian hospital ship, the *Vita*, that arrived shortly afterwards and rescued most of the survivors, while a few had managed to swim the short distance to the shores of Ceylon.

The Japanese hadn't had it all their own way, even at this early stage of the war in the Pacific. However, the period from victory to defeat was to be very short in the East, and within six months of Pearl Harbor the Japanese were to be on the defensive.

The USN Strikes Back

By this time, the United States Navy was already proving its resilience and its ability to strike back. The war in the Pacific was the ultimate aircraft carrier war. Without the aircraft carrier the Japanese could not have attacked Pearl Harbor, but without the aircraft carrier the Americans could not have taken the war back to Japan as it was not until Saipan was captured in June 1944 that the United States Army Air Force's long-range bombers came within striking distance of the Japanese home islands.

As mentioned above, on 1 February 1942 Vice Admiral W.F. 'Bull' Halsey had taken the aircraft carriers *Enterprise* and *Yorktown*, escorted by five cruisers and ten destroyers, to attack Japanese bases on the Marshall and Gilbert Islands.

Something more ambitious was needed, however, and the idea came from a USAAF officer, Colonel James 'Jimmy' Doolittle. The plan was to fly twin-engined North American B-25 Mitchell bombers from an aircraft carrier to mount a raid on Japan itself. There were objections to the idea because the aircraft would have to remain on deck and that would leave little space for taking off, and also from the leader of the Chinese Nationalists, Generalissimo Chiang Kai-shek, who feared reprisals by Japan against the Chinese. Nevertheless, the sheer nerve of the idea and the impact it would have on Japanese morale, forcing them to divert resources to protect their cities, made it too attractive to reject.

Two carriers were assigned to the operation. The *Hornet* was to carry the bombers, while her sister ship *Enterprise* would provide fighter and anti-submarine protection. The plan was that the bombers would not return to their ship, which would have been impossible anyway, but would fly on to bases in mainland China, which gave the operation the code-name of SHANGRI-LA, the fictional 'earthly paradise'.

The plan was so audacious that when *Hornet* left Pearl Harbor with sixteen B-25s crowded on her flight deck, observers simply assumed that she was being used as an aircraft transport. Even the Japanese were not alarmed when they picked up signals on 10 April as the two ships attempted to rendezvous, as two US carriers could easily be handled by Japanese forces and a network of picket ships had been established 700 miles off the Japanese islands. Once the picket line was crossed, Japanese aircraft could deal with the carriers.

Radio silence was maintained after 10 April. Halsey knew about the picket line and assumed that once it was crossed the Japanese would know his position. On 18 April the B-25 bombers were launched 550 miles from Tokyo, allowing the carriers to withdraw. Halsey had been wise not to hazard his ships, but in fact his crossing of the picket line was not noticed by the Japanese. Even when a patrolling aircraft radioed that it had spotted sixteen twin-engined bombers in the air, the Japanese did nothing as they knew that the USN had no carrier-borne twin-engined bombers.

The Japanese did have fighters patrolling at 10,000 feet but they missed the bombers as they raced across the coast at just 150 feet, heading for Tokyo, Yokosuka and Nagoya. The bombers caused considerable alarm as they dropped their bombs and fired their machine guns before flying on to land in China. This was the weak spot in the planning as the bases chosen were unsuitable for such relatively large aircraft. One which overflew and landed in the Soviet Union had its crew arrested, while another two crash-landed near Japanese-occupied Hankow where they were taken prisoner by the Japanese. Taking prisoners gave the Japanese a propaganda coup, enabling them to claim that nine bombers had been shot down. The prisoners were taken to Tokyo where they were prosecuted for the deaths of two schoolchildren killed in the attack, before being executed. In China, as Chiang Kai-shek had feared, the Japanese brought forward an operation and slaughtered 250,000 men, women and children.

The operation has been dismissed as worthless bravado, but it boosted American morale. The real problem was that the small force was spread across too many targets, and had all sixteen aircraft headed for one target, such as the Imperial Palace in Tokyo, it could have been far more successful. Even so, at this stage of the war the Allies had much to learn about the concentration of force, especially in the air.

Nevertheless, what was to happen over the next two months was to change the entire course of the war. Yamamoto, that most realistic of senior Japanese officers, had hoped to have a year in which the Japanese armed forces could run free, but he was to be proved over-optimistic.

The setbacks were not simply at sea. The Japanese advance had finally been stalled in Burma and New Guinea; two places a considerable distance apart and that showed the limitations imposed on Japanese logistics. The problem was made worse by the Japanese placing far greater emphasis on fighting units at the cost of neglecting the support units, which armed forces elsewhere in the world knew directly affected the efficiency of the fighting units. At sea, convoy protection was poor and seen as a duty to be avoided. The Japanese had what the Royal Navy would have regarded as auxiliary aircraft carriers; however, these were not used as convoy escorts but as aircraft transports for the Japanese Army Air Force.

By today's standards, aircraft of the day had limited range and airlift capability, so the one vital strategic asset possessed by the Japanese was their carrier force, but it was an asset also enjoyed by the United States Navy, which had the industrial base to renew and expand its carrier force as necessary.

Further landings were planned by the Japanese, both in New Guinea and much further north in the Aleutians. New bases were planned in the Solomons and at Midway Island. The Aleutians and Midway were seen as important points in an outer defensive ring.

Returning from operations over and around Ceylon, Nagumo was ordered to detach the Fifth Carrier Division and send it towards Truk. The Fifth was commanded by Vice Admiral Takagi and had two of Japan's newest and finest aircraft carriers, *Zuikaku* and *Shokaku*, with a total of 125 aircraft between them. The actual landings at Port Moresby would be covered by aircraft from the smaller *Shoho*, a converted submarine depot ship of just 13,000 tons. The two large Japanese carriers were supported by two heavy cruisers and six destroyers, while other ships covered *Shoho*. Meanwhile, Admiral Chester Nimitz, the new commander-in-chief of the US Pacific Fleet, sent Rear Admiral Frank Fletcher with Task Force 17, which included the aircraft carriers *Yorktown* and *Lexington* with 141 aircraft, to the Coral Sea. Task Force 17 also included five American heavy cruisers and nine destroyers, as well as three British cruisers and two destroyers.

On 3 May Japanese forces landed unopposed on Tulagi and Guadalcanal in the Eastern Solomon Islands, but on the following day aircraft from *Yorktown* surprised Japanese warships lying off Tulagi and sank a destroyer and three minesweepers as well as destroying several seaplanes. Both fleets refuelled at sea on 6 May, for some hours not realizing that they were just 70 miles apart in the Coral Sea, despite both fleets mounting aerial reconnaissance. It was not until later in the day when USAAF aircraft located the Japanese Port Moresby assault force and passed this information to Fletcher that the Americans realized how close the Japanese were.

The next day, aircraft from both the American carriers found the Port Moresby invasion force and concentrated their efforts on the *Shoho*, which despite desperately circling was sunk within three minutes at the cost of three American aircraft. The Japanese immediately recalled the assault force, including the troopships. Next a Japanese reconnaissance aircraft discovered a tanker being escorted by a destroyer, and mistook the tanker for an aircraft carrier and the destroyer for a cruiser, which encouraged Takagi to send no fewer than sixty bombers to attack both ships, which were sunk within minutes.

That night, both fleets were so close that six Japanese aircraft attempted to land on *Yorktown* in the dark. On 8 May reconnaissance aircraft from both fleets finally found each other almost simultaneously, 200 miles apart. Both admirals hastily arranged air strikes, with the Japanese sending ninety aircraft against the Americans, who sent seventy-eight aircraft against the Japanese. *Zuikaku* escaped into a rainstorm but *Shokaku* was not so fortunate, being hit by three bombs which forced her to return to Truk, although she missed the torpedoes dropped by Douglas Devastators from the *Lexington*, almost certainly due to the problems the Americans were suffering with their torpedoes at this stage of the war.

Anticipating an attack, Fletcher had ordered fighter cover and sent reconnaissance aircraft out to warn him of any approach by the Japanese. They were spotted at 17,000 feet and at a range of 60 miles. The two American carriers each had a cruiser and a destroyer screen, with *Lexington* steaming some 2 miles ahead and to starboard of *Yorktown*. The Japanese torpedo bombers attacked in three groups of six aircraft each, with two groups attacking *Lexington* on both sides and a third group attacking *Yorktown*. Captain Sherman aboard *Lexington* took violent evasive action while his AA gunners put up a curtain of fire, blowing up a Nakajima B5N 'Kate' on its run towards the ship. It has been claimed that as many as eleven torpedoes were dropped before two finally hit the ship, with the first striking the port bow at 1120 and the second amidships on the port side shortly afterwards.

Stanley Johnson, a war correspondent with the *Chicago Tribune*, was later to recall:

> I arrived on the main deck – two below the flight deck – to find dust and smoke drifting through the passageways coming from further aft. In the passageway amidships, I found four men who were nearly naked...they were horribly burned. A Filipino cook... assisted me to get the men on to the cots in the passageway and take off the remainder of their clothes, give them a drink of water and a morphia injection. A hospital corpsman...treated their burns with tannic acid jelly and took over their care. Men kept coming in from the 5in gun galleries, sometimes alone, others with the help of comrades. We had about twelve men on the cots and during a brief lull I went to the gun galleries to see what had happened. There I saw several bodies, they seemed to have been frozen or charred into grotesque statues.

Elsewhere aboard the crippled carrier, men were fighting to stop her from sinking and at first they seemed to be succeeding. Commander Healey, in charge of damage control, reported to his commanding officer that they had the damage shored up and would soon have the ship on an even keel, suggesting flippantly that any further torpedo strikes should be taken on the starboard side. These were almost certainly his last words, for no sooner had he stopped speaking than a massive blast swept through the ship as an aviation fuel tank blew up close to Healey's damage-control station. Streams of flame and sparks swept through the ship, killing many men and opening up decks and deckheads, leaving the surviving damage-control parties overwhelmed. Worse was to come when a second aviation fuel tank exploded twenty minutes later, wrecking the water mains and making further fire-fighting impossible. After this, the electricity failed and plunged the ship into darkness, with the only means of communication throughout the ship being by messenger. A chain of men had to be arranged so that instructions from the bridge could be sent 500 feet aft and four decks down to the auxiliary steering position.

Despite this, at first the ship's plight was not apparent and returning aviators attempted to land on the carrier, but by 1345 the smoke over the flight deck was so dense that all operations were suspended, with *Yorktown* recovering *Lexington*'s aircraft. At 1430, all damage-control and fire-fighting parties were withdrawn with the fires left to burn behind watertight doors. At 1445 the engine and boiler rooms had to be abandoned as a further major explosion wrecked the ventilation system. By this time the ship was dead in the water, but it was not until 1500 with all hope lost that other ships were asked to come alongside and provide assistance. At first the destroyer USS *Morris* attempted to fight the fires, but her capabilities were not up to the task as fuel-fed fires raged out of control and finally the order was given to abandon ship. At 2000, the destroyer *Phelps* torpedoed the wrecked carrier. Incredibly, more than 2,700 men survived but she took another 216 down with her. *Yorktown* did not escape unscathed, but the one bomb that did hit her exploded close to the island and operations were not affected.

Having lost one of the world's two largest aircraft carriers, it would seem that the United States was the loser in the Battle of the Coral Sea, but the USN had sunk the *Shoho* and so damaged the *Shokaku* that she would not be available for the planned invasion of Midway Island (in actuality little more than a coral atoll or reef). More importantly, Japanese expansion had come to an end within just five months of the war starting in the Pacific. Having abandoned the assault on Port Moresby, there was no question of Japan isolating Australia from the United States.

The great significance of the Battle of the Coral Sea was that this was the first naval battle in which the opposing fleets did not come within gunnery range. The supremacy of the battleship had ended.

The Tide is Turned

Even if one takes the view that the Battle of the Coral Sea was a draw, what happened next was an overwhelming defeat for Japan from which the Imperial Japanese Navy could never recover.

It did not help that among the Japanese high command there were serious disagreements over the strategy to be adopted. Many wanted to stick to the original strategy and drive a wedge through the Pacific, separating Australia from the United States, but a growing number wanted to adopt a defensive strategy, worried by the Doolittle raid that had done much to undermine Japanese confidence. It was the latter strategy that saw the occupation of Midway as being important. A diversionary raid in the Aleutians, close to Alaska, was also planned to draw American attention away from Midway.

Despite the debate over strategy, no one sought the opinions of Nagumo, with his experience of carrier warfare, or of Minoru Genda, who had largely planned the raid on Pearl Harbor, or Mitsuo Fuchida. These last two officers were concerned that the Japanese Naval Air Force had already lost too many experienced pilots, while those that had survived needed to be rested and time taken to train new arrivals up to combat readiness. Not all the experienced pilots had been casualties, as some had been transferred to other operations after the attacks on Ceylon. The ships themselves also needed to be refitted rather than just refuelled and replenished.

Even the fact that a diversionary raid was being mounted in the Aleutians was a problem as it meant that two aircraft carriers and their aircraft were not available for the Combined Fleet.

Variously known as the Battle of Midway, the Battle of Midway Island or the Battle off Midway, since all three are correct, this was the battle that marked the turning-point in the Pacific War. Yamamoto had serious concerns about Japan's ability to achieve its objectives in the war, but after Midway few in the Imperial Japanese Navy could have seen any outcome other than defeat.

Unknown to the Japanese, the Americans had broken their codes and knew that the Aleutian raiding force was simply a diversionary tactic. They knew the real target and the date, early June 1942. This meant that unlike the Japanese who had divided their forces, Admiral Chester Nimitz, commander-in-chief of the US Pacific Fleet, could concentrate his forces to defend Midway Island. Japanese hopes of a major clash between opposing fleets were to be fulfilled, except, of course, that the fleets would once again not come within gunnery range.

On 3 June, aircraft from the carriers *Junyo* and *Ryujo* attacked Dutch Harbour in the Aleutians, while the United States Army Air Force sent Boeing B-17 Fortress bombers to attack the Midway invasion force. However, the bombers enjoyed little success as ships at sea were a difficult target for heavy bombers as they could manoeuvre even while the bombs were falling.

Aboard *Akagi*, Mitsuo Fuchida was recovering from an operation for appendicitis, having refused the offer of a destroyer to take him to a naval hospital as he wished to be around to advise his superiors. At that time a more dangerous and difficult operation than today, on 4 June he was still in the ship's hospital, below the waterline. Although he had had his stitches removed on the previous day, he was still weak from the operation but anxious to get to the flight deck to see his airmen before they took off. This was no easy task as the ship was closed up for action stations and all the watertight bulkheads were closed. The only way through the ship was to pass through the small manhole on each watertight door, which entailed unlocking the manhole using a small wheel, clambering through and then locking the manhole again. There were ten manholes between the sickbay and Fuchida's cabin, where he rested briefly before shaving and changing into his uniform. He then had to get from his cabin to the flight deck, which meant passing through several more manholes.

Despite this, and his still frail state, Fuchida arrived at the ship's operations centre before the aircraft took off. In his absence, Lieutenant Tomonaga was to lead the attack. The bad news was that the reconnaissance sorties had already been put into the air, and when Fuchida was shown their search patterns, he realized that large areas of sea would not be covered. Despite expecting a strong American defence, the Japanese had not thought carefully enough about the likely presence of American aircraft carriers.

At dawn, more than 100 Japanese aircraft left the four carriers, *Akagi, Kaga, Hiryu* and *Soryu*, to attack Midway. The carriers were supported by the battleships *Haruna* and *Kirishima*, three cruisers and twelve destroyers. A fifth carrier, the *Hosho*, was with the battle fleet's 7 battleships, while a sixth, the *Zuiho*, was with the assault group, which had 2 battleships, 10 cruisers, 21 destroyers and 12 troopships.

While the Japanese were attacking Midway, shore-based aircraft of both the USN and USAAF found the Combined Fleet and attacked, breaking up the fleet's formation and killing many crewmen on deck in strafing attacks, at the cost of seventeen aircraft lost to intense Japanese AA fire.

The Japanese attack on Midway caused considerable damage to shore installations, but failed to put the airfield or its AA defences out of action. Tomonaga radioed a report to the carriers and Nagumo decided to send a second wave to keep the Americans under pressure. A problem then arose as the second wave was fitted with torpedoes, expecting to be sent to attack American warships. These had to be removed and replaced by bombs, but no sooner than had this been done than a reconnaissance aircraft finally discovered American warships, reporting that there were ten, causing Nagumo to reverse his order and demand that the bombs be removed and the torpedoes put back on the aircraft. It was then decided to delay the second wave until the first-wave aircraft, by now short of fuel, had returned. Down on the hangar decks, the armourers had left the bombs on the deck as they frantically worked to obey first one order and then the counter-order.

The first reconnaissance report had not mentioned an aircraft carrier among the American ships, and it was not until 0900 that a further report mentioned an American aircraft carrier, believed to be the *Yorktown*.

The first wave finally landed on and the aircraft were struck down into the hangar while the second-wave aircraft were brought up from the hangar deck onto the flight deck and ranged ready for take-off. None of the Japanese ships had radar and there was no time to react when the first American aircraft were spotted. The USS *Enterprise* and *Hornet* had sent all of their aircraft, while the *Yorktown* had sent half of hers, making 156 aircraft in all. Leading the first wave of the attack were forty-one Douglas Devastator torpedo-bombers, seen as the ideal means of attacking ships under way at sea. Even if the Japanese carriers had radar, the low-flying torpedo-bombers might still have escaped attention, but even so, no fewer than thirty-five of the Devastators were shot down, mainly by AA fire, with the crews having little time to escape before their aircraft plunged into the sea. A few Zero fighters managed to get into the air and accounted for some of the American losses.

Radar would have caught the second wave of American aircraft, but the Douglas Dauntless dive-bombers remained undetected as they approached at 19,000 feet and the Japanese remained distracted by the torpedo attack, with their fighters milling around at low altitude. At 1022, the first dive-bomber peeled off and began its dive towards the *Kaga*. Twelve 1,000lb bombs were aimed at the ship and four hit her. The first bomb to hit the carrier went straight through the amidships lift and into the hangar, while the second went straight through the flight deck, unarmoured in contrast to the British *Illustrious*-class ships, and straight into the hangar. Both bombs exploded in the hangar among aircraft that had returned from the first strike and still had some fuel in their tanks, and among the bombs, each of 1,750lbs, that had been hastily taken off the aircraft for the second strike and were still lying on the hangar deck. On the flight deck, aircraft ranged, fuelled and armed for the second strike were caught by other bombs, and soon fires were raging across the flight deck and in the hangar deck below.

Wounded airmen from the aircraft and sailors who had been on the two decks could not be taken down to the sick bay as no one could carry them through the flames. Fuchida thought of going to his cabin to rescue some of his belongings, but even this was impossible.

Akagi was not the only carrier to suffer, as exactly the same sequence of events had struck *Kaga* and *Soryu*, both of which were huge balls of flame, belching thick smoke into the atmosphere. Only *Hiryu*, steaming ahead of the other carriers, was unaffected. The three crippled aircraft carriers were abandoned while, at 1100, aircraft took off from *Hiryu* to attack the *Yorktown*. Just eight Aichi D3A 'Val' bombers managed to penetrate the American carrier's fighter screen and intense anti-aircraft fire, but they managed to drop three 500lb bombs on the carrier. The first of these exploded among aircraft parked on the flight deck, setting them alight. The second bomb hit the funnel and blew out the fires in five of her six boilers. The third actually penetrated the wooden flight deck and then plunged through three decks to explode on an aviation fuel tank. Prompt damage control saw the fuel fire smothered in foam, while the ship's magazines were flooded as a precautionary measure. At first it looked as if *Yorktown* would survive.

That afternoon, a second strike was ordered against *Yorktown*, which was again operational and had aircraft being refuelled on her flight deck. Ten Nakajima B5N Kate torpedo-bombers were accompanied by six Zero fighters and led by Tomonaga, who had led the first wave against Midway and managed to return safely to land on *Hiryu*. As soon as the Japanese aircraft were spotted, refuelling stopped and as a further precautionary measure, the carrier's aviation fuel system was drained. Nevertheless, these prudent precautions meant that just six Grumman F4F Wildcats were left to provide fighter cover and then only with whatever fuel was left in their tanks. This wasn't easy, as Lieutenant (later Captain) J.P. Adams recalled in a BBC television documentary, *Pilots at Sea*:

> We only had forty gallons of gas apiece, but nonetheless they wanted us off to try to oppose the torpedo attack. Lieutenant [later Admiral] Thatch and myself and four others manned the planes... All the guns in the Fleet were firing. I vividly remember taking off, trying to crank up my wheels and charge the guns, which we had to do manually, and then trying to catch the torpedo planes. I did catch one and possibly another.

In all, the fighters shot down four torpedo planes, but four got within range of the carrier. *Yorktown* avoided two torpedoes, but two hit her on the port side. Three bombs also found their target. Adams saw the torpedoes strike the ship and realized that there was no way he could land on, but managed to get to the deck of the *Enterprise*, 40 miles away, with just a few gallons of fuel.

While *Yorktown*'s commanding officer gave the order to abandon ship, Tomonaga reported the hits on the carrier, and his superiors immediately jumped to the conclusion that a second American carrier had been hit and this meant that there were no American carriers left in the Pacific. *Hiryu* prepared another strike but before this could be flown off, aircraft from *Enterprise* and *Hornet* found her and attacked, with four dive-bombers hitting their target and another four only narrowly missing, leaving her with flames spreading across the flight deck and her hangar a raging inferno.

Later that afternoon *Soryu* blew up, followed fifteen minutes later by *Kaga*. *Akagi* survived the night before being torpedoed by Japanese destroyers at dawn and soon after *Hiryu* received the same treatment, taking her commanding officer and Rear Admiral Yamaguchi with her as she sank beneath the waves.

With all four carriers lost, Yamamoto ordered that the invasion of Midway be abandoned. Rear Admiral Raymond Spruance, in command of the US Task Force 16, then ordered *Enterprise* and *Hornet* to give chase, hoping to catch the Japanese battleships at sea. On 6 June two heavy cruisers, *Mikuma* and *Mogami*, collided and were badly damaged. Aircraft from Midway attacked but caused little damage; however, *Mikuma* was later sunk by US carrier-borne aircraft that also badly damaged *Mogami* and two destroyers.

The following day, the Japanese submarine *I-168* found the crippled *Yorktown* as efforts to save her continued and sank her and an escorting destroyer.

The outcome of the Battle of the Coral Sea was close, but there would be no doubt that the Battle of Midway was a resounding victory for the USN. The USN had lost a carrier, but the Imperial Japanese Navy had lost 4 carriers, 250 aircraft and around 3,500 personnel. The poor training regime meant that those personnel would be hard to replace, and in front-line roles the losses among newly-trained personnel were always higher than among the more experienced.

The Battle of Midway was later succinctly summed up by Admiral Ernest King:

The Battle of Midway was the first decisive defeat suffered by the Japanese Navy in 350 years. Furthermore, it put an end to the long period of Japanese offensive action, and restored the balance of naval power in the Pacific. The threat of Hawaii and the west coast was automatically removed, and except for operations in the Aleutian area, where the Japanese had landed on the islands at Kisku and Attu, enemy operations were confined to the South Pacific. It was to this latter area, therefore, that we gave our greatest attention.

Chapter 13

The Siege of Malta

Malta was the Royal Navy's main base in the Mediterranean; more than that, it was its Mediterranean 'home', a popular posting and somewhere that virtually every sailor visited at least once in his career. Malta – in reality four main islands: Malta, Gozo, Comino and the uninhabited Fifla – occupied a central position in the Mediterranean across the routes between Italy and North Africa and almost midway between Gibraltar and Alexandria. The island's importance had grown after becoming a British colony because the opening of the Suez Canal in 1869 had meant that the Mediterranean was no longer a pleasant backwater but on the main shipping route from Western Europe to the Gulf, East Africa, India, Malaya and, of course, Australia.

Uniquely in the British Empire, the Maltese had virtually volunteered to join it when they sought the Royal Navy's help in evicting the French in 1798 after Napoleon's defeat at the Battle of the Nile (sometimes known as the Battle of Aboukir Bay). The anti-religious and anti-clerical attitudes of post-revolutionary France had displeased the pious Maltese.

It could fairly be said that whoever controlled Malta commanded the Mediterranean, but in the Second World War that situation came perilously close to being lost.

The British Mediterranean Fleet was the second most important command in the Royal Navy; only the Home Fleet was larger or more important.

The situation in the Mediterranean had been tense since Italy had invaded Abyssinia in 1935. There had been plans laid for a war with Italy that would have included blockading the Suez Canal to Italian shipping and attacking the Italian navy's forward base at Taranto, in the instep of Italy. These plans came to nothing as France was not interested in a war with its neighbour, despite there having been a naval arms race between the two countries during the 1920s and 1930s, and the League of Nations was not prepared for action. The United States was not a member of the League, despite it having been the brainchild of an American president; generally American policy was that of isolationism.

Italy was not the only problem. The United Kingdom had remained neutral during the Spanish Civil War, unlike Germany and Italy who had supported the Nationalists and the Soviet Union and France who had supported the Republicans, although in the case of France the relationship was more businesslike than ideological. Nevertheless, the outcome had been victory for the Republicans, a Fascist party on good terms with Germany and Italy. Whether or not Spain and its new dictator, Franco, would enter the war was at first a great concern for the United Kingdom and for its colony and naval base at Gibraltar. Fortunately, Spain was too weakened by the conflict to consider taking part, although it provided a convenient and congenial base for German agents who were able to watch British and later Allied shipping movements with ease.

The German dictator, Adolf Hitler, had been an admirer of his Italian counterpart, Benito Mussolini but their relationship began to change when Italy did not enter the Second World War on 3 September 1939. Germany and Italy had signed the Axis Treaty in June 1936, followed in 1939 by the so-called Pact of Steel. It was not until 10 June 1940, shortly before the French surrender, that Italy entered the war, sending troops over the border into southern France in the hope of taking a share of the spoils but this plan failed as the area became part of Vichy France, administered by the French themselves until late 1942. For many Germans, Italy's late entry into the war caused the Italians to be known as the 'harvest hands', ready for the rich pickings after the main work had been done.

To some extent, Italy's delay in entering the war could have been due to a lack of preparedness. Many Germans, especially those in the navy, had not expected war in 1939, as mentioned in the introduction to this book. Italy also would have had good reason not to expect war so soon. Nevertheless, from the time that he came to power in 1922, Mussolini had made it clear that the Mediterranean was *Mare Nostrum* ('Our Sea'), that the Maltese were part of the Italian race and that the islands really belonged to Italy. There was some cause for this as Malta had once been part of the Kingdom of Sicily, but that had been centuries earlier and there was now little Italian blood in the Maltese and even less that was Italian about their Maltese language (more properly, Phoenician Maltese).

Malta had strong defences that dated from the Great Siege of Malta in 1565, but these were inadequate for the age of the bomb, the bomber and the artillery shell. Efforts had been made to create a strong anti-aircraft defence during the Abyssinian crisis of 1935, but little else followed. Part of the problem was that neither the British Army nor the Royal Air Force believed that Malta could be defended. There were good reasons for this, including the fact that the islands – small and even at that time over-populated – could not feed themselves, even with an ideal harvest, as Maltese farms could only provide around a quarter of the food needed. Vital items such as seed potatoes had to be imported as Maltese farmers could not grow a surplus to provide their own. It was not just a case of over-population; the soil was thin and poor, and the long summers dry. Worse, as bombing got under way, the chemicals used in the explosives poisoned the soil. The total area of the Maltese islands amounted to 122 square miles, and in 1940 there were approximately 280,000 inhabitants, although this did not include British service personnel and their dependants.

The views of the two shore-based services could also have reflected the fact that the British government had decided it could not defend the Channel Islands and shortly before the fall of France had abandoned these, evacuating as many of the local inhabitants who wanted to leave as possible. True, Malta was bigger than all the Channel Islands combined and further from Italy than they were from France but even so, the 80 miles or so from Sicily was little enough in the age of the aeroplane.

The sole dissenting voice in this analysis of Malta's fate in wartime was that of the Admiralty, which saw Malta as being a base for offensive operations by submarines and aircraft. It was the Admiralty view that prevailed with the British government, and the RAF and army units deployed in Malta throughout the war were there to ensure that the islands remained available for the Royal Navy.

The main base for the Royal Navy in Malta was in the Grand Harbour, with the famous dockyard on the eastern shores opposite Valletta, the capital. There was also a base for submarines on the other side of Valletta in Sliema Creek at Manoel Island, a small islet separated from Sliema by a few yards of water. The Royal Navy had establishments ashore including an important signals centre, but during the war years it had no naval air station, simply having what were known as 'lodging rights' at what was then RAF Hal Far, which post-war became RNAS Hal Far, HMS *Falcon*.

The army's main base was at St Andrew's Barracks, although other barracks were scattered around the island including those for the two locally-raised regiments, the King's Own Malta Regiment and the Royal

Malta Artillery. The army also had a hospital at Mtarfa, near Rabat, while that for the Royal Navy was in the dockyard at Bighi.

As already mentioned, the RAF's main air station was at Hal Far, and close to Hal Far was the seaplane and flying boat base of Kalafrana. A second base for the RAF was at Ta' Qali, close to the walls of Rabat and Mdina, the old capital. Ta' Qali had been selected not as an RAF base but as a prospective airport for Imperial Airways, which even in the later 1930s had been planning to substitute landplanes for flying boats on its long services to the Empire. Among the first users were Italian air services to Malta. A third RAF base at Luqa, the present-day civil airport, was under construction when war broke out in 1939.* The RAF also had a major radar station at Dingli, overlooking the cliffs and the island of Fifla. This radar station was to be the saviour of Malta, but in 1940 it had just nine personnel.

War Reaches Malta

With the heavy pressures on the Royal Navy in 1940 with operations off Scandinavia and France as well as the vital North Atlantic convoys to protect, the British Mediterranean Fleet was not at its strongest. Once France surrendered, the balance of naval power in the Mediterranean was firmly in Italy's favour. Italy had six battleships while the Mediterranean Fleet had three, and although it had an aircraft carrier, this was the elderly *Eagle* that had been transferred from the Indian Ocean when the ill-fated *Glorious* had been transferred to the Home Fleet to take part in the Norwegian campaign. All three of the British battleships were veterans of the First World War and while all three had been modernized to some extent, only *Warspite* had received a complete programme of improvements and the other two, *Malaya* and *Royal Sovereign*, were far too slow by the standards of 1939.

It was not until April 1940 that the Italian armed forces were told that they could expect to fight alongside the Germans. Clearly, they must have anticipated the possibility of war from the start of the Abyssinian adventure in 1935 and also realized that the United Kingdom was the most likely opponent. Italy's armed forces were controlled by the Supreme Command which was dominated by the army, effectively leaving the sailors and airmen to do as they were told.

---

*Of the three main RAF bases, only Luqa survives. Ta' Qali and later Hal Far were both taken over for general industrial use.

Admiral Domenico Cavagnari, Chief of the Italian Naval Staff, should have had considerable influence and to have expected Mussolini to heed his advice but this was not the case, despite the admiral also holding the political post of Under Secretary of State for the Navy. He warned Mussolini in a letter that entering a war once it had already started meant that any chance of surprise was gone. He continued by pointing out that Italy was in a weak position and that the United Kingdom could cut off the country by blockading the Mediterranean at both ends, Gibraltar and the Suez Canal, starving Italy of the fuel and raw materials necessary for the country to survive, let alone fight a war.

While the leaders of both the German and Japanese navies had been pessimistic about their countries' chances in a war and especially the probable fate of their services, Cavagnari seems to have been even more pessimistic. His worst fears were immediately dispelled by the collapse of French resistance. On the other hand, he was far more realistic than the Italian army that had claimed to have six months' supplies in Libya but once fighting started and then Marshal Graziani, Italy's commander in North Africa, invaded Egypt in an attempt to reach the Suez Canal, the demand for supplies of all kinds soared and a convoy system across the Mediterranean had to be hastily instigated. The so-called 'convoy' system showed Italy's poor preparations for war, as just one or two warships would guard a number of merchant vessels.

The British expected the war to reach the Mediterranean sooner than later and had in fact expected Italy to be engaged in hostilities from the start. Admiral Sir Andrew Cunningham, C-in-C of the British Mediterranean Fleet, moved the fleet from its main base in Malta to Alexandria in Egypt. This was a wise move as it vastly reduced the chances of the fleet being bombed in port, but it did mean that his ships were now 1,000 miles from Malta and twice that from Gibraltar. A partial solution was the creation of what was in reality a fleet for the Western Mediterranean, Force H, based on Gibraltar and under the command of Vice Admiral Sir James Somerville, which could also operate in the Eastern Atlantic when required. Force H was a powerful fleet, more than just a squadron, and included the new aircraft carrier *Ark Royal* that had joined the Royal Navy in 1938.

Yet, despite these moves, the situation was difficult. The Mediterranean Fleet lacked fighters other than the obsolete Gloster Sea Gladiator, a biplane, and worse still, Malta was completely without fighter aircraft.

The mainstay of the fleet's aircraft was another biplane, the Fairey Swordfish, much loved by those who flew it but slow and plodding, with many claiming that it had difficulty flying at 100 mph! The Sea Gladiators had been found by *Eagle*'s Commander Flying C.L. Keighley-Peach, who flew one himself and trained two Swordfish pilots in fighter tactics so that they could fly the other two. The Sea Gladiators could tackle Italian reconnaissance seaplanes hampered by the drag and weight of their floats, but were no match for modern bombers, let alone fighters. It was fortunate that the Italians lacked a fighter as potent as the German Messerschmitt Bf 109, and explains why the Mediterranean Fleet was so pleased when it was eventually joined by *Illustrious* with her Fairey Fulmar fighters, even though these were hampered by the Royal Navy's insistence on having a two-man crew.

Other precautions were set in hand by Cunningham before Italy entered the war. Many British civilians including dependants of British service personnel were sent home aboard the Orient Lines ship *Oronsay*, *en passage* to the UK from Australia, while the Mediterranean and the Bay of Biscay were still relatively safe. This was not a popular move as many army wives in particular felt that they were being forced to leave, so the liner was dubbed the 'slave ship'. However, in truth not only were they being moved out of harm's way, they were also easing the pressure on the island's food and fuel supplies.

Those taking passage in *Oronsay* were in fact the fortunate ones. A further set of civilians was moved on 10 July, their ship joining a convoy bound for Alexandria and the start of a very long voyage home via the Suez Canal and Cape Town. Another convoy, even slower, carried naval stores regarded as being superfluous on Malta, but needed in Alexandria. Both convoys were protected by the Mediterranean Fleet.

Realizing that Malta would be a thorn in the side of the Axis operations in the Mediterranean and North Africa, the Italian navy pressed for the island to be invaded but for some reason Mussolini held back. Instead of sending warships to bombard Malta, Mussolini prepared to use his air force, the *Regia Aeronautica*, to bomb the island.

Defending Malta

Malta had been lightly garrisoned in the years between the two world wars. Until the late 1930s, there had been no real threat and the crowded island did not offer a great deal in the way of training opportunities. Once Italy entered the war, extra troops were soon sent to the island and on 12 August, despite the pressing needs of Britain's air defences, a squadron of twelve Hawker Hurricane fighters was flown off to the island by the elderly aircraft carrier *Argus*. Additional Fairey Swordfish were supplied to the island's resident 830 Naval Air Squadron, while the RAF received a reconnaissance flight of four Martin Baltimore bombers, a fast twin-engined aircraft that was to provide aerial reconnaissance not just for Malta, but for the British Mediterranean Fleet as well.

In addition to the arrival of the new fast armoured aircraft carrier, HMS *Illustrious*, the Mediterranean Fleet also received the recently-refitted and modernized battleship *Valiant* and the two anti-aircraft cruisers *Calcutta* and *Coventry*, former First World War cruisers that had been modernized and refitted for AA work. The new ships provided Admiral Sir Andrew Cunningham with two fresh advantages. For the first time he now had radar, providing early warning of an attack and so reducing the amount of time his AA gunners had to stand by waiting for an attack that might not develop. The second was that he now had more modern fighters. True, despite having the same Rolls-Royce Merlin engine as the Hurricane and the Spitfire, the Fulmar was slower and burdened by the need to carry a second crew member – an observer, regarded at the time as essential for naval aircraft – but it was an improvement on the Sea Gladiator biplane. Nevertheless, *Eagle*'s three Sea Gladiators had done well, shooting down eleven Italian aircraft.

The defences of the Grand Harbour had not been neglected. Ships inside the harbour were protected by a form of boom defence, with chains and nets positioned in the entrance. These included a double chain of cylindrical buoys and the nets transferred from Alexandria after the Abyssinian crisis had passed; a guard ship, HMS *Westgate*; a second double chain linking Fort St Elmo with the mainland; and a number of spiked rafts and underwater obstructions.

Attention had also been paid to improving the anti-aircraft defences around the Grand Harbour and at the airfields, with additional guns including the new 4.5in-calibre weapons capable of shooting higher than 40,000 feet and intended to provide a box barrage to defend the port and the dockyard facilities.

Malta on the Offensive

Despite moving the Mediterranean Fleet from Malta to Alexandria, the Royal Navy was determined to continue making the most of its bases on the island. Malta remained an offensive base, not only for submarines but for the Fleet Air Arm as well. The campaign against Axis shipping started slowly, there being so many other demands on the Royal Navy. During the first six months after Italy entered the war, from June to November 1940, they lost just four ships carrying supplies to North Africa, with a total tonnage of 11,104. The level of losses rose during the winter: from December 1940 to March 1941, Italy lost thirty ships with a total tonnage of 109,089. This was not enough to stop the two divisions of Rommel's *Afrika Korps* from reaching North Africa with few losses.

Initially two destroyers, *Lance* and *Lively*, operated from Malta, attacking Axis shipping. In October 1941 they were joined by two light cruisers, *Penelope* and *Aurora*, forming Force K under the command of Captain W.G. Agnew. Malta was also sheltering the cruiser *Ajax*, one of the victors in the Battle of the River Plate, which was out of action. Force K was a small force with which to face the might of the Italian *Regia Marina*. Had the Italians sent their battleships and cruisers to sea, not to mention their substantial fleet of submarines which on Italy's entry into the war had outnumbered those of Germany, the situation for Malta would have been hopeless. The Germans had expected the Italian fleet to bombard Malta within hours of Italy entering the war and follow this up with an invasion, but the opportunity passed. After the Fleet Air Arm's attack on Taranto, the Germans were astonished that three of the Italian battleships had been put out of action without being engaged in a major naval battle.

Force K soon proved its worth. Luftwaffe intelligence persuaded the Italians that the two cruisers were damaged so badly that they were out of action, and on 9 November 1941 the Italians sent a convoy of seven ships to North Africa with an escort of two cruisers and ten destroyers. Instead of being confined to port, Force K arrived on the scene and in the ensuing engagement, all seven merchantmen were sunk as well as a destroyer, while another destroyer was so badly damaged that she sank later. Eleven days later, on 20 November, another convoy was spotted with four ships escorted by two cruisers and eight destroyers. Both cruisers were badly damaged by torpedoes and the entire convoy beat a hasty retreat into Taranto. Two other ships were spotted steaming to join the convoy, and these were promptly sunk by *Penelope* and *Lively*. In all, the Italians lost 54,900 tons of shipping that November.

Among the other forces operating from Malta at this time were the Swordfish of No. 830 Naval Air Squadron, while the Royal Air Force bombed targets in Sicily and mainland Italy. With such bleak prospects, at one stage the Italians gave up trying to get convoys through to Libya, and on other occasions they used what they euphemistically called 'white ships' – meaning hospital ships that would not be attacked by the British – to smuggle supplies through. Despite the frequent air attacks on Malta, Italian intelligence seems to have been poor since the two cruisers in Malta were classified as battleships, or possibly this was an attempt to explain away the fact that on at least one occasion, Force K managed to sink every ship in a convoy.

Despite the damage done in the attack on Taranto, the Italians remained reluctant to risk a major fleet engagement, or perhaps they felt too weakened after Taranto. There was a gallant attempt to attack Force K in the Grand Harbour using fast small craft packed with explosives. Next, they turned their attention to the Mediterranean Fleet at Alexandria. Nevertheless, the most serious damage to the Royal Navy was inflicted by the Germans, including the occasion on 25 November 1941 when *U-331* torpedoed the battleship *Barham* off the coast of Libya; the ship rolled over and sank rapidly, and 862 officers and men died as she blew up. Cunningham had earlier rejected an Admiralty order that *Barham*, which had not been modernized to the same extent as *Warspite* and others of the *Queen Elizabeth* class, should be scuttled in Tobruk harbour to stem the Axis advance, preferring to see her continue in an active role with the fleet.

These setbacks apart, the Mediterranean Fleet continued to have its victories, inflicting serious damage on the Italians. On the night of 12/13 December 1941, off Cap Bon, three British and one Dutch destroyers used the dark coastline behind them to make identification difficult and torpedoed and sank two Italian light cruisers, the *Alberico da Barbiano* and *Alberto da Giussano* in a brilliant action as the enemy guns should have been able to keep the destroyers at bay.

The paradox was, of course, that the British were finding it increasingly difficult to get supplies through to Malta and had to supply their forces in Egypt with ships from the UK sailing around the Cape of Good Hope and along the coast of East Africa, through the Red Sea and then through the Suez Canal.

At the same time, both sides were forced to take increasingly desperate measures to protect their convoys, with ever-stronger convoy escorts. A good example was on 17 December when 4 Italian battleships, *Littorio, Caio Duilio, Andrea Doria* and *Giulio Cesare* escorted by 5 cruisers and 20 destroyers met Rear Admiral Philip Vian with 5 cruisers and 20 destroyers escorting a Malta-bound merchantman. After a brief gunnery exchange, the Italian admiral Iachino broke off as darkness fell. As so often, the balance of armament was weighed in favour of the Italians but they failed to make the most of their advantage.

Even so, the luck of anyone heavily outnumbered and outgunned in wartime can only defy the odds for so long. As mentioned earlier in Chapter 11, on 18 December Force K found itself in serious trouble when it ran into an Italian minefield off Tripoli. The cruiser *Neptune* and a destroyer were sunk, while two other cruisers, *Aurora* and *Penelope*, were badly damaged. That same night an Italian submarine surfaced in the darkness just over a mile from the entrance to the harbour at Alexandria and released three two-man human torpedoes into the water, badly damaging the battleships *Valiant* and *Queen Elizabeth*, a tanker and a destroyer.

For the island of Malta, a more serious problem was looming as 1941 drew to a close. German forces were advancing across the Soviet Union but had faltered and stopped under the crushing cold of the Russian winter, for which they were woefully ill-prepared with severely stretched lines of communication and inadequate winter clothing. Many of their aircraft were grounded, while others could only get airborne after fires had been lit under their engines. Faced with such terrible odds, the Germans transferred many aircraft westwards where they could still operate. As winter closed in, the Luftwaffe returned to Sicily. British forces based on Malta could not be allowed to strangle Rommel's campaign in North Africa. The Germans and Italians knew that if they could reach the Suez Canal, Britain's position in the war would be seriously weakened and such a success might even persuade Turkey, a First World War ally of Germany, to enter the conflict on the Axis side.

As we will see later, submarines played an important role in ensuring that supplies to Malta never dried up completely, while some British minelayers such as the ships of the *Abdiel* class were large, almost the size of light cruisers, and fast at almost 40 knots, and ships of this class did much sterling work in helping to keep supplies flowing to Malta.

The Malta Convoys

It had been clear even before Italy entered the Second World War on 10 June 1940 that Malta would be a target, sitting roughly halfway between Gibraltar and Alexandria, and between southern Italy and Italian forces in North Africa. Malta was a fortress, but a fortress of the past not the present, built for earlier conflicts and armaments. The high population density and thin soil meant that the islands could only grow a quarter of the food needed for the peacetime population, but in wartime this requirement was increased by the presence of military reinforcements, and Malta had no fuel or raw material resources at all, other than stone. These factors led the British Army and the Royal Air Force to believe that Malta could not be defended, but the Royal Navy saw the island as being of strategic importance and as a base for light forces and submarines. The Royal Navy won the argument and the armed forces stayed, while most British civilians were evacuated well in advance of the Italian declaration of war.

Convoys to Malta were far smaller than on the North Atlantic route or to the Arctic. This was not only a reflection of the small size of the population – around 280,000 in 1940 – but also of the limited port facilities. In peacetime, most supplies had arrived on small ships; a case of little and often. At the outset, there were no RAF fighters and fighter defences were based on three Gloster Sea Gladiators left behind by the carrier *Eagle* which were flown by RAF flying boat pilots and became famous as 'Faith, Hope and Charity'. Someone at the Admiralty sent a signal demanding to know why Fleet Air Arm assets had been handed over to the RAF! This caused Cunningham to muse whether the official concerned was aware that there was a war on!

Later aircraft were flown from carriers, including the USS *Wasp* which made two trips into the Mediterranean to provide Malta with a fighter defence, but at first these fighters were often destroyed as they landed to refuel and re-arm in the middle of almost continuous Axis air attack.

The infamous convoy Operation EXCESS of January 1941 that saw the aircraft carrier *Illustrious* crippled by the Luftwaffe did nevertheless deliver all of its merchant ships safely to Malta. This was not always to be the case. It was also obvious that Malta did not have the port facilities to receive and discharge the cargoes of a number of ships at once. Large cargo ships had to moor in the centre of the harbour and discharge their cargo into lighters to be taken ashore. When four ships were sent to Malta in March 1942, a tanker was so badly damaged that she had to be towed into Marsaxlokk and the two ships that managed to reach the famous Grand Harbour were sunk at their moorings with most of their invaluable cargo unloaded. Such was the degree of desperation that grain damaged by sea water was salvaged and made into bread. One serviceman in Malta at the time recalled in a letter to the author that the resulting bread tasted like putty, 'but we would have eaten putty', and that they were rationed to two slices each, for which they had to sign.

Most famous of the Malta convoys was that of 10–15 August 1942, known to the Allies as Operation PEDESTAL but to the devout Maltese as the 'Santa Marija Convoy', that arrived in Malta on 15 August, the feast day of the Assumption of the Virgin Mary.

This was the largest of the Malta convoys with fourteen merchant vessels, reflecting not only the desperate plight of those on Malta but also the cruel reality that not all the ships would make it. Under the command of Vice Admiral Syfret, there was also a massive escort led by the battleships *Nelson* and *Rodney* with their 16in guns mounted in three triple turrets forward; the 4 aircraft carriers *Eagle*, *Furious*, *Indomitable* and *Victorious*; 7 cruisers and 27 destroyers. *Furious* was carrying forty-two Supermarine Spitfire fighters to be flown off to augment Malta's defences.

This strong force was itself largely dependent on forty-three Hawker Sea Hurricanes for its air defence, although it also had a number of Fairey Fulmars and Grumman Martlets. After passing Gibraltar on the night of 10/11 August, *Eagle* was torpedoed at 1315 on 11 August by *U-73*. All four torpedoes hit the carrier, sinking her quickly, and her four Sea Hurricanes flying a combat air patrol (CAP) at the time had to land on the other carriers. The elderly carrier, regarded as too slow for further front-line duty, was no stranger to the Malta run and had previously flown 183 fighters safely to the island from her deck, as well as earlier having been part of the Mediterranean Fleet.

Later that day, the Luftwaffe started the series of heavy aerial attacks that the convoy was to suffer on its run across the Mediterranean. The escort vessels sank a U-boat at 1500, before another combined strike of 100 aircraft attacked at 1900, sinking a merchantman and so seriously damaging *Indomitable* that her aircraft had to be recovered by *Victorious*. Later, in a further attack, the Luftwaffe sank the cruiser *Cairo* and two more merchant vessels, as well as damaging the cruiser *Nigeria* and three other ships including the fast tanker *Ohio*. Darkness brought no relief, but instead an attack by E-boats that sank another five ships and so damaged the cruiser *Manchester* that she had to be sunk later.

The next day was typical with another ship lost to air attack and further damage inflicted on the *Ohio* whose master ordered her to be abandoned, but before the crew could be picked up, they re-boarded the ship as she was still afloat. The leading ships reached Malta on 13

August but the *Ohio*, aided by an escorting destroyer, did not arrive until 15 August, one of just five merchant vessels to survive the ordeal. Undoubtedly those aboard the ships in the convoy and the naval escort showed outstanding courage, but luck also played a part as another straggler was promptly despatched by a U-boat and, strangely, the ships that reached Malta were not bombed as they unloaded. *Ohio's* cargo of fuel was to prove invaluable in the defence of Malta, but shortly after she was unloaded her back broke and she sank to the bottom of the Grand Harbour.

Yet the overall price was high as the convoy cost one aircraft carrier, two cruisers and a destroyer, with serious damage to two carriers and a cruiser as well as nine merchant ships lost, including *Ohio*, while another left the convoy to seek refuge.

Chapter 14

Fighting the Weather and the Enemy in the Arctic

In September 1939, it seemed clear to the British and French Allies that the Soviet Union and Germany were allies. The Soviet Union was able to occupy the eastern part of Poland some weeks after the German invasion that started the war. It was clear that the two countries had agreed a division of territory in the east, while Germany was heavily reliant upon the Soviet Union for many items including timber, food and, most important of all, oil.

Finland was next to feel the might of Soviet ambition and military strength as the two countries were at war throughout the winter of 1939–40 but although far stronger, the Soviet Union was unable to break Finnish resistance. In the end, Finland was forced to make some territorial concessions to the Soviet Union, but retained most of its territory.

All of a sudden, this changed overnight with the German invasion of the Soviet Union on 22 June 1941. The Soviet Union had been supplying Germany with many of its vital war needs up to the day before the invasion. To observers in the West it was no surprise, and indeed they had done their best to warn the Soviet dictator, Joseph Stalin, of German intentions. Warnings had come from elsewhere as well; however, Stalin refused to heed any warnings. Russia's armed forces were largely equipped with weapons, aircraft, vehicles and ships that were obsolete, while pre-war purges and trials had removed half the senior officers, especially from the army and air forces (of which there were several, including Frontal Aviation), meaning a great loss of experience. Even the more modern Soviet equipment was inferior to that of the other belligerent nations.

Operation BARBAROSSA, the German invasion of the Soviet Union, had been delayed by the need for Germany to assist Italy in Yugoslavia and Greece, although a late thaw and wet spring also played a part as the terrain was too soft for a massive armoured thrust. This delay was to affect the success of the operation as it proved impossible to take the main objectives before the Russian winter set in and, as Napoleon had discovered almost 130 years earlier, 'General Winter' was Russia's most successful general! As it was, the actual attack came as a surprise to the Russians and it caught most of their aircraft in the west on the ground and troops not deployed in the right defensive positions.

In the years of war that followed, the Soviet Union was to be heavily dependent on the United Kingdom and the United States for supplies and for upgrading the country's armed forces. It proved to be a difficult relationship. Stalin was a demanding and unreliable ally. He fully expected the Allies to ease the pressure of the Germans fighting the Russian armies by opening a so-called 'second front', ignoring the practical problems that this entailed, and also ignoring the fact that the Allies were first engaged in fighting in North Africa and then in Italy, and at the same time fighting at sea, not least in protecting the vital convoys across the Atlantic, and that from December 1941 the United States was also engaged in war against Japan.

On the plus side, the start of Operation BARBAROSSA eased the pressure on the British. The blitz on British towns and cities ended, far too soon from the point of view of the Luftwaffe, and the pressure on Malta eased as well. On the debit side, Soviet preoccupation with Germany also allowed Japan to concentrate on fighting the Americans. While the Soviet Union did not declare war on Japan until August 1945, Japan's presence in China had been the cause of much friction.

On balance, the British welcomed their new-found Russian allies. It also eased the political situation in the United Kingdom where many on the left of politics and who were sympathetic to the Soviet Union had been lukewarm in their support for the continuation of the war against Germany. The British felt the need to support their new ally and stiffen Russian resolve. There were fears that Stalin might have been tempted to cede territory to the Germans in order to make peace; this would have freed German forces to return to their attacks on the British Isles and Malta, as well as in North Africa.

Petsamo and Kirkenes

German occupation of the ports of Petsamo and Kirkenes, north of the Arctic Circle, made it more difficult for supplies to be sent. The most direct route, through the Baltic, was out of the question. Kirkenes was a key location at the northern tip of Norway; Petsamo (or modern Pechanga) in Russia was originally part of Russia before passing to Finland, but was ceded to Russia again as part of the price of peace in the Russo-Finnish War of 1939–40, and then regained when Finland joined Germany in the invasion of the Soviet Union, which to the Finns was a continuation of the 'Winter War'.

Given the distances involved, the only possible means of making an impact on the German forces invading the Soviet Union lay with the Royal Navy and especially with naval air power. The Commander-in-Chief, Home Fleet, Admiral Sir John Tovey, was urged by Britain's wartime leader, Winston Churchill, to carry out an attack that would be 'a gesture in support of our Russian allies to create a diversion on the enemy's northern flank'. At the time, an aerial attack on the two ports seemed to be the only way forward. The Royal Navy deployed one of its newest aircraft carriers, *Victorious*, and its oldest, *Furious*.

Aircraft for the attack were Fairey Albacore torpedo-bombers, complemented by Fairey Swordfish, escorted by Fairey Fulmar fighters. *Victorious* sent twenty Albacores from Nos 827 and 828 Naval Air Squadrons, escorted by Fulmars from 809 NAS. *Furious* sent nine Swordfish of 812 NAS and nine Albacores of 817, escorted by the Fulmars of 800 NAS.

Unlike the raid on Taranto, the operations had to take place in daylight because of the almost twenty-four-hour summer daylight of the far north. German aerial reconnaissance was far more methodical than that of the Italians; the carriers soon became known to the enemy and the nature of the operation also became clear. The final approaches to the targets were also far more difficult than at Taranto.

Aircraft were flown off late on the afternoon of 30 July 1941, with those from *Victorious* going to Kirkenes, while *Furious* sent her aircraft to Petsamo. The operation was jeopardized from the start as the aircraft from *Victorious* had to fly over a German hospital ship en route to the target and were ordered not to attack it, although, of course, those aboard could warn the authorities ashore. The approach to Kirkenes was over a mountain at the end of the fjord, before diving into the bay where they found just four ships. After enduring heavy anti-aircraft fire from gun installations on the cliffs, the attackers were themselves attacked by German fighters and most of them had to jettison their torpedoes in a desperate bid to escape. They managed to sink just one cargo vessel of 2,000 tons and set another on fire. The slow and lumbering Fulmars did well to shoot down four Luftwaffe aircraft. Petsamo was even worse, for the harbour was empty. Frustrated aircrew could do nothing more than aim their torpedoes at the wharves, hoping at least to do some damage.

Afterwards the attackers attempted to escape, which was easier said than done, especially for the torpedo-bombers that were obviously much slower than the German fighters. Swordfish and Albacore pilots and aircrew were trained in a defensive drill that entailed taking their aircraft as low as possible over the water and waiting to be attacked. The telegraphist-air-gunners would watch for the cannon shells hitting the water and at the last second call out to the pilot 'hard-a-starboard' or 'hard-a-port'. Flying just above the surface of the water also forced the fighters to pull out early or risk a high-speed dive into the sea.

Inevitably, even when these defensive measures worked, they could only last so long if the aircraft were to return to their ships. Altogether forty-four aircrew were lost; seven of them killed and the remainder taken prisoner. Had the losses at Taranto been on a similar scale, seven aircraft would have been lost rather than just two. 'The gallantry of the aircraft crews, who knew before leaving that their chance of surprise had gone, and that they were certain to face heavy odds is beyond praise,' remarked Tovey. 'I trust that the encouragement to the morale of our allies was proportionately great.'

The Arctic Convoys

Grimmest of the many Second World War convoy routes were those to Russia, sailing past enemy-occupied Norway and north of the Arctic Circle where the weather was as much of an enemy as the combined efforts of the *Kriegsmarine* and the Luftwaffe. Not for nothing are the veterans of these convoys singled out at Remembrance Day parades with their distinctive white berets. The Malta convoys were also grim but the weather was less cruel and, of course, far fewer ships and personnel were involved. A total of 811 ships sailed in the Arctic convoys to Russia, of which 720 completed their voyages, another 33 turned back for one reason or another, and 58 were sunk, giving a loss rate of 7.2 per cent. Of the ships that reached Russia, 717 sailed back (some were being delivered to the Soviet Union), and of these 29 were sunk, a loss rate of 4 per cent. This was the price of delivering some 4 million tons of war stores, including 5,000 tanks and more than 7,000 aircraft. The sinking of a 10,000-ton cargo ship was the equivalent, in terms of matériel destroyed, of a land battle.

The problems of keeping the Soviet Union, industrially and technologically backward and ill-prepared for war, in the conflict were many. Both the United States and the United Kingdom went to great lengths to keep the Soviet Union supplied. Most of the aid went via the Indian Ocean and Persian Gulf and then overland from an Iranian port, with Soviet troops occupying Northern Iran. Very little took the short route from the west coast of the United States to Siberia, partly because the Soviet Union did not enter the war with Japan until August 1945, and partly because of the limited capacity of the Trans-Siberian Railway to move matériel to the western USSR where it was most needed against German forces. Most attention has centred on the Arctic convoys from Scotland and Iceland to Archangel and Murmansk.

In summer, the almost constant daylight left the ships open to attack from the air and from U-boats and surface raiders. In winter, the almost constant darkness provided just three hours of weak twilight in the middle of the day, and the weather was another hazard. One naval officer having difficulty eating a meal as his cruiser rolled to angles of 30 degrees consoled himself with the thought that life must be even more difficult in the destroyers and corvettes, which rolled as much as 50 degrees and sometimes even more! For the airmen, life was hard. The cold meant that they had to wear as much as possible, limited only by their ability to get in and out of the cockpit. Metal became so brittle that tail wheels could break off on landing.

The first convoy to suffer heavy losses was PQ13, which sailed on 20 March 1942 and was attacked not just by U-boats and aircraft but also by destroyers based on Kirkenes. Despite Ultra intelligence warning of the impending attack, which led to one German destroyer being sunk and two damaged by the cruiser *Trinidad*, the convoy lost five ships. The scale of the Luftwaffe attacks was considerable, with Convoy PG16 being attacked by no fewer than 108 aircraft on 27 May 1942, contributing to the convoy's overall loss of seven ships.

Most famous of the Arctic convoys was the ill-fated PQ17, which sailed from Hvalfjordur in Iceland on 27 June 1942 without an aircraft carrier among its escorts which might have prevented the tragic events that occurred. The original cause of the disaster was the German battleship *Tirpitz* that was lying in Norway's Altenfjord and was observed moving by Norwegian resistance who thought that she was preparing to go to sea on 4 July, although in fact she was simply moving from one berth to another. In London, the Admiralty had been aware that an attack was likely and the convoy was given a heavier escort than usual, but with nothing heavier than cruisers in the distant escort, Ultra intelligence had revealed that the cruisers *Admiral Scheer* and *Hipper* and possibly *Scheer*'s sister ship *Lutzow* were also in the Altenfjord.

Faced with the strong possibility that this powerful force could overwhelm the convoy escorts, First Sea Lord (the service head of the Royal Navy) Admiral Sir Dudley Pound ordered the convoy to scatter and the escorts to return to base. This left the thirty-seven ships of the convoy at the mercy of U-boats and the Luftwaffe. In the ensuing attack, just eleven ships of the thirty-seven originally in the convoy reached their destination. This meant the loss of 153 lives, 2,500 aircraft, 430 tanks and almost 1,000 lorries and other vehicles. *Tirpitz* meanwhile had remained in harbour, believing that a British battleship was included in the distant escort. When aerial reconnaissance confirmed that no battleship was present, she left port with the other ships during the afternoon of 5 July, but returned to her berth when it was clear that the convoy was already destroyed.

The order to scatter the convoy remains one of the most controversial of the war, especially the war at sea. With hindsight, the entire convoy should have been turned back and brought under the protection of the heavy units of the Home Fleet. On the other hand, had it tried to continue without scattering, the entire convoy and its escort would have been at the mercy of the *Tirpitz* battlegroup which would have destroyed both the convoy and the escort.

The disaster was a clear indication that the convoys, and not just those on the Arctic run, needed good air support and that meant having an aircraft carrier present at all times.

PQ18 – The First Air Support for the Convoys

PQ17's fate could not be ignored. It was necessary to maintain the link between the Western Allies and the beleaguered Soviet Union. Four British destroyers were despatched to Archangel loaded with ammunition and replacement anti-aircraft gun barrels, as well as interpreters in an attempt to improve liaison with the Russians. The ships arrived on 24 July 1942. On 13 August the American cruiser USS *Tuscaloosa* sailed for Russia, escorted by a British destroyer and two American destroyers, carrying RAF ground crew and equipment as well as aircraft spares for two squadrons of Handley Page Hampden bombers destined to be based in northern Russia, as would be photo-reconnaissance Supermarine Spitfires and a squadron of RAF Coastal Command Consolidated Catalina flying boats. Also included in the cargo carried by these warships was a demountable medical centre with medical supplies, but while the Soviets took the medical supplies, they rejected the hospital that would have done so much to improve the lot of Allied seamen in need of medical attention on reaching a Russian port.

Survivors from PQ17 were brought home to the UK aboard the three American ships plus three British destroyers. Ultra intelligence led the three British destroyers to Bear Island where they discovered the German minelayer *Ulm*, and while two of the destroyers shelled the ship, the third, *Onslaught*, fired three torpedoes with the third penetrating the magazine, which exploded. Despite the massive explosion, the commanding officer and fifty-nine of the ship's company survived to be taken prisoner.

Less successful were the Hampden bombers. Already obsolescent, several were shot down on their way to Russia by the Germans and, perhaps due to mistaken identity, by the Russians, who may have confused the aircraft with the Dornier Do 17. Unfortunately, one of those shot down by the Germans crashed in Norway and contained details of the defence of the next pair of convoys, PQ18 and the returning QP14. QP14 was to be the target for the *Admiral Scheer*, together with the cruisers *Admiral Hipper* and *Köln* and a supporting screen of destroyers. This surface force moved to the Altenfjord on 1 September.

PQ18 was the first Arctic convoy to have an escort carrier, the American-built *Avenger*. The ship had three radar-equipped Swordfish from No. 825 NAS for anti-submarine duties, as well as six Hawker Sea Hurricanes, with another six dismantled and stowed beneath the hangar deck in a hold, for fighter defence. These aircraft were drawn from 802 and 883 Squadrons. Another Sea Hurricane was aboard the CAM ship *Empire Morn*. Other ships in the convoy escort included the cruiser *Scylla*, 2 destroyers, 2 anti-aircraft ships converted from merchant vessels, 4 corvettes, 4 anti-submarine trawlers, 3 minesweepers and 2 submarines. There was a rescue ship so that the warships did not have to risk stopping to pick up survivors, and three minesweepers* being delivered to the Soviet Union also took on this role.

The convoy had gained an escort carrier but the Home Fleet, which usually provided the distant escort – a much heavier force than that providing the close escort – had lost its fast armoured fleet carrier, *Victorious*, damaged while escorting the convoy Operation PEDESTAL to Malta and being refitted as a result. Also missing were the American

---

*Many accounts maintain that the minesweepers were ex-US vessels, but a survivor of the convoy has assured the author that they were in fact ex-British.

ships, transferred to the Pacific. The C-in-C, Home Fleet, Admiral Sir John Tovey, also made other changes. This time he would remain aboard his flagship, the battleship *King George V*, at Scapa Flow where he would have constant telephone communication with the Admiralty, while his deputy, Vice Admiral Sir Bruce Fraser, went to sea in the battleship *Anson*. Both PQ18 and QP14 had a strong destroyer escort with the freedom of action to leave the close escort to the corvettes, armed trawlers, AA ships and minesweepers if the situation warranted it. To save fuel, the officer in command of the destroyers, Rear Admiral Robert Burnett aboard the light cruiser *Scylla*, ordered that no U-boat hunt was to exceed ninety minutes.

In addition, the convoy would have the support of Force Q and Force P, both comprising two fleet oilers, or tankers, and escorting destroyers, which were deployed ahead of the convoy to Spitzbergen, Norwegian territory not taken by the Germans but that had Russians ashore working on a mining concession dating from Tsarist times. A re-supply operation for the garrison in Spitzbergen was linked with Force P and Force Q.

Iceland was the main rendezvous, but getting there was difficult despite it being summer. Seas were so rough that a Sea Hurricane was swept off *Avenger*'s deck, and the steel ropes securing aircraft in the hangars failed to stop them breaking loose and crashing into one another or the sides of the hangar. Fused 500lb bombs stored in the hangar lift-well broke loose and had to be captured by laying down duffel coats with rope ties, which were secured as soon as a bomb rolled onto one of the coats. Fuel contamination with sea water meant that the carrier suffered engine problems. It also seems that remote Iceland was not remote enough, or safe enough, for the carrier was discovered and bombed by a Focke-Wulf Fw 200 Condor long-range maritime-reconnaissance aircraft that dropped a stick of bombs close to *Avenger* but without causing any damage.

The engine problems meant that the convoy, already spotted by a U-boat while *en passage* to Iceland from Scotland, had to sail without the carrier and, on 8 September, the convoy was discovered by another Condor. Low cloud then protected the convoy from German aircraft until 12 September when a Blohm und Voss BV 138 flying boat dropped through the clouds. By this time, *Avenger* had caught up with the convoy and was able to launch a flight of four Sea Hurricanes, but not in time to catch the German aircraft before it disappeared.

Swordfish were extremely vulnerable on the Arctic convoys which, unlike those across the Atlantic, also had to face German fighters. As a result, the fighters from *Avenger* not only had to protect the ships in the convoy from aerial attack, they had to protect the Swordfish as well. At 0400 on 9 September, the Sea Hurricanes were scrambled after Swordfish on anti-submarine patrols were discovered by a BV 138 flying boat and a Junkers Ju 88 reconnaissance aircraft, but both disappeared into the clouds before the Hurricanes could catch them. Another Swordfish patrol discovered that the BV 138s were laying mines ahead of the convoy.

PQ18 was repeatedly attacked from the air, which meant that the ships had to make mass turns and put up heavy anti-aircraft fire, all of which made life for the returning Swordfish crews very interesting as aircraft recognition was not as good as it could be and the single-engined biplane Swordfish were often mistaken for twin-engined monoplane Ju 88s. Ditching in the sea was never something to be considered lightly but in Arctic waters, even in summer, survival time could be very short indeed.

The Sea Hurricanes attempted to keep a constant air patrol over the convoy with each aircraft spending twenty-five minutes in the air before landing to refuel, but with just six operational aircraft, keeping a constant watch over the Swordfish as well as the convoy was impossible.

On 14 September, the first Swordfish of the day found *U-589* on the surface, but she dived leaving the Swordfish to mark the spot with a smoke flare. Once the aircraft had gone, the submarine surfaced and continued charging her batteries, but alerted by the Swordfish the destroyer *Onslow* raced to the scene. Once again *U-589* dived, but the destroyer attacked with depth-charges and destroyed her. As a result the Germans, so far not accustomed to a convoy having its own air cover and aerial reconnaissance, were forced to change their tactics. Reconnaissance BV 138s and Ju 88s were sent to intimidate the Swordfish, forcing them back over the convoy until the Germans were so close to the ships that they were driven off by AA fire. The Swordfish would then venture out, only to be driven back again.

Later that day, another attack by Ju 88s was detected by the duty Swordfish. This time, *Avenger* herself was the target. Her maximum speed was just 17 knots, much slower than an ordinary aircraft carrier, but fortunately the Sea Hurricanes broke up the attack and no ships from the convoy were lost, while most of the eleven Ju 88s shot down had succumbed to anti-aircraft fire. Further attacks followed that day, again without any losses to the convoy, although another German aircraft was shot down. In a final attack, three of the four patrolling Hurricanes were shot down by friendly fire from the convoy's ships but all three pilots were saved. In this last attack of the day, *Avenger's* commanding officer Commander Colthurst successfully combed torpedoes dropped by the Germans. A bomb dropped by a Ju 88 pilot, who flew exceptionally low to make sure he did not miss the target, hit the ammunition ship *Mary Luckenbach*, which blew up, taking her attacker with her. The sole survivor from the ship was a steward who had been taking the master a cup of coffee, was blown off the upper deck by the explosion and found himself in the sea half a mile down the convoy.

Not all rescues were left to the rescue ships. At the height of the battle for PQ18, the destroyer *Offa* saw a cargo ship, the *Macbeth*, hit by two torpedoes and beginning to sink with her cargo of tanks and other war matériel. *Offa's* commanding officer, Lieutenant Commander Alastair Ewing, took his ship alongside *Macbeth* and, at the cost of some guard rails and stanchions, took off all her ship's company before she sank. One Sea Hurricane pilot had been very lucky to be snatched out of the sea within minutes of baling out by the destroyer *Wheatland* which was acting as close escort for *Avenger*, her role also being what became known as a 'plane guard', fishing unfortunate naval aviators out of the sea.

The next day, the remaining Sea Hurricanes and the Swordfish were again in the air, with the former breaking up further attacks. It was not until 16 September that the Swordfish were relieved of their patrolling by shore-based RAF Consolidated Catalina flying boats of No. 210 Squadron operating from Russia. However, the break was short-lived. Later that day the convoy passed the homeward convoy QP14 with the survivors of the ill-fated PQ17 and *Avenger*, with her aircraft and some of the other escorts transferred to this convoy. The interval had been used by the ship's air engineering team to assemble five Sea Hurricanes, more than replacing the four lost on the outward voyage. In all, the Sea Hurricanes had accounted for a total of 5 enemy aircraft and damaged 17 others out of a total of 44 shot down. It was fortunate that the three Fairey Swordfish remained serviceable as no replacement aircraft were carried.

During the convoy, *Avenger's* commanding officer had changed the operational pattern for the Sea Hurricanes in order to get the maximum benefit from his small force, having a single aircraft in the air most of the time rather than having all of his aircraft, or none of them, airborne at once.

Once the Sea Hurricane flight had been so depleted, it fell to the CAM ship *Empire Morn* to launch her Hurricane, flown by Flying Officer Burr of the RAF. The launch was accompanied by friendly fire from other ships in the convoy until he was finally out of range. Despite problems with the barrage balloons flown by some of the merchantmen, he managed to break up a German attack, setting one aircraft on fire. Once out of ammunition, he saved his precious aircraft by flying it to Keg Ostrov airfield near Archangel. As previously mentioned, this 'one-off' use of aircraft from the CAM ships was a major drawback as convoy commanders were reluctant to use them in case a more desperate situation emerged later in the convoy's passage. Cases of CAM ship fighters being saved were very rare.

Clearly, even an escort carrier with a mix of fighters and anti-submarine aircraft was hard-pressed to provide adequate air cover. It is hard to escape the conclusion that two escort carriers would have been needed, or a larger ship such as *Nairana* or *Vindex* with up to fourteen Swordfish and six Wildcat fighters, a much better aircraft than the Sea Hurricane. Again, even with these two ships one might suggest that the balance between fighters and anti-submarine aircraft was wrong for an Arctic convoy.

Inevitably, as the convoy approached its destination there was no sign of the promised Red Air Force air cover. This was typical of the experiences of those on the convoys to Russia, with neither Russia's air forces nor her navy providing any support. Indeed, apart from some coastal bombardment as the Red armies swept westwards, the main achievement of the Russian navy was for its submarines to sink the merchantmen carrying German refugees away from the Russians and one of these attacks resulted in the greatest recorded loss of life at sea as the Germans struggled to evacuate more than 1.5 million civilians.

Homeward Bound – QP14

With convoys, it was always important to 'bring home the empties': those ships that had delivered their cargoes safely and were needed for the next consignment of supplies. Little came out of the Soviet Union at this time but on some routes, such as that across the North Atlantic, there was some export traffic from the UK as goods that were not available on the home market were still produced to send abroad to earn some foreign currency and, above all, retain a traditional export market. Although it was available on the home market, Scotch whisky and similar products continued to be exported.

The main point was, of course, that ships and their crews were valuable and difficult to replace. For this reason, even ships sailing in ballast (important to ensure that an 'empty' ship retained her stability) were important targets for the enemy.

On 17 September 1942 the homeward convoy QP14 took over the destroyer escort and several other ships from PQ18, including *Avenger*. The convoy had left Archangel on 13 September escorted by 6 British minesweepers, 4 of which then detached leaving the convoy with the remaining minesweepers, 2 destroyers, 2 AA ships, 4 corvettes and 4 anti-submarine trawlers, as well as *Avenger*, the cruiser *Scylla*, AA ship *Alynbank*, 2 submarines and 17 destroyers from PQ18 under Burnett's command.

Initially there was little trouble from the Germans as the Luftwaffe was concentrating on PQ18, but the convoy was shadowed by reconnaissance aircraft that edged to within AA range before moving away again. A number of destroyers were detached to lay a false trail, while the convoy was joined by Force Q. Despite U-boat sightings, the first sign of trouble came at 0520 on 20 September when *U-435* put two torpedoes into the ocean minesweeper *Leda*, a veteran of the convoys. Commander A.H. Wynn-Edwards and eighty-six of his crew were rescued, along with two Merchant Navy officers who were survivors of PQ17. Those rescued from *Leda* were spread over three of the rescue ships, but six died from wounds or hypothermia afterwards. That same day a Swordfish depth-charged a U-boat, and the destroyer *Ashanti* went in pursuit of another U-boat which it also depth-charged, at the time believing it had destroyed it. An attempt by the submarine *P614* to torpedo *U-408*, caught on the surface, failed when one of the torpedoes blew up prematurely, setting off the other one and allowing the U-boat to dive and escape.

At 1745 *U-255* torpedoed a PQ17 survivor, *Silver Sword*, and the ship burst into flames, with her ship's company only managing to escape with difficulty. She was later sunk by gunfire from the destroyer *Worcester*.

As the U-boat threat intensified, Colthurst aboard *Avenger* had to signal Burnett, warning him that his Swordfish crews were at the limit of their physical endurance. Realizing the problem, and that both *Avenger* and the cruiser *Scylla* were fast becoming liabilities rather than assets, Burnett transferred his flag to the destroyer *Milne*. Three destroyers were detailed to provide an anti-submarine screen for the two ships, which were then sent home. Burnett's decision was logical as the German aerial threat had diminished, leaving little for the Sea Hurricanes to do. In addition, if the Swordfish crews were beyond the limits of their physical and mental endurance, they were more likely to be a danger to themselves and the convoy than provide additional protection. A Swordfish crash-landing could have resulted in considerable damage to the carrier as at this time unused depth-charges were not dropped before landing.

Somali, one of the Tribal-class destroyers, was torpedoed by *U-703* later that day. Her commanding officer had attempted to comb the torpedo, without success. While two destroyers attempted to hunt down the culprit, another destroyer and a trawler came alongside to take off survivors. Five men were killed and four wounded in the engine room. The stricken destroyer's commanding officer signalled that he thought his ship could be towed with just a skeleton crew aboard, and her sister ship, *Ashanti*, was ordered to her assistance.

The following morning, 21 September, saw a Catalina flying boat from the RAF's No. 330 Squadron, based in Shetland, over the convoy. The aircraft was just in time to spot *U-378* on the surface, but was spotted and came under accurate anti-aircraft fire from the submarine that ripped into the fuel tanks. As it crash-dived, it dropped four depth-charges before making a forced landing. The crew were picked up by the destroyer *Marne*, which then destroyed the aircraft as it was still afloat.

Dropping depth-charges before an aircraft crashed was essential for the survival of the crew. The charges were pre-set to explode at a certain depth, and once the aircraft sank were almost certain to explode and anyone on the surface nearby would be killed.

Despite renewed air cover at 0630 on the morning of 22 September, *U-435* managed to get within the screen. In one of the most successful actions by a U-boat during the Second World War, within minutes three ships were sunk, two merchantmen and the fleet oiler *Grey Ranger*, although without loss of life. One of the ships sunk was the *Bellingham* carrying the convoy commodore, Captain J.C.K. Dowding, RNR, who joined the other survivors aboard the minesweeper *Seagull* and handed over command to his vice commodore Captain Walker aboard *Ocean Freedom*, another survivor from PQ17.

On 23 September the rescue ships and some of the destroyers headed for Seidisfjord to refuel, while the rest of the convoy continued towards

Cape Wrath on the north-western tip of Scotland as the weather deteriorated and a gale approached.

The remaining ships of the convoy were to make a safe landfall, but on 24 September the gales that had been a nuisance for the surviving ships were dashing all hopes of salvaging *Somali*. The destroyer had already slipped her tow once, and her condition was perilous. Most of her port side was holed, although most of the compartments apart from the boiler room and engine room were dry. As the rising sea tortured and stressed the stricken ship further, the inevitable happened and her back was broken, splitting the ship in two. Almost immediately the bow and stern sections went vertical and sank beneath the feet of her skeleton crew as they scrambled into life-rafts and Carley floats. Out of eighty-two men aboard, just thirty-five survived, with many of those lost being swept under the bows of *Ashanti* as she returned to their rescue with the trawler *Lord Middleton*. Some of those picked up from the water died from hypothermia.

The U-boat menace had not completely gone away, however, and a Catalina from No. 210 Squadron spotted *U-253* less than a mile from the rear of the convoy. The U-boat crash-dived but the Catalina dropped six depth-charges as the submarine went down. As the depth-charges exploded, the U-boat was blasted back to the surface before submerging for a second time and then suddenly reappearing on her beam ends before her bows dived and her stern lifted to the vertical, hanging there for a moment and then disappearing for good.

The efforts of the destroyer escort seemed to be disappointing at the time, but unknown to their crews, they did inflict damage on five U-boats. The escort carrier had proved itself beyond doubt, but these did not become more widely available until 1943 so there were to be many more convoys without any air cover at all once beyond the range of shore-based aircraft.

There were many more convoys to Russia still to come at this stage, but PQ17 and PQ18 were two of the most famous. The convoys were a demanding operation for both the Royal Navy and the Merchant Navy, one that Stalin never recognized and there was no Soviet contribution to the escorts. The convoys continued, despite German attacks and the weather, until the war's end, with the exception of the period immediately before, during and after the Normandy landings when a massive effort was required that demanded the escorts and especially the larger ships. That finally gave Stalin the only battlefront that he would recognize as being a 'second front'.

Chapter 15

The Submarine War

Submarines figured prominently in both world wars but in each case attention has focussed mainly on the role of the German U-boats, ignoring the work of British submariners and for that matter their American counterparts who did so much to interrupt supplies from Japan's newfound empire to the home islands. British submariners wreaked havoc in the Baltic and the Bosphorus in the First World War, and maintained an outstanding campaign in the Mediterranean in the Second World War. So much of this has passed by unremarked and with little attention.

As in the Fleet Air Arm, the Royal Navy's submariners received extra money, but while the former described it rather nobly as 'flying pay', the submariners were blunt and to the point; to them it was 'danger money'. Both these sections of the Royal Navy had been regarded as not very respectable when first formed, and indeed one First World War submariner was turned down for an important posting despite being favoured by an Allied government because the Admiralty thought he was 'something of a pirate'.

Submariners and airmen were a breed apart. They had come together briefly between the two world wars with the ill-fated M2, the Royal Navy's only attempt at an aircraft-carrying submarine whose aircrew, flying the diminutive Parnall Peto seaplane, were reputed to have received both danger money and flying pay. The extra money was necessary to attract men into the submarine service, for apart from the extra dangers there were many other hardships including cramped accommodation with the smell of diesel oil always present and a shortage of fresh water, which was why beards, known as a 'full set' in the Royal Navy, were so common among submariners. The Submarine Service was organized in flotillas for control and administrative convenience. There was never a set size for a flotilla; it could be just two or many more vessels, but they were usually grouped around a base such as the headquarters, HMS *Dolphin*, a stone frigate at Haslar, Gosport, or a depot ship such as HMS *Forth*.

Submarines were more than just another means of striking at enemy shipping. In contrast to the nuclear-powered submarine that spends most of its operational life submerged, Second World War submarines spent much of their time on the surface, only diving when threatened or when needing to be concealed before making an attack. Many attacks were made on the surface, using the deck gun rather than a more expensive torpedo, of which only replenishment stocks could be carried. The submarines of the day could cruise at a reasonable speed on the surface, but were very slow when submerged unless they made a high-speed dash, itself still not very fast, in which case their batteries would need recharging after about an hour.

Submarines could be used for mine-laying, inserting special forces and for reconnaissance or guiding an attacking force towards a landing area and also to carry urgent supplies. They had a greater radius of action than a destroyer and made use of much less manpower. In theory, they could get much closer to an enemy warship than a destroyer without being detected. The Royal Navy's submarines varied greatly, ranging from the larger boats (submarines were never ships) for mine-laying and smaller craft for operations in confined or shallow waters, and of course there were the X-craft, the midget submarines.

Among the more notable successes of British submarines were the torpedoing and sinking of the German light cruiser *Karlsruhe* off Kristiansand during the Norwegian campaign by *Truant* on 9 April 1940. Later the 'pocket battleship' or *Panzerschiff Lutzow* was caught by *Spearfish*, commanded by Lieutenant Commander John Forbes, as the German ship was on her way from Norway to Germany for repairs to bomb damage. Although not sunk, *Lutzow* was disabled and had to be towed into harbour at Kiel.

This was not the last British success against a major German warship. The heavy cruiser *Prinz Eugen*, believed by many to have fired the fatal shell that destroyed HMS *Hood* and which had participated in the celebrated Channel Dash in February 1942, was discovered in Norwegian waters by Lieutenant Commander George Gregory in *Trident* on 23 February 1942 and a well-placed torpedo blew off part of her stern. A slow crawl with a temporary rudder to Trondheim was needed for temporary repairs before the ship could go to Kiel for permanent repairs, putting her out of service for the rest of the year.

British Submarine Strategy

Submarine strategy and tactics varied greatly between the belligerent nations during the Second World War. In 1939, the British Admiralty decided that the priority target for British submarines would be enemy warships. Submarines were to wait in their individual patrol areas, submerged, waiting for enemy warships to appear. By 1941 this strategy had been amended, especially in the Mediterranean where submarine commanders were given what amounted to a roving commission to attack anything that appeared worthwhile and, of course, merchantmen supplying Axis forces in North Africa or the Balkans were very worthwhile. The same approach later applied in the Far East.

The Royal Navy did not neglect specialized craft, including the midget submarine. After experimenting with a one-man design known as the Welman – basically a cross between a midget submarine and a human torpedo – British midget submarines evolved into the X-craft with a four-man crew. One or two members of the crew had to leave the craft in wet suits with breathing apparatus to place explosive charges on the target. This was a different approach from the Axis navies, who used midget submarines armed with torpedoes carried externally. The finest hour for the X-craft was on 20 September 1943 when six of these vessels penetrated the defences around the Altenfjord in Norway and placed explosive charges on the hull of the German battleship *Tirpitz*, damaging her machinery and main armament so that she was out of action for seven months. *Tirpitz* had earlier been the target for British human torpedoes, known to the Royal Navy as 'chariots', that had mounted an unsuccessful attempt to sink the ship in October 1942.

Later, on 6 June 1944, two X-craft undertook beach reconnaissance before the Normandy landings and then provided guidance to the British beaches.

Other targets included a floating dock in Norway, while a development of the X-craft, the XE-craft, was used in the Far East to disable Japanese communication cables and they also damaged a cruiser.

During the Second World War, British submarines sank 169 warships, including 35 U-boats, and 493 merchant vessels, but at a high cost with no fewer than 74 British submarines sunk, a third of the total number deployed during the war. A third of British submarine losses were due to enemy minefields. Just one submarine, *Triumph*, survived contact with an enemy mine and her survival was all the more remarkable as she lost her bows as far back as frame eight, which meant that she also lost her torpedo tubes and ten torpedoes!

The Malta Submarines

Before the outbreak of war, the Admiralty saw Malta as a base for submarines and other forces able to attack the Italian supply lines supporting their forces in North Africa. Yet, the battle was far from one-sided and within three days of Italy entering the war on 10 June 1940, three British submarines, *Grampus*, *Odin* and *Orpheus*, had been sunk by Italian warships. As the bombing of Malta intensified, submarines in port had to lie submerged on the harbour bed in the hope of being missed.

In 1941 Malta became an operational base for submarines. This was not without difficulty as most of the necessary supplies had been taken to Alexandria, but submarines operating from Gibraltar to Malta overloaded with torpedoes and other supplies until stocks were built up. The use of Malta as an offensive base was helped by the introduction of the new U-class submarines, smaller than many of the other classes but ideal for the clear waters of the Mediterranean in which, all too often, sonar is not needed to spot a submerged submarine.

These clear waters often proved fatal for larger submarines, but the U-class was better suited to the conditions, although the class had had its origins in plans for a smaller training submarine. Nine of the U-class were deployed to Malta as the 10th Submarine Flotilla: *Undaunted*, *Union*, *Upholder*, *Upright*, *Utmost*, *Unique*, *Urge*, *Ursula* and *Usk*. *Usk* and *Undaunted* did not survive long, but their place was soon taken by others of the same class. In addition to attacking Axis convoys and warships, these submarines were also ideal for landing raiding parties on the Italian coast and on one occasion wrecked a railway line along which trains carrying munitions for the Luftwaffe bases in Sicily travelled.

The submarines were based at Manoel Island, which lay in the Marsamxett Harbour and was approached by a causeway off the main road from Valletta to Sliema, the island effectively dividing Sliema Creek from Lazaretto Creek. Originally a fort designed to cover the outskirts of Valletta which towered over the other side of the harbour, Manoel Island became a naval base with workshops and accommodation for resting submariners and for artificers, the Royal Navy's term for skilled tradesmen, who were often senior ratings. The submarines were moored alongside. Substantial anti-aircraft defences were placed on Manoel Island, as being on the opposite side of Valletta from the Grand Harbour did not spare the base from heavy aerial attack.

Offensive submarine operations based on Malta started in February 1941 with patrols by *Unique, Upright* and *Utmost*. The first significant engagement was later that month when *Upright*, commanded by Lieutenant E.D. Norman, sank the Italian cruiser *Armando Diaz*, one of two cruisers escorting a large Axis convoy. No doubt the Italians had put on two cruisers to impress their German allies, but there were no major British warships in the area and the cruiser, which posed no threat to a submarine, proved an ideal target.

Reconnaissance reports of large-scale shipping movements were received on 8 March and resulted in three boats being sent to sea. This was despite *Utmost*, commanded by Lieutenant Commander R.D. Cayley, having only been in harbour for twenty-four hours. The following day she found and sank the Italian merchantman *Capo Vita*. On 10 March *Unique* sank another merchantman, the *Fenicia*. Later in the month these submarines were at sea again, with *Utmost* finding a convoy of five ships on 28 March and torpedoing and sinking the *Heraklia*, while the *Ruhr* had to be towed into port. The return voyage for the depleted convoy was no less eventful when *Upright* torpedoed and severely damaged the *Galilea*, reported as being a straggler.

In April *Upholder* joined the Malta flotilla, and for almost a year she and her commander, Lieutenant Commander Malcolm Wanklyn, played havoc with the Axis convoys. From April 1941 to March 1942, this one submarine accounted for three large troop-carrying liners each of more than 18,000 tons, seven other merchant ships, a destroyer and two German U-boats, as well as damaging a cruiser and three merchant ships. The first two troopships had been in a convoy of three approached by Wanklyn steering on the surface and skilfully firing a spread of four torpedoes at the ships. Two of the troopships managed to zigzag into the path of the torpedoes with one sinking immediately, leaving the other to be finished off by Wanklyn when he returned the following morning. *Ursula* missed the third troopship which managed to reach Tripoli safely. For his time in the Mediterranean Wanklyn was awarded the Victoria Cross, the highest British service decoration, and the DSO. It was a sad day when *Upholder* was lost off Tripoli with all hands in April 1942.

So successful was the Malta-based 10th Flotilla in disrupting the supplies for Rommel's *Afrika Korps* in the Western Desert campaign that his chief of staff, Lieutenant General Fritz Bayerlein, later admitted: 'We should have taken Alexandria and reached the Suez Canal had it not been for the work of your submarines.'

For about a year the Malta-based submariners exacted a high price from the enemy, but even so, opportunities were missed. More than any other type of warship, submarines needed to practise 'deconfliction', largely because of the difficulty of recognizing other submarines. Deconfliction is the deliberate separation of friendly forces. In British submarine practice, this meant placing submarines to operate independently within designated patrol zones known as billets, and any other submarine found in that area was to be regarded as hostile. Off Malta there were often so many British submarines that it was necessary to impose an embargo on night attacks on other submarines because of the difficulty in accurate recognition.

Early one morning in 1942, *Upright* was on the surface when her lookouts spotted another larger submarine on a reciprocal course and it was not until the two boats had passed that they realized the other submarine was a large U-boat. There were many U-boats off Malta at the time and no one will ever know whether the Germans were working to the same rules or whether their lookouts failed to spot the smaller British submarine. This almost certainly wasn't the only occasion on which two submarines from opposing navies met and passed each other by. Another instance was when an Italian and a British submarine encountered one another on the surface at night and after exchanging mutually unintelligible signals, both dived.

Even with such missed opportunities, the submarines from Manoel Island accounted for 54,000 tons of Axis merchant shipping between October 1941 and February 1942, as well as a destroyer, two submarines and two other ships off Taranto.

The 'Magic Carpet'

During the First World War, the Germans had established a company to operate merchant submarines to carry much-needed strategic materials and bring them past the increasingly effective British blockade of German ports. While there was no equivalent British submarine 'line', given the strategic importance of Malta and the desperate plight of the islanders and the forces garrisoned there, British submariners were keen to show just what they could do. The submarine supply line that was established became known as the 'Magic Carpet'.

While at first the Axis hold on Malta had been relatively light, by 1941 the situation was becoming increasingly difficult. Many convoys did not get through at all, and all suffered serious losses. It became the practice for every submarine heading to Malta from Gibraltar or

Alexandria to carry at least some items of stores in addition to their usual torpedoes or mines. The true Magic Carpet submarines were the larger vessels, especially the mine-laying submarines *Cachalot* and *Rorqual*, as well as the fleet submarine *Clyde* and the larger boats of the 'O', 'P' and 'R' classes. An even better supply-carrying submarine would have been the Royal Navy's sole aircraft-carrying submarine, M2, whose aircraft hangar would have made a good cargo hold, but she had been lost in an accident some years before the war. An alternative could have been the French submarine *Surcouf*, a large 2,800-ton boat also with a hangar and in service with the Free French, but she was eventually lost in the Caribbean.

The 'P' or *Porpoise*-class minelayers and *Clyde* all proved to be especially efficient supply vessels with plenty of room between their casing and the pressure hull for stores, and sometimes one of the batteries would be removed to provide extra space; the mine stowage tunnel was another good cargo space. *Rorqual* on one occasion carried 24 personnel, 147 bags of mail, 2 tons of medical stores, 62 tons of aviation spirit and 45 tons of kerosene. Inevitably there was also much unofficial cargo, such as gin for the wardrooms and other officers' messes on Malta, and even Lord Gort, the island's austere governor, was not above having a small consignment of gramophone records brought out to him in this way. Cargo was sometimes carried externally in small containers welded to the casing of a submarine.

Impressive though the efforts of the submariners were, they could not compare with a merchant ship which at this time could carry as much as 7,500 tons of cargo compared with the 200 tons or so of a large submarine. For the submariners, there were problems as well, as the cargo gave rise to problems with buoyancy. Once *Cachalot* had so much sea water absorbed by wooden packing cases that her first lieutenant (i.e. on a smaller warship, the second-in-command) had to pump out 1,000 gallons of water from her internal tanks to compensate. Fuel was another hazard. In July 1941, *Talisman* carried 5,500 gallons in cans stowed beneath her casing, while on other occasions fuel could be carried in external fuel tanks. When carrying petrol in cans, submarines were not allowed to dive below 65 feet, while high-octane aviation fuel in the external tanks meant that fumes venting in the usual way constituted a fire hazard so smoking was banned on the conning tower and pyrotechnic recognition signals were also banned. These problems were in addition to conditions in the Mediterranean favouring smaller submarines rather than larger.

A good example of what could be done was the case of *Saracen*. She reached Malta via Gibraltar, sailing with a Malta-bound convoy. Smaller than the mine-laying submarines, *Saracen* had two of her fuel tanks cleared of diesel and filled with aviation fuel instead, while every space aboard was filled with food with priority being given to medical supplies and powered or tinned milk for children and babies. After reaching Malta, *Saracen* left to search for Italian merchantmen, but instead sank a destroyer and an Italian submarine.

In peacetime, Malta had been one of the most popular postings for the Royal Navy and an equally popular place to call. In wartime, despite the miserable conditions aboard submarines that had to remain submerged during daytime when in harbour, there was little enthusiasm for a 'run ashore', visiting the bars and other attractions of Valletta. Ashore, there was little to eat and not much to drink. Things were so bad that one army officer recalled his pleasure at being invited to dinner aboard a submarine.

In addition to the tradition of flying her 'Jolly Roger' at the end of a successful patrol, *Porpoise* added a second flag beneath the Jolly Roger's tally of ships sunk. This was marked 'PCS' for 'Porpoise Carrier Service' with a white bar for each successful supply run, and this boat alone had at least four of these.

After delivering supplies to Malta, the Magic Carpet submarines would take mines from the island's underground stores and proceed north to lay them off the main Italian ports, such as Palermo, before returning to Egypt or Gibraltar. They also torpedoed Axis shipping, and on one occasion an Italian submarine was torpedoed and sunk before an Italian merchant ship was also torpedoed, and as this stubbornly refused to sink, the submarine surfaced and sank her with gunfire.

The arrival of the famous Malta convoy Operation PEDESTAL in August 1942 reduced the pressure on the submarines to supply Malta and allowed increased offensive patrolling.

Despite this, by October 1942 the situation was again becoming difficult, with a renewed German air offensive. At this time, five submarines – *Unbending, Unbroken, United, Utmost* and *Safari* – attacked a convoy of five merchant ships including a tanker escorted by seven destroyers south of the Italian island of Pantelleria, co-ordinating the attack with aircraft from Malta.

The role of the submarine was varied. On 21 April 1941, the British Mediterranean Fleet ventured west for an attack on the Italian-held port of Tripoli. Accuracy was usually a great difficulty when attacking a land target from the sea in the dark, so Cunningham had the submarine *Truant* positioned exactly 4 miles off the harbour, showing a light to seaward as a navigation mark for the bombardment. Then in July, two submarines helped to confuse the enemy and assist a convoy *en passage* to Malta. The convoy was code-named Operation SUBSTANCE. While the Mediterranean Fleet steamed west from Alexandria to Malta and Force H escorted the convoy east from Gibraltar, the two submarines were west of Crete making fleet signals to indicate that the Mediterranean Fleet was operating in the area while the fleet itself maintained radio silence.

Truant was one of the new 'T'-class submarines intended for operation in distant waters, which was to prove useful once Japan entered the war. The class could handle the long Pacific distances. It displaced 1,571 tons while submerged and had eight bow torpedo tubes as well as another aft and two amidships, with a 4in gun and light anti-aircraft weapons. Surface speed was just over 15 knots, but while submerged these boats could manage 9 knots, although the batteries needed to be recharged after an hour so the usual submerged speed was around 2 or 3 knots.

Originally *Truant* and her sisters had a range of 8,000 miles but on later boats this was extended to 11,000 miles by the use of welding to strengthen the boats during construction and by using some of the ballast tanks to carry fuel. However, this still compared badly with the range of more than 32,000 miles of the German Type IXD U-boat.

Chapter 16

Changing Ships and Aircraft

The appearance of the Royal Navy in 1945 differed greatly from that in 1939, and not just because of the widespread adoption of camouflage to disguise the shape of ships and aircraft. In 1939 the battleship was still all-important, and while the Royal Navy had seven aircraft carriers, four of these were already regarded as being ready for replacement. By 1945 the Royal Navy had seven large aircraft carriers, mainly the fast armoured variants, but the first aircraft carrier, *Furious*, had survived along with the *Argus*, by this time a hulk, and there was also the maintenance carrier *Unicorn* that was also used operationally when needed. There were five light fleet carriers of the *Colossus* class with more building, and no fewer than forty escort carriers.

In 1939 the Fleet Air Arm, only just handed back to Admiralty control from the Air Ministry, had 232 aircraft in 19 squadrons, but in 1945 there were 1,336 aircraft in 78 combat squadrons. More than half the 1945 aircraft had been built in the United States. The service that had been without high-performance aircraft in 1939 was in 1945 the proud possessor of high-performance fighters and bombers that were among the best available.

The fast armoured carriers of which *Illustrious* had been the first had proved themselves under the most demanding conditions in the Mediterranean and in the Far East. They were the most successful aircraft carriers of the Second World War.

Yet, the growth in naval air power and the decline of the battleship did not mean that surface vessels were unimportant and their development had not been neglected. Destroyers had been found to be too narrow in the beam and perhaps too delicate for convoy escort duties in the most demanding sea conditions, while their high speed was of little use sitting alongside a convoy that usually managed much less than 10 knots. Something slower and sturdier was required, and so the corvette appeared. When something bigger than a corvette with better habitability in high seas was required, the frigate was reinvented, mainly for anti-submarine duties but anti-aircraft versions also followed.

In Nelson's day, the frigate had been the mainstay of the Royal Navy. The large ships of the line, the predecessors of the battleship, came together for the major fleet actions but routine patrols, convoy escorts, anti-piracy and anti-slavery patrols were all carried out by frigates. With communications with higher command and even the Admiralty being very slow and so poor as to be almost non-existent, the commanding officers of these useful ships had to use their initiative and on their shoulders had rested the fate of the British Empire. The new frigates of the mid-twentieth century often operated in flotillas and the freedom enjoyed by the commanding officers of their ancestors was much curtailed, but the frigate was to become the most common warship of the late twentieth century and take this position into the twenty-first century when defence cuts meant that once again they were to be found often on their own and again commanding officers found themselves with great responsibilities, even though communications had improved.

This is to leap ahead by more than half a century. What happened between 1939 and 1945?

The Ships

Improvisation was very much to the fore as war loomed. There was nothing new in this. The Royal Navy was accustomed to taking merchant vessels 'up from trade' in wartime, and fishing vessels were also used. In times past, the difference between merchant vessels and naval vessels had been small and many merchant vessels had been fitted with cannon as a precaution against pirates. The dawning of the steam age had coincided with a period when merchant ship and warship design had started to differentiate. Nevertheless, armed trawlers made good convoy escorts or minesweepers, and drifters could be used for all manner of work inside harbours and anchorages. In the First World War, Irish Sea and English Channel packet ships were the first choice for conversion to seaplane carriers. Liners were taken up for use as armed merchant cruisers to help protect convoys, but these proved to be inadequate for the task when confronted by a battleship, battle-cruiser, *Panzerschiff* or even a cruiser, be it heavy or light, as the armed merchant cruiser lacked the firepower, speed and armour of a warship. One of the most famous of these ships was the *Rawalpindi*, a former P&O liner, but she was lost when she was confronted by the German battle-cruisers *Scharnhorst* and *Gneisenau* off Iceland. The

Germans had also used armed merchant cruisers in both world wars, but as commerce raiders rather than convoy escorts.

Before the war, recognizing that there was a shortage of flight decks, the Admiralty considered converting into aircraft carriers two of the world's largest and fastest ocean liners, RMS *Queen Mary* and the even newer *Queen Elizabeth*, still completing, but decided that they would be needed as troopships. The size and speed of these two ships would have made them excellent aircraft carriers, but conversion would have taken some time and armour would have been difficult, leaving them vulnerable. Even with the benefit of hindsight, leaving them to be used as troopships was the right decision.

No doubt the decision was also taken with full knowledge that the Royal Navy had four new fast armoured aircraft carriers building. Before the war this order was increased to six ships, while those that were due to be replaced – *Furious*, *Argus*, *Eagle* and *Hermes* – were all retained in service but of these, only the first two survived the war. All four ships would have been more useful escorting convoys while the first escort carriers were awaited rather than on other even more exposed tasks, although it was on a convoy, Operation PEDESTAL, that *Eagle* was lost.

The escort carrier and the MAC ships and CAM ships that preceded them showed that improvisation was taken to greater lengths during the Second World War than in any earlier conflict. While the Royal Navy's first escort carriers were British conversions, for the rest of the war most of the conversions came from the United States, although a small number of ships were also converted in British yards as the Admiralty believed, wrongly, that the welded hulls of the American ships would be inadequate for Arctic waters.

Progress was made, and British submarine designs were soon strengthened and improved when welded hulls became commonplace. Habitability also improved, with submarines intended for the Far East having air-conditioning. The arrival of American ships in the Royal Navy also started another change: the move from hammocks to bunks. This was not always welcomed, as old hands preferred the hammock in bad weather conditions.

There can be no doubt that the fast armoured carriers were the best aircraft carriers of the Second World War. The American carriers were often larger, but had wooden flight decks rather than steel. This was a serious weakness when Japanese kamikaze attacks became frequent. As one American naval officer put it succinctly: 'When a kamikaze hits an American carrier, it is six months in Pearl; when he hits a limey carrier, it is "sweepers, man your brooms".' A bit of an exaggeration perhaps, but quick-drying cement to smooth out the dent in the steel plate kept the ship operational without dockyard help.

Even so, these ships were costly and took time to produce. While the Americans had their *Independence*-class light carriers based on the hull of the *Cleveland*-class light cruisers, these ships were too narrow in the beam. Instead of converting ships, the British could be said to have converted their shipyards by designing the *Colossus*-class light fleet carrier, built to merchant shipping standards so that they could be built in yards with no history of warship construction. Five of these ships were available before the war ended but reached the Far East too late to see action.

These ships were cheaper and smaller than *Illustrious* and her sisters and half-sisters, while the *Majestic* class that followed was an enlarged version. Sometimes criticized for being too slow at 24 knots as jet aircraft became the norm for carrier work, they were nevertheless the most widely-used aircraft carrier classes of all time, with ships of these two classes used not only by the Royal Navy but also by the Royal Australian Navy, Royal Canadian Navy, Indian Navy and the navies of Argentina, Brazil, France and The Netherlands.

The wartime navy was hampered by decisions taken by interwar British governments, with the *King George V* class of battleships having 14in guns instead of the planned 16in and heavy cruisers having six 8in guns instead of eight. The folly of these decisions was recognized and the last battleship to be built for the Royal Navy, HMS *Vanguard*, had 15in guns. Completed too late to see action, at one stage consideration was given to completing her as an aircraft carrier, although she would not have been broad enough to make a good carrier. The idea was dropped, but one wonders why a battleship was still regarded as necessary by this time.

Destroyers continued to be built during the war, with large-scale building of 'war emergency destroyers'. The United States provided First World War-vintage destroyers that became the Royal Navy's Town class in return for the use of British naval bases in the Caribbean but, as mentioned earlier, these ships were wasted as convoy escorts and were also not sturdy enough for the worst weather conditions. The answer lay in the corvette, based on the design of a commercial whaler but slightly longer. Some of these were transferred to the United States Navy under what became known unofficially as reverse lend-lease, providing the USN with sonar-equipped ships. Larger corvettes were also built before the frigate was reinvented.

Completely new arrivals in the Royal Navy were the midget submarine or X-craft, and the human torpedo, the latter being an Italian idea that was adopted by the Royal Navy. As mentioned before, the Royal Navy was much kinder about its human torpedoes than the Italians, calling them 'chariots' while the Italian name for them was 'pigs'.

More widely used were other innovations: the landing craft and the larger landing ship. It is doubtful whether the series of invasions across the Mediterranean and then at Normandy could have been made without these vessels. In the First World War, converted cargo ships and barges were used as well as large rowing boats, confusingly also known as 'whalers' in the Royal Navy. The Germans had used barges, or caiques, for the invasion of Crete and had suffered heavy losses at the hands of the British Mediterranean Fleet, which never lost control of the seas but sadly air control was missing at the time.

Most landing craft were stowed on the sides of ships, rather as large and ungainly lifeboats would have been, but the first ships with floodable stern docks also appeared, making the transfer from ship to landing craft easier.

Protecting Home Waters
While a classic 'blue water' or deep-sea navy, the Royal Navy also had to defend Britain's long coastline. Surprisingly, despite the success of British coastal motor boats (CMBs) during the First World War, these craft were neglected between the two world wars, possibly due to severe budget restrictions. By contrast, the *Kriegsmarine* had done much to develop their E-boats, the cover-all term used for German motor torpedo boats and gunboats. The reasons for German interest were the small manpower requirement of these inexpensive craft and their ability to harass enemy shipping in waters too shallow for U-boats to operate. The best defence against such small fast-moving craft were small fast-moving craft of one's own; apart from the difficulty of hitting such a small and fast-moving target, another problem was that larger ships could not depress their guns sufficiently to hit back at the E-boats.

It was not until 1935 that orders were placed with small boatyards specializing in fast small craft. The problem that then affected production was the lack of a small high-speed diesel engine, so the early examples were petrol-engined with the consequent risk of fire and explosion. Initially, all were motor torpedo boats (MTBs) but these were later joined by motor gunboats (MGBs), which were longer and often exceeded 100ft in length.

The MTBs were used mainly for attack, but the motor gunboats could be used for defence against German raids on ports on the south and east coasts or for landing or picking up agents off enemy-held coastlines. By 1944 the Royal Navy was operating a highly-effective force of MTBs and MGBs in the Channel. British experience was later used by the United States Navy in the Pacific as the Americans had also neglected this branch of naval warfare, believing that there was no need for such craft in the wide reaches of the Pacific. In fact, while the Pacific may be wide, these small craft proved useful in operations among the many island groups that had to be captured as the war progressed across the Pacific to Japan. British designs were obtained by the USN and developed into the famous PT (Patrol Torpedo) boats. The most successful type of MGB was the Fairmile 'D',* otherwise known as 'Dog Boats'.

The first small fast British craft for what became known as Coastal Forces were the MTBs and the first MGBs appeared in March 1941. Small bases were built around the coast for Coastal Forces and while each base had an experienced RN captain as commanding officer, the flotillas as well as the individual craft were largely commanded by officers from the Royal Naval Volunteer Reserve; at least one historian has credited the verve of Coastal Forces to the originality brought to the operation by young people freed from naval tradition.

Despite the term 'Coastal Forces', these craft were not confined to home waters, and especially in the Mediterranean proved effective at hit-and-run raids on Axis shipping and for putting ashore small groups of commandos for attacks alongside partisans in Greece and Yugoslavia. In the Tyrrhenian Sea, they attacked German coastal shipping that was used to keep German land forces supplied.

Not all the work of Coastal Forces was glamorous. Keeping British ports and shipping lanes open was another important task, and a dangerous one. Much has been written about convoys and the threat to Allied shipping from U-boats and surface raiders, but initially the biggest threat to British shipping while the U-boat fleet built up was from mines laid by German ships, U-boats and aircraft. The British carried out similar operations, with shore-based units of the Fleet Air

---

*Fairmile was one of the leading designers and builders of such craft.

Arm helping the Royal Air Force in laying mines, termed 'gardening' by the RAF as previously mentioned.

At the time, most mines were known as 'contact mines', i.e. a ship had to hit one to set it off. Many will be familiar with this type of mine as over the years numbers of them have been painted red and used as large collection boxes at seaside resorts, having first had their explosives removed, of course. Such mines were swept using special equipment called paravanes, towed behind a ship, which would usually cut the mine free from its mooring and let it float to the surface to be detonated by gunfire. This was also known as the 'Oropesa Sweep', named after the first ship to use it.

The real problems began when the Germans began using 'influence type' mines. These had originally been developed by the British at the end of the First World War, but they had still to find a means of detonating them. The first of these was the magnetic mine but pressure mines were also introduced later. A German magnetic mine was accidentally dropped on land in November 1939 and in an act of outstanding courage, Lieutenant Commander J.G.D. Ouvry dismantled it, providing enough information for a magnetic sweep to be developed. Despite this, by November 1939 enemy mines had almost brought the east coast convoys to a halt, with seven ships totalling 120,958 tons lost. In the first seven months of the war, mines accounted for 128 ships totalling 429,899 tons.

One reason for having coastal or light forces was that it was wasteful to deploy seagoing ships for operations in offshore waters. The greater speed and manoeuvrability of such small craft was another factor and the use of wooden hulls in many classes also meant that they had a poorer radar image and were less susceptible to magnetic mines. The low crewing requirements also meant that they could be built in greater numbers, often in small boatyards where the necessary skills and experience to build small craft in wood could be found rather than in the overworked shipbuilding yards. This was, of course, in the days before glass fibre construction of small craft, something which in recent years has spread to mine countermeasure vessels in many navies, including the Royal Navy.

Aircraft
The Royal Navy had taken an interest in the aeroplane as early as 1910. During the First World War, First Lord of the Admiralty Winston Churchill volunteered the Royal Naval Air Service for the air defence

of the United Kingdom and this and the operations over France must have been its undoing as there was considerable duplication of effort with the British Army's Royal Flying Corps; as a result a report was commissioned that proposed a merger. On 1 April 1918, with the war still far from won, the two air arms were merged to form the Royal Air Force, the world's first autonomous air force that inherited 2,500 aircraft and 55,000 officers and men from the RNAS. The RNAS thus comprised about a sixth of the new service on its formation. By contrast, in 1939 the Fleet Air Arm had 232 aircraft.

Given the still early development of military aviation, all that can be said was that the decision was naturally taken without any benefit of hindsight, but also with little understanding of the different requirements of naval and army aviation or of the concept of organic air power. At the time, so few people understood the potential of air power. Not least of the problems was that overnight the Royal Navy was deprived of senior officers who understood air power and the way it could be used to support the fleet.

Thus it was that when the Royal Navy used its first aircraft carrier operationally for the only time in the First World War in a raid on the Zeppelin sheds at Tondern, the operation was carried out by members of the Royal Air Force. A small number of naval personnel flew seaplanes from battleships and cruisers, while there was also a sprinkling of naval personnel among the carrier fighter and bomber flights that were later organized into squadrons, but otherwise the air-crew and maintainers were all members of the Royal Air Force.

In 1923, the RAF units serving with the Royal Navy became the Fleet Air Arm, part of what was then known as RAF Coastal Area which became RAF Coastal Command in 1936. It was not until the following year that it was proposed that the Fleet Air Arm be handed over to full Admiralty control, but even then this did not actually take place until 24 May 1939. In the meantime, Parliament authorized a 300 per cent increase in Fleet Air Arm personnel. Most of the RAF personnel serving with the Fleet Air Arm were transferred to other units in the service, by this time itself expanding as quickly as it could, but around 1,500 transferred to the Royal Navy, forming what became known as the 'Air Branch'. This left them outside the mainstream of the Royal Navy as 'airmen who went to sea' rather than 'sailors who fly', which became the case post-war.

One decision taken by the RAF that survived the handover and continues to this day was the squadron numbering system, which can be described briefly as having numbers in the 7XX series for non-combatant squadrons and 8XX for combat squadrons. Under the pressures of wartime expansion this did not provide sufficient numbers, so eventually there were also squadrons in the 17XX and 18XX series.

Naval Aircraft and the Stark Reality of 1939
The simple transfer from Air Ministry as the sponsoring government department for the RAF to the Admiralty, which had the same role for the Royal Navy, was not the end of the story. The fast-expanding RAF needed all the bases and training facilities it could find, and so there were few naval air stations. The most important was HMS *Daedalus*, also known as RNAS (Royal Naval Air Station) Lee-on-Solent on the Hampshire coast between Portsmouth and Southampton. In addition to runways, it also had a slipway for seaplanes and flying boats, sheltered from the English Channel weather by the Isle of Wight.

An emergency programme of airfield construction was put in hand, using sites that were unsuitable for the RAF's bombers and fighters. One of the most important was HMS *Heron*, RNAS Yeovilton in Somerset. The Fleet Air Arm also had what were known as 'lodging facilities' at many RAF stations, including RAF Hal Far in Malta which had been used by the RAF squadrons serving with the Mediterranean Fleet and was handed over to the Fleet Air Arm after the war, becoming HMS *Falcon*. Despite this, more air stations were needed and many of the original air stations soon found themselves joined by a satellite airfield to relieve the pressure with, for example, that for Yeovilton being nearby at Zeals.

The Fleet Air Arm was still dependent on the RAF for training, this at a time when the RAF was so hard-pressed to meet its own needs that British heavy bombers were flown by a single pilot rather than the two for which they were designed. The solution came from the United States under the so-called 'Towers Scheme', named after the American admiral, which enabled the Fleet Air Arm's pilots and observers to be trained in the USA at the massive USN flying school at Pensacola in Florida. This also had the advantage that training was not interrupted by the weather or enemy activity. As mentioned earlier, having been trained by the USN, the new airmen then moved north to Canada to learn the British way of doing things!

As an aside, the RAF also conducted much of its training abroad under the Empire Air Training Scheme, again because of better weather and to avoid the danger of raw pilots and unarmed training aircraft meeting enemy fighters.

One of the problems facing the Fleet Air Arm in 1939 was that it had no high-performance aircraft. Some of this was the fault of the RAF in being ultra-conservative and ordering biplanes when monoplanes were already available, but it was also the fault of senior naval officers who, lacking experience, believed that high-performance aircraft could not be flown off aircraft carriers. They clearly hadn't looked at the United States Navy or the Imperial Japanese Navy!

To be fair, the first generation of aircraft carriers was small and had short flight decks, while what might be described as the next 'half-generation', *Glorious* and *Courageous*, had a second flight deck running from the hangar deck to allow take-offs while aircraft were landing on the flight deck above it but both decks were still too short for high-performance aircraft. *Furious*, in her final rebuilt form, suffered from the same drawback. All three ships had originally been sisters, light battle-cruisers designed to cover the invasion of Pomerania and the march on Berlin during the First World War. Yet, in HMS *Ark Royal*, the last of the interwar carriers and only the second British aircraft carrier to be designed as such from the keel upwards, there was a ship capable of handling high-performance aircraft. The fast armoured carriers, of which *Illustrious* was the first, could also handle high-performance aircraft and indeed they did, especially in the Pacific.

For the first two years of war, the Fairey Swordfish was the mainstay of the fleet for offensive operations, being able to act as a dive-bomber or a torpedo-bomber. The Blackburn Skua was officially a 'fighter-dive-bomber', but this unexciting aircraft was described by the wits of the fleet as 'more dive-bomber than fighter'. For fighter defence, there was the Blackburn Roc, burdened by the extra weight of a rear gunner in a turret, and the Gloster Sea Gladiator, which was a biplane. The new addition to the Fleet Air Arm was the Fairey Fulmar, a monoplane fighter with the same Rolls-Royce Merlin engine as the Supermarine Spitfire, but the weight of an observer meant that the performance was nothing like that of the latter. For a poorer performance the Fulmar cost about a third more than a Spitfire, at more than £8,000 each.

Aircraft such as the Blackburn Roc and the RAF's Boulton Paul Defiant with a rear-facing gun turret were favoured by Winston Churchill, who was First Lord of the Admiralty until he relieved Chamberlain as prime minister in June 1940. The trouble was that by the late 1930s such a configuration, although common during the First World War, was outdated. By this time, the fighter was a highly manoeuvrable fast-moving aircraft that did not need to be burdened with an extra crew member and the rear gunner was not an asset as enemy aircraft knew that there were still blind spots, such as attacking from below, and so no advantage was gained by their presence.

The fault with the Fulmar was not so much the fault of the manufacturer but that of the Admiralty, which insisted that naval aircraft needed two crew including an observer, as the navigator was called (in 1939 and 1940, the RAF also called its navigators observers). The Swordfish had a crew of three comprising a pilot, observer and telegraphist/rear-gunner, each with their own open cockpit.

The first attempt to provide the Fleet Air Arm with a more effective fighter was the Sea Hurricane, a navalized version of the Hawker Hurricane. In RAF service, the Hurricane was an improvement on anything that had been provided earlier and was more manoeuvrable than the Spitfire as well as being easier to repair. Nevertheless, despite having the same engine as the Spitfire, the Hurricane was slower and during the Battle of Britain whenever possible the Hurricane was left to deal with the bombers while the Spitfire faced the German Messerschmitt Bf 109 fighters. A skilled pilot could confront the Bf 109 in a Hurricane, but he entered the dogfight at a disadvantage. The Hurricane's finest hour was possibly on tank-busting duties, fitted with rockets, over North Africa.

As a naval aeroplane, the Sea Hurricane lacked that most essential feature for aircraft carrier operation: folding wings. It had the knobs for attachment to an accelerator – a hydraulic device that preceded the steam catapults of post-war years – and an arrester hook so that it could 'hook on' when landing aboard a carrier, but without folding wings, the numbers that could be carried were reduced. More serious still was the fact that the number of aircraft carriers that could operate the Sea Hurricane was limited by the size of their lifts. As we saw in the withdrawal from Norway, the elderly *Glorious* could strike the RAF's Hurricanes down into her hangar deck, but the modern *Ark Royal* could not. During the famous Malta convoy, Operation PEDESTAL, those on the aircraft carriers watched in despair as Hurricanes tried to chase Axis aircraft away without success.

Eventually a naval version of the Spitfire arrived: the Seafire. This was the aircraft the Fleet Air Arm needed, except for one thing: the aircraft had a high performance but wasn't really strong enough for the rough and tumble of carrier deck landings. It also tended to bounce on landing and could even pitch forward onto its nose. Its weakness was the undercarriage. Ironically, the tendency to bounce and pitch forward was also a characteristic of the Vought Corsair, which many regarded as the best naval fighter-bomber of the war.

It was the United States aircraft industry that provided the best aircraft of the war years, although in the immediate post-war period there were a number of excellent British versions.

First of the American aircraft was the Grumman Wildcat, known at first to the Fleet Air Arm as the Martlet until after American entry into the war when aircraft designations started to be standardized, except for the C-47 Dakota, of course!

As an example of what could be done, the Wildcat showed how far ahead the USN was. This single-seat, single-engined fighter first flew in 1937 and was powered by a Pratt & Whitney Twin Wasp radial engine that could produce 1,200hp on take-off. It had a range of 722 nautical miles – more if drop tanks were fitted – and four or six 0.5in machine guns. Drawbacks included the need to manually crank up the undercarriage after taking off, which was a nuisance if enemy aircraft were approaching fast. The unusual fuselage-mounted undercarriage could also have the aircraft bouncing from one undercarriage leg to the other in bad weather. The aircraft first entered service with the Fleet Air Arm in September 1940.

Better still was the next aircraft from Grumman, the Hellcat. Another single-seat, single-engined fighter, this first flew in June 1942 and joined the Fleet Air Arm in July 1943. A 1,675hp Pratt & Whitney P-2800-10W engine gave a maximum speed of 330 knots and a range of 950 nautical miles. Armament was four 0.5in machine guns augmented by two 20mm cannon, and two 1,000lb bombs could be carried.

The Spitfire had first flown in 1936, but the Seafire did not join the fleet until June 1942. The single Rolls-Royce Merlin engine provided 1,415hp and a maximum speed of 352 knots, but was short on range at 440 nautical miles. It had four 0.303 Browning machine guns and two 20mm cannon.

The Vought Corsair fighter-bomber had a long nose and was prone to bounce on landing and could topple forwards. To some it was 'the bent wing bastard from Connecticut', to others the best naval fighter-bomber of the war; the bent wing referred to their unusual shape. Designed for the USN, it was regarded as too heavy for carrier operation but the United States Marines and the Fleet Air Arm were only too pleased to have this aircraft. First flown in May 1940, it joined the Fleet Air

Arm in June 1943. A single 1,700hp Pratt & Whitney P-2800-18W engine provided 393 knots and a range of more than 1,000 nautical miles, more with drop tanks, while six 0.5in machine guns were fitted and two 1,000lb bombs could be carried.

Intended as a replacement for the Swordfish, the Fairey Albacore was another biplane, albeit with an enclosed cockpit, but its Bristol Taurus engine was unreliable and so the Swordfish soldiered on and some of the final examples were intended to have enclosed cockpits. Next from Fairey was the Barracuda, a high-wing monoplane intended to be used mainly as a dive-bomber but with the unfortunate habit of all too often not pulling out from a dive. Even so, its best warload was a 1,620lb torpedo or three 500lb bombs, making it inferior to the American fighter-bombers. One ex-Fleet Air Arm man described it as a 'maintenance nightmare'.

The best wartime bomber for the Fleet Air Arm was the Grumman Avenger, which first flew in August 1941 and entered service with the Royal Navy in April 1943. Despite having a crew of three, the Wright Cyclone engine could deliver 1,800hp on take-off and provided a range of almost 1,000 miles, double that with drop tanks. It could carry a 2,000lb bomb or two of 1,000lb.

One reason for the longevity of the Swordfish was its role on anti-submarine operations when flying from a MAC ship or escort carrier. The Swordfish could loiter and also flew slowly enough for operation from these ships to be possible. It is also possible that the Barracuda's terrible reputation as a dive-bomber was due to poor training as dive-bomber pilots had to acquire the knack of knowing when to pull back on the control column: the steeper or faster the dive, the more time and space were needed to recover from it. In theory the altimeter should have told the pilot just what his altitude was, but as one German Stuka pilot discovered during his training, during a steep dive the altimeter could not keep pace with the dive and so always gave the impression that the aircraft was higher than in reality.

These were the days before operational aircraft also came with conversion trainer variants, although twin-seat Hurricanes were later provided for what was at the time the Imperial Iranian Air Force and twin-seat Spitfires were supplied to the Irish Air Corps. Pilots had to learn how to fly a new aircraft type, even though many of them may have been inexperienced and had only recently finished training. Maintainers were usually just given a manual during the early days, and the first aircraft that they were given training for was the Seafire.

American aircraft seemed to have their major components arranged more logically and usually in roughly the same places. One British pilot also noticed this with the controls and instruments on American aircraft, saying that the layout of many a British cockpit 'looked as if it had been done by the cleaning lady'.

Chapter 17

The Invasion Fleets

Wars are not won by defensive measures alone. Defence can only continue for so long. The war has to be taken to the enemy and where territory has been taken, it has to be won back, no matter how difficult that might be. Stalin recognized this, which is why he constantly demanded a 'Second Front' to relieve the pressure on his forces but, of course, he failed to accept that the Allies already had a second front on the North Atlantic, perhaps a third on the Arctic convoys or in the fighting in North Africa and later in Italy. To his mind none of these mattered, and what he wanted was a repeat of the First World War strategic situation with a Western Front in France and an Eastern Front in Russia.

Clearly North Africa was a good place to start and to exercise the growing Allied amphibious capability. Without the industrial support of Metropolitan France, resistance by Vichy forces, no matter how determined, was bound to be overcome sooner rather than later. That opposition was likely demonstrated not just by the Vichy refusal to surrender the French fleet at Mers-el-Kébir and Oran, but by the fact that in May 1941 the Vichy regime had signed the Paris protocols with Germany. These allowed the Germans to use French bases in Syria – which prompted the British-led invasion of that country – and in Tunisia and French West Africa, as well as releasing almost 7,000 French prisoners of war for service with the Free French in North Africa.

Operation Torch
Another factor in the choice of North Africa was that British and British Empire forces were already engaged in the Western Desert, in Libya and Egypt, and landings further west would help them by squeezing the Italians and Germans between two large Allied forces. The British had become increasingly successful in North Africa with the capture of El Alamein, but more was needed if the Mediterranean was to be secured. The Royal Navy and Royal Air Force had certainly helped

to weaken the Axis forces in North Africa, attacking and sometimes cutting the supply lines from Italy to Libya.

For many this was the 'Second Front', landing almost 100,000 men in French Morocco and Algeria behind the Axis lines. The operation, code-named TORCH, had to take into account that Morocco included Spanish-held territory to the south and east of Tangier. The Allied naval commander was Admiral Andrew Cunningham of the Royal Navy, while the Supreme Commander was General Dwight Eisenhower of the United States Army.

The division of territory in Morocco between France and Spain meant that the invasion forces had to be divided into three. The Western Task Force, designated TF34, came from the United States with twenty-three transports to land 34,000 troops commanded by Major General Patton to the north and south of Casablanca. The force had covering fire from 3 US battleships as well as the aircraft carrier USS *Ranger* and 4 escort carriers, 7 cruisers and 38 destroyers.

The Centre Task Force came from England and was commanded by Commodore Troubridge, RN, with 2 escort carriers, 3 cruisers and 13 destroyers escorting and then supporting 28 transports and 19 landing craft, landing 39,000 soldiers commanded by Major General Fredendall at Oran in Algeria.

Near Algiers, 33,000 British and American troops under the command of Major General Ryder were landed from 16 transports and 17 landing craft with the aircraft carriers HMS *Argus* and *Furious* (the world's first two aircraft carriers), 3 cruisers and 16 destroyers commanded by Rear Admiral Sir Harold Burrough, RN.

Good communications are essential in any such operation but with the forces divided as they were, communications were more important than ever. Commodore Troubridge had his signals team in the ex-armed merchant cruiser *Large*, which had been converted so hastily that the sleeping accommodation for staff officers, just aft of the bridge, was unfinished and umbrellas provided the only protection from the weather.

The landings all took place on 8 November, starting an hour or so after midnight at Oran and then shortly afterwards at Algiers, while those at Casablanca started at 04.30. Many of those involved were very inexperienced, and this told most with the pilots aboard the US ships. The escort carrier USS *Santee* had just 5 experienced pilots aboard and during the operation she lost 21 of her 31 aircraft, of which only one was 'just possibly' due to enemy action.

The invasion showed confusion among Vichy leaders. Admiral Darlan, in Oran and in overall command of Vichy French forces, agreed to a ceasefire if Marshal Philippe Pétain, the dictator of Vichy France, agreed, but Pétain was desperately trying to prevent German forces from entering unoccupied France. Darlan then decided to change sides and ordered his forces to side with the Allies, but a number of his subordinate commanders disagreed and allowed German forces to enter Tunisia.

Meanwhile, British and American ships attacked the Vichy positions with gunfire and carrier-borne air power. Several of the British Fleet Air Arm pilots were engaged in air-to-air combat with French fighters. Another was shot down by anti-aircraft fire, but while his captors decided what to do with him the Vichy French forces surrendered and he was back on board his ship within two days of being shot down. One of the shortest spells as a prisoner of war on record!

Operation Husky

Eight months were to pass before the next Allied invasion; that on Sicily, Operation HUSKY, on 10 July 1943. The delay was necessary because Axis forces in North Africa were still capable of fighting and it took until May 1943 before resupply became completely impossible and they surrendered to the Allies.

At this stage the United States would have preferred to start planning an invasion of France, but the British saw the taking of Sicily as more important. It would not only lead to the invasion of Italy, through which Churchill hoped to reach Germany, but more importantly it would ease the pressure on Malta and also enable the Mediterranean to be used by convoys once more. The saving in fuel and time of using the Mediterranean and the Suez Canal rather than sailing via the Cape was one consideration, but another was that this provided a massive one-off boost in both merchant shipping tonnage, estimated by some to be the equivalent of having an extra 1 million tons of shipping, and naval vessels, all of which could be used to ease the pressure elsewhere.

Invading France – or as Churchill insisted, landing in France, as he believed that as allies, the UK and USA could not 'invade' France to liberate it – was in any case going to be the hardest of all. While the so-called 'Atlantic Wall' was not as well-built and defended as Hitler liked to believe, it was still a formidable obstacle and the Germans had substantial air and ground forces in the country. Even the Americans began to realize that an invasion of France would take time to prepare, with rehearsals and training. A good indication of the size of the problem was that the original idea was for simultaneous invasions of Normandy and the south of France, but the resources simply were not available.

The decision to invade Sicily was taken at the Casablanca Conference held between 14 and 24 January 1943. Code-named SYMBOL, this was one of the most important conferences of the war, planning future strategy, and was attended by the British and American leaders, Churchill and Roosevelt, as well as Generals Alexander and Eisenhower. However, there was one noticeable absentee: Stalin. The Soviet leader was invited but he declined because of the critical situation at Stalingrad. It was at Casablanca that the Allies first decided to demand unconditional surrender and also planned a combined USAAF and RAF bomber offensive against Germany. A determined effort was also made to reconcile the different factions of the French armed forces represented by de Gaulle and Giraud, and this led to them forming a French National Committee for Liberation.

Stalin's failure to attend the Casablanca Conference was yet another instance of his lack of logic, especially since he missed the opportunity to demand an Allied invasion of France and his much-desired 'Second Front'. The Battle of Stalingrad was almost over, the Germans having been encircled and an attempt to relieve them foiled by the Russians. While final surrender did not come until 2 February, any other leader would have had the strategic perspective and the confidence to leave matters in the hands of trusted military commanders.

Much of the problem lay in Stalin's policy of, in modern terms, micro-managing the war. He knew who was in command and where they were situated, down to middle-ranking officers. His close colleagues, in effect his war cabinet, were constantly harassed and bullied, humiliated in front of their peers. Often a close member of their family would be held in a gulag (prison camp), usually on rations that were not even at subsistence level. There was no trust, no semblance of being part of a team, but instead the rule of fear. In short, Stalin felt vulnerable.

Operation HUSKY was more akin to the Normandy landings than TORCH had been, with a combined amphibious and airborne assault. First, on 11 and 12 June 1943, the garrisons on two small Italian islands, Pantelleria and Lampedusa to the west of Malta, surrendered after bombardment by the Royal Navy and raids from Malta-based squadrons of the RAF and Fleet Air Arm.

For some time the Royal Navy had maintained what amounted to a second Mediterranean Fleet in what was officially known as Force H, based on Gibraltar, while the Mediterranean Fleet had been forced to withdraw to Alexandria in Egypt from the beginning of 1941. Force H had grown in strength and its successes had included participation in the sinking of the German battleship *Bismarck*. By mid-1943 it had 6 battleships and 2 modern aircraft carriers – HMS *Indomitable* and *Formidable* – plus 6 cruisers and 24 destroyers. Designed to be a fast-moving task force, it did not have escort carriers. Force H was to act as the covering force for Operation HUSKY. The landings were by an American Western Naval Task Force and a British Eastern Naval Task Force. There were 2,590 ships altogether with 2,000 landing craft, including the new landing ship tank (LST), with the intention of landing 180,000 men under General Dwight Eisenhower who had to face more than 275,000 men in General Guzzoni's Italian Sixth Army.

Where the Allies were strongest was in the air, as well as at sea. The Allies had 3,700 aircraft, mainly operating from land bases in North Africa as well as the three airfields on Malta, while the Axis powers had 1,400 aircraft.

The Western Naval Task Force was to land the US Seventh Army on the south coast of Sicily, while the British Eastern Naval Task Force would land the British Eighth Army on the south-eastern point of the island. The Americans had to take the port of Licata and the British the port of Syracuse. After this, they were to seize the airfields around Catania.

The assault was launched from North Africa as the forces assembled would have overwhelmed the facilities available on the small island of Malta. On the eve of the invasion, bad weather nearly caused the landings to be postponed. This did at least lull the Axis commanders into a false sense of security, apart from which many of them had been led to believe that the Allies would head for Sardinia. The result was that the amphibious assault was a great success, but in the high winds the airborne assault was less so, with many paratroops landing in the seas while many of the Horsa gliders suffered the same fate having been released too early by their towing aircraft. More than 250 troops were drowned.

On 11 July a strong counter-attack was launched by German Panzer divisions, but this was broken up by Allied air power and a heavy bombardment from Force H.

Italian resistance virtually ended when Mussolini fell from power on 25 July, after which Hitler dropped his opposition to German troops being withdrawn and some 40,000 German and 62,000 Italian troops crossed the Straits of Messina to the Italian mainland starting on the night of 11/12 August, with much of their equipment and supplies intact.

Only the invasion of Normandy, Operation OVERLORD, was larger than HUSKY. More than any other operation, the invasion of Sicily provided the Allies with vital experience and many lessons were learned that would prove invaluable later.

Operation Avalanche
The logical move was for the Allies to follow the retreating Axis forces across the Straits of Messina and this is what Montgomery's Eighth Army did on 3 September 1943. That same day, the Allies and the Italians signed a secret armistice at Syracuse.

The next step was to cut off as much of the German forces as possible and also shorten the advance towards Rome. This was done at Salerno on 9 September, the day after the armistice was announced. The landings at Salerno were co-ordinated with a British airborne landing at Taranto to enable the remains of the Italian fleet to escape to Malta. The airborne landing was covered by the guns of the six Force H battleships.

On learning of the armistice, the Germans moved quickly to seize Italian airfields. Salerno was chosen instead of a landing site further north because it was close to Allied airfields in Sicily but it was only just within range for fighter aircraft, meaning that they could spend very little time patrolling the area, usually no more than twenty minutes, and if combat occurred could not return to Sicily. The solution was to deploy aircraft carriers.

The United States Navy provided an *Independence*-class light carrier and four escort carriers. The Royal Navy once again deployed Force H to cover the landings with HMS *Illustrious* and *Formidable*, as well as creating an escort carrier fleet known as Force V with escort carriers HMS *Attacker, Battler, Hunter* and *Stalker* augmented by HMS *Unicorn*, a maintenance carrier but here, not for the last time in her career, used as an active fleet carrier with fighter sorties flown from her. Force V provided thirty Supermarine Spitfire fighters aboard each escort carrier and no fewer than sixty aboard *Unicorn*.

The British ships sailed from Malta as if to attack Taranto, but instead headed north to Salerno. Once off Salerno, Force V was given a 'box' in which to operate, flying off and recovering their aircraft. The trouble was that with so many other ships in the area, the box was too small, giving the carrier commanders great difficulty as they steamed from one end to another and then had to turn. This was nothing compared to the difficulties facing the pilots, trying to land on ships steaming close to one another and avoiding mid-air collisions. Worse still, the weather on this occasion was good, too good in fact. The Seafire needed a headwind of 25 knots over the flight deck for a safe take-off but in still air conditions the escort carriers could only provide 17 knots. Arrester wires and crash barriers had to be kept as tight as possible. Most escort carriers lacked catapults – known at the time as accelerators – and even when fitted, these hydraulically-powered aids lacked the punch of a modern steam catapult. The amphibious assault and the covering force on this occasion were much smaller, at 627 ships.

In contrast to the landings in North Africa and Sicily, the Luftwaffe mounted heavy attacks against the carriers and these were sustained until 14 September. The need for air cover meant that the carriers were asked to remain on station longer than originally planned, and their frantic racing up and down with the 'box' meant that fuel began to run low so they had to resort to using their reserve tanks. In addition to conventional bombing, the German response was augmented by the first use of radio-controlled glider bombs that damaged two British cruisers and the veteran battleship HMS *Warspite*.

The difficulties faced by the carrier pilots meant that deck landing accidents accounted for a higher loss rate than the Luftwaffe with Force V's 180 aircraft reduced to just 30 by 14 September. Meanwhile, the Germans had organized a massive counter-attack between 12 and 14 September.

As the campaign ashore moved slowly, a further amphibious assault was planned for Anzio further up the coast. For this, shore bases near the Salerno landing site were available and carrier air support was not needed, but even in January 1944 the landings at Anzio faced strong German opposition and it took four months for the Allies to break out of their beachhead. While Salerno and Vietri were captured, they remained too close to the German front line for either to be used as ports.

Operation Shingle
Convalescing at Marrakesh in French Morocco after an illness, Churchill convened two conferences at his villa to discuss the situation in Italy

where the hopes of a rapid advance on Rome following the Salerno landings had been foiled by strong German resistance. The first was held on 7 and 8 January 1944 with Churchill in the chair, accompanied by Lord Beaverbrook and attended by senior British and American officers. The second was on 12 January when Churchill and de Gaulle met.

Although the need for a second landing further north had been agreed in late 1943, the initial plan was cancelled in favour of landings at Anzio, code-named Operation SHINGLE, which was decided at the Marrakesh conferences. Little time was lost in mounting the operation which took place on 22 January but suffered accordingly as the force used was too small, simply the 6th US Corps of the Fifth US Army. The 6th US Corps was augmented by the 1st British Infantry Division and a British Commando brigade, which landed north of Anzio. Other forces landed at the port or to the south. Just 378 ships took part and air support was provided mainly by the USAAF with the Mediterranean Allied Tactical Air Force. The Germans deployed radio-controlled explosive boats and human torpedoes against the ships but with little effect while German air power was also weak in the area.

There was confusion over the objectives and instead of exploiting the initial surprise, the 6th US Corps found itself consolidating its position. Bad weather meant that the Allies had difficulty in reinforcing those ashore and by 26 January, Kesselring, the German commander in Italy, improvised a Fourteenth Army with a core of six divisions. This force surrounded the Allies, and attempts to break through saw both the British and the Americans suffer heavy casualties with 2,100 and 3,000 respectively. As the month drew to a close, Ultra intelligence warned the Allied commanders of a German counter-attack, to which they were able to respond effectively.

Fierce fighting in the second half of February saw the Germans suffer very heavy casualties with 5,389 men killed or wounded as the Allies moved heavy artillery and massive air power into position. Nevertheless, Kesselring managed to keep the Allies contained until they were able to break out and link up with the US Fifth Army on 25 May and begin the final advance on Rome.

Anzio was a big disappointment to the Allies. Churchill later wrote that he had 'hoped that the Allies were hurling a wild cat onto the shore but all they got was a stranded whale.' The US Navy's official historian was equally blunt, writing that 'putting such a small force ashore was akin to sending a boy on a man's errand.'

The landings in the Mediterranean were not over until the Allies invaded the south of France in August, and even then there were further minor operations to re-take Axis-occupied territory. Nevertheless, Normandy was next and the Allies had learned much about amphibious operations both in the Mediterranean and in the Far East by this time. Two points were clear. The first was that the Germans might be losing the war, but they were still capable of mounting a formidable defence and still possessed the capability of fighting a highly mobile war so that large and well-equipped forces could be assembled quickly when needed. The second was that any assault had to be meticulously organized and assembled in such force that the defences could be overwhelmed, while the force ashore needed to be sustained and supported, regardless of the weather.

Nevertheless, there was much to be done and much to be learned before the Normandy landings.

St Nazaire
One idea that appealed to the British in particular was the idea of raids on enemy-held Europe. The Royal Navy had two successful raids during the First World War at Zeebrugge and Ostend, and so plans for such raids started soon after the withdrawal from Europe.

The first such raid was at St Nazaire on the night of 28 March 1942. This was the one major French Channel port that had a dry dock capable of accommodating the German battleship *Tirpitz* that occupied so much time of the Royal Navy and Royal Air Force. If the Normandie Dock (built for the French ocean liner of that name) was put beyond use, there would be no chance of the battleship being brought south from Norway to begin a career of commerce raiding. St Nazaire had been the intended destination for the *Bismarck* when she was sunk by the Royal Navy.

In an operation code-named CHARIOT, the destroyer *Campbeltown*, one of fifty Town-class ships provided by the United States Navy in 1940, was to be loaded with 3 tons of explosives and used to ram the dock gates before exploding 150 minutes later. *Campbeltown* was to be escorted by two destroyers, *Atherstone* and *Tynedale*, an MGB, an MTB and sixteen motor launches carrying army commandos led by Lieutenant Colonel Charles Newman of the Essex Regiment, who were to land and blow up the dock and other shore installations. In all, there were 44 army officers and 224 other ranks as well as 62 naval officers and 291 ratings. Overall command lay with Commander Robert Ryder in

MGB314, with Lieutenant Commander Stephen Beattie in command of the *Campbeltown*. The two escorting destroyers were to pick up the raiders after the operation, assisted by further MTBs.

Leaving Falmouth in Cornwall before dawn on 27 March 1942, the timing of the operation was dictated by the spring tide and the need to cover 410 miles of open sea and 5 miles of the Loire estuary to reach St Nazaire. To help with the operation, *Campbeltown* was remodelled to look like a German destroyer and wore the German naval ensign. Despite being spotted by a U-boat, the small force was within 2 miles of St Nazaire before being picked up by German searchlights, but Ryder gained an extra three minutes by offering German identification signals; however, the small force was then extensively illuminated and came under heavy fire. Beattie continued at 20 knots, full speed for his elderly destroyer, and at 0134 on 28 March he rammed the dock gates, just four minutes later than scheduled. The ship penetrated the caisson to a depth of 36 feet.

Ryder landed under heavy fire to find that the destroyer was in exactly the right position and then ordered *MTB74* to fire her torpedoes, which were also set to go off later, at the dock gates. Commandos ran ashore from *Campbeltown* to destroy the pumping house, anti-aircraft positions and a fuel tank, while those aboard the launches set up a diversionary raid on the Old Mole and the Old Entrance. The commandos also seized the Ile de St Nazaire, from which the withdrawal was to be made. In the ensuing fire-fight the commandos suffered heavy casualties as the Germans struck at their launches, and by the time Ryder ordered the withdrawal, just seven out of the sixteen were available.

During the withdrawal, heavily laden with wounded, they were intercepted by E-boats and an MTB sent to help with the rescue was sunk and another three damaged before the destroyers *Atherstone* and *Tynedale* were able to pick up the survivors and speed them to Falmouth. The cost of the operation was 144 men killed – 23 per cent of the raiding force – and another 215 captured, with 271 returning safely to Falmouth.

Campbeltown's explosives did not go off on time and were not discovered by the Germans, so many German officers took their wives and mistresses aboard to see the ship. Around noon the following day *Campbeltown* finally blew up, taking 380 Germans with her. The next day, 30 May, the torpedoes also blew up, prompting French dockyard workers to attempt to take over the dock from the Germans, causing panic among the German gun crews who opened fire and in addition to killing eighty French dockyard workers also killed many of their own men.

Three VCs were awarded to the naval personnel involved and two to the army commandos, including their commanding officer. Commander Ryder received the VC for commanding the attack under heavy fire and ensuring that its objectives were met before ordering and organizing the withdrawal while his MGB was severely damaged. Beattie also received the VC for his coolness under fire and determination in ensuring that *Campbeltown* fulfilled her mission. Able Seaman William Savage aboard *MGB314* showed great skill and determination as well as devotion to duty, maintaining fire while under heavy fire himself, but was fatally wounded as *MGB314* attempted to withdraw. He died the following day.

Dieppe

The raid, originally known as Operation RUTTER but later renamed Operation JUBILEE, was to be launched from five ports in the south of England with Southampton as the most westerly and Newhaven the most easterly. There would be 5,000 Canadian troops, 1,000 British and 50 US Rangers, supported by 237 ships and aircraft from 74 squadrons, of which no fewer than 66 would be fighter squadrons. The heavy Canadian involvement was due to their commanding general wanting them to see action.

Given the complexity of the exercise and the lack of experience among the men and their commanders as the first of the Mediterranean landings was still some months away, an exercise was conducted to provide training and also to ensure that the arrangements were workable. This was just as well as the first exercise was a complete disaster, but ten days later all went well with the second. A date still had to be fixed and it was not until 1 July 1942 that the Dieppe operation was set for 4 July, or the first day after that date with favourable weather conditions.

The weather was bad and on 7 July the operation was postponed. General Montgomery in command of forces in the south of England wanted it cancelled as the troops involved had been briefed and he feared that security would be compromised. His objections were ignored and planning continued; he was then removed from the operation and posted to Egypt to command the British Eighth Army.

One of the changes made after his departure was that of the name to Operation JUBILEE, but more serious was the decision to cancel the planned aerial bombardment which it was feared could cost heavy French casualties. Instead, eight British destroyers would bombard the port but battleships, which could have made a difference with their guns of 14, 15 or even 16in calibre, were held back because they would be vulnerable to German shore-based artillery once they were in coastal waters. This was being overly cautious as the guns of these ships could easily fire over ranges of 20 miles, outside the range of German coastal artillery. Meanwhile, Montgomery's concerns about security were soon justified as French double agents warned the Germans about British interest in Dieppe, while the commanding officer of the 1st Parachute Battalion was later to comment that from the start 'security was abysmal'. In any case, increased radio traffic and the growing concentration of landing craft in the south coast ports were also detected by the Germans. The next change, as the weather continued to be poor, was that the planned paratroop landings were cancelled as the use of airborne forces was even more vulnerable to weather conditions. This decision was reversed.

In command of combined operations, Admiral Louis Mountbatten was anxious to see action and impatient for a landing on enemy territory, although this would be just another 'hit and run' raid. In this he was not alone. Churchill felt that there was much to be gained both in raising morale among the Allies and in showing Stalin that the British were taking the war to the enemy. In fact, by this time Stalin was already on the offensive in northern Russia, but his main concern was that the main German thrust had turned southwards towards Stalingrad.

Churchill later recalled:

> I thought it most important that a large-scale operation should take place this summer, and military opinion seemed unanimous that until an operation on that scale was undertaken, no responsible general would take the responsibility of planning the main invasion...
>
> In discussion with Admiral Mountbatten it became clear that time did not permit a new large-scale operation to be mounted during the summer (after 'Rutter' had been cancelled), but that Dieppe could be remounted (with the new code-name 'Jubilee') within a month, provided extraordinary steps were taken to ensure secrecy. For this reason no records were kept but, after the Canadian authorities and the Chiefs of Staff had given their approval, I personally went through the plans with the C.I.G.S.,

Admiral Mountbatten, and the Naval Force Commander, Captain J. Hughes-Hallett.

The initial plan for the attack was an unimaginative frontal assault, but this was developed with the use of British paratroops to attack the German artillery positions mounted on the headlands either side of the town and the port. There were plans for an aerial bombardment before the raid to soften up the target.

The special troops who were still assigned to the operation were Royal Marine, and Royal Navy Commandos, although the idea was not that they should lead the operation but instead they would follow the main force ashore from motor gunboats and destroy the harbour installations. There was even an ex-burglar on their strength who was supposed to break into a port office and burgle the safe, expecting to find important documents.

If security was poor before the raid, so too was intelligence about the target area. Allied air reconnaissance missed the German gun positions embedded in the cliff faces, while the suitability of the beach for tanks was assessed using holiday postcards and amateur photographs. In addition to poor knowledge of the terrain and the defences, there was little knowledge of enemy strength.

Although Mountbatten was in command of special operations, he was not going on the raid; the assault force would be led by Major General Roberts and the naval force by Captain Hughes-Hallett. Mountbatten did, nevertheless, address at least some of the troops before they embarked, as recalled by Sergeant George Cook of No. 4 Commando, which was to attack the artillery batteries at Varengeville-sur-Mer, to the west of Dieppe:

> Mountbatten gave us a lecture – said he wished he was coming with us. Once we realised where we were going, I think 200 blokes thought, 'I wish he were going instead of us.' But yes, very nice talk. We cheered him – off he went. Then we started priming grenades, drawing ammunition. Our troop were doing the demolitions, so we drew explosives and we'd a fair amount of stuff which we packed up...Then we had a meal and we sailed – a beautiful evening, as we went down the Solent and past the Isle of Wight.
> Suddenly an officer said, 'Oh – they've got all the harbour lights lit.' I looked over the prow of the boat and you could see lights

on the shore. The lighthouse at Varengeville-sur-Mer was flashing, so I thought, Cor blimey – everybody awake. We're going to have a pretty bad welcome here.

When we landed, there was some barbed wire. We'd a roll of wire netting which we threw over the barbed wire so we could run over it. The Germans were firing tracers from their pill-boxes, and Lord Lovat said, quite casually, 'They're firing too high.' He was about six foot – I'm five foot four – so I thought, 'If they're firing over his head, there's no danger they're going to hit me' – but they did fire their mortars and four or five blokes were killed on the beach.

Cook and his comrades advanced, firing. One of them shot a man out of an ack-ack tower, who 'did a lovely swallow dive off the top', before they reached an orchard accompanied by one of Cook's friends, another sergeant, Geordie Horne, who was almost immediately shot dead, before Cook himself was hit in the face and shoulder.

Even before the raid began at 0450 on 19 August, the cover was blown completely as a number of the escorting warships had already engaged warships accompanying a German convoy off Puys and Berneval at 0348.

To avoid confusion, the landings were at four beaches each given a colour designation for the operation. One of these, the most easterly, was Blue Beach, where the assault started badly. After leaving the converted Belgian cross-Channel ferry *Princess Astrid*, the 10th Landing Craft Assault Flotilla started off in the wrong direction and eventually reached the beach sixteen minutes late as dawn was breaking and the element of surprise had been lost. The initial attacks were on the coastal batteries. The attack at Varengeville-sur-Mer by No. 4 Commando was successful, but this was the only unit to meet all of its objectives during the operation. The Royal Regiment of Canada landed at Puys, where they were virtually wiped out with just 60 of the regiment's 543 men being evacuated from the beach after many were cut down on the ramp where the bodies piled up, while others were mown down by machine-gun fire as they attempted to cross the pebbled beach to the shelter of the sea wall 40 feet away.

Those offshore could not see what was happening ashore because the ships covering the landings had laid a dense smokescreen. This did nothing at all to protect those involved in the landings, but made command and control more difficult.

In the ensuing chaos, most of the landing craft carrying the marines were hit by gunfire on the run-in and the few men who reached the shore were killed or taken prisoner. In an attempt to regain control and end the suicidal mission, their CO stood up in the stern of his craft and signalled to those behind that they should turn back; he was then killed by German gunfire.

The RAF had allocated aircraft, including many fighters, to the operation but Squadron Leader 'Johnnie' Johnson leading No. 616 Squadron recalled that there was supposed to be a headquarters ship, HMS *Calypso*, with radar and RAF controllers aboard that was meant to be controlling air operations. On four sorties over Dieppe that day, he could never establish communications:

> We could see very little except for a bloody great pall of smoke over the town, and lots of shelling going on down below. But we could do nothing about it because the attackers and defenders were all within a hundred yards of each other. We couldn't help the army. When we got home after the first patrol, we knew that the whole thing had been a disaster, but there was nothing we could do to help them.

Withdrawal began at 1100 as the heavy fire continued. It took until 1400. When the assault force left, it left behind 3,367 Canadians who had been killed, wounded or taken prisoner, as well as 275 RM Commandos. The Royal Navy lost a destroyer and 33 landing craft, with 550 men killed or wounded. The RAF lost 106 aircraft. Compared to this, the Germans lost just 591 men killed or wounded, and 48 aircraft.

The surviving landing craft had been ordered to the main beach at Dieppe at 1030. When the first of them arrived there, it was met by a solitary soldier and it was only after he had been handed a Lewis gun with which to defend himself that someone realized he was a German soldier attempting to desert. Once the withdrawal started in earnest, the few landing craft were overcrowded and in danger of being swamped. One of them was hit by a shell and capsized, but the crew managed to get their passengers aboard another vessel.

In the inevitable enquiry into what went wrong, many tried to blame Mountbatten, but as there was no reprimand and he remained in post, it seems that it was not his fault and he did not act alone, although there is no written record of the operation being given the go-ahead. General Sir Alan Brooke was abroad at the time and many believe that had he been at home in the War Cabinet, he might have persuaded Churchill to cancel the operation; however, this is conjecture.

Some believe that the disaster at Dieppe was necessary so that lessons could be learned in time for the Normandy landings but even so, there were many avoidable failings. Either there had to be a heavy aerial bombardment before the operation, or it should have been called off. Some form of reconnaissance from the sea was necessary: this would have noted the gun positions in the cliff face, and could also have assessed whether the shingle on the beach would have damaged the tank tracks, although the latter would have required reconnaissance parties to land on the beach and take samples without being noticed. In addition, much heavier naval firepower was needed and had to continue right up to the moment when the landing craft hit the shore.

Chapter 18

NEPTUNE and OVERLORD

Operation OVERLORD was the code-name given to the Allied landings in Normandy by air and by sea, but the naval aspect of the landings was so important that it was given its own code-name, Operation NEPTUNE. This was the largest operation ever undertaken by the Royal Navy, which provided more than 79 per cent of the warships involved on D-Day. The largest maritime invasion in history required almost 7,000 ships of all kinds to land 75,215 British and Canadian troops and 57,500 US troops – a total of 132,715 men – plus armoured vehicles, artillery, motor vehicles and supplies on the first day.

Some say that to those aboard the ships in this massive armada, it *seemed* to stretch to the horizon but the truth is that it almost certainly did, as once assembled at the rendezvous point at 'Piccadilly Circus', actually some miles to the south of the Isle of Wight rather than the centre of London, the assembled fleet covered 5 square miles of sea. There were more than 4,000 landing ships and landing craft, preceded by 287 minesweepers in line abreast clearing the English Channel ahead of the invasion fleet. Escorting the convoys (but not the landing ships and craft) were 6 battleships; 4 monitors (shallow draft ships with a heavy armament that would join the battleships in giving naval gunnery cover); 22 cruisers; 104 destroyers and another 152 escort vessels such as corvettes and frigates; 80 patrol craft including anti-submarine trawlers and gunboats; and 360 motor launches. No less than 79 per cent of the warships were British or Canadian, 16.5 per cent were American, and the remaining 4.5 per cent manned by crews from France, Greece, The Netherlands, Norway and Poland. The US contribution consisted not just of United States Navy warships, but also those of the United States Coast Guard, which in wartime passed from the US Department of Transportation [sic] to the USN, although today its peacetime home is the Department of Homeland Security.

Missing from the vast armada of ships was the aircraft carrier. There was no need for carriers, with the landing zones only around 80 miles from the south coast of England. Equally important, there was no room, as with so many ships in a relatively small area of water, aircraft carriers would not have been able to charge around at full speed, heading into the wind ready to launch aircraft or recover after a sortie.

Even though the strength of the Royal Navy, Royal Canadian Navy and the United States Navy had increased massively since the outbreak of war, assembling such a vast armada was no easy task and operations elsewhere were seriously affected. The most obvious change was the decision to postpone the invasion of the south of France until August, but less obvious was the suspension of a number of convoys for the Soviet Union. The navies concerned were stretched to the limit, especially as the war in the Pacific moved steadily towards Japan. Perhaps Stalin did not appreciate that this would happen when he insisted on a 'second front' but naval strategy was never his strong point.

An indication of just how the Normandy landings differed from any invasion before or since was the fact that they required more than just shipping.

First, two harbours – the Mulberry harbours, built from prefabricated parts – had to be towed across the Channel and assembled, one for the British zone and one in the American zone. A bad storm hit the area before the harbours could be completed and the American Mulberry was so badly damaged that it had to be abandoned. This left the British harbour as the main supply point. Such harbours were important because landing ships had a much lower cargo space than conventional cargo ships, and the latter could carry supplies all the way from the United States and Canada without the need for transhipment. While strenuous efforts were made to capture ports in France, these were not immediately available for use as the Germans took care to damage and sabotage as many of the facilities as possible.

Next, fuel was another problem for heavily-mechanized Allied armies and for the intense air support that they needed from aircraft of the two tactical air forces, one American and the other British and Empire, which had their first aircraft land in France late on D-Day. A pipeline, known as PLUTO for 'pipeline under the ocean', was laid from Shanklin on the east coast of the Isle of Wight with the initial single line being joined by others and meeting the fuel needs of the Allied armies.

Most of the minesweepers used to prepare the way for the landing fleet were of the Royal Navy's *Bangor* class, with a displacement of 672 tons and a complement of sixty men. They were capable of up to 16 knots. Armament consisted of a 3in gun and one 40mm cannon, as well as four .303 machine guns. Clearly such ships had little chance of standing up to a German destroyer had any chanced upon them, but the Allies had never lost naval supremacy in the war against Germany.

The navies of the day knew how to sweep contact mines and the Royal Navy had discovered a means known as degaussing (or demagnetizing) to protect ships from magnetic mines, but acoustic mines that reacted to the sound of ships' propellers or machinery were more difficult. Worst of all were the new pressure mines known as 'oysters', which responded when a ship passed over the mine, creating an increase in water pressure. Acoustic mines had the unpleasant characteristic of being able to be set not to explode the first time a ship passed but instead waiting for the second or third vessel, all of which made mine clearance more difficult.

Not all the minesweepers were British as many were American and on the afternoon before the landings at 1757 one of these ships, the USS *Osprey*, was to discover just how necessary minesweeping was to be to the landing force. The *War Diary* of Mine Squadron 7, part of Force U covering Utah beach, tells the tale:

> USS *Osprey* (Lt Charles Swimm, captain) was struck by an underwater explosion, under forward engine room; explosion is believed to be from a moored contact mine. Position 50 degrees 12.9N, 01 degrees, 20.4W – about 35 miles south of the Isle of Wight. USS *Chickadee* came alongside *Osprey* to assist. Fire that broke out onboard *Osprey* was under control in 3 to 5 minutes and extinguished in 10 minutes... In view of the list and irreparable damage and lack of watertight integrity, as a result of the blast, the order to abandon ship was given at 18.15. *Chickadee* took all survivors onboard. (Casualties were six dead, twenty-nine wounded.)

Such a loss in broad daylight and 20 miles north of where the nearest enemy minefield was charted was a sobering warning of what might lie ahead.

Potentially the most serious casualty from hitting a mine was the Royal Navy's *Queen Elizabeth*-class battleship HMS *Warspite*, a veteran of the First World War that had seen action at Narvik during the Norwegian campaign in 1940 and later at the Battle of Cape Matapan. This mighty warship, with a full load displacement of 36,450 tons and eight 15in guns, had been repaired in the United States after being damaged at Matapan and then operated in the Far East before returning to Europe for the Mediterranean landings, but was not fully repaired after being struck by a glider bomb off Salerno. Playing an important part in the Normandy bombardment, she hit a mine and damaged her propulsive system to the extent that when needed for further bombardment duties at Brest, Le Havre and later at Walcheren, she had to suffer the indignity of being towed into position by tug. Even then her 'X' turret, one of the two aft turrets, was inoperable.

Combined naval personnel and men from the Allied merchant navies, a total of 195,701 seafarers took part, actually outnumbering those landed ashore.

Overall command of this vast armada was given to a British naval officer, Admiral Sir Bertram Ramsay. His signal on 31 May to all the ships under his command summed up the situation, and the task, perfectly:

> Our task in conjunction with the Merchant Navies of the United Nations, and supported by the Allied Air Forces, is to carry the Allied Expeditionary Force to the Continent, to establish it there in a secure bridgehead and to build it up and maintain it at a rate which will outmatch that of the enemy.
>
> Let no one underestimate the magnitude of this task.

The absence of aircraft carriers did not mean that naval aviation did not play a part. At any one time, a number of the Royal Navy's Fleet Air Arm squadrons would be based ashore, often under the control of RAF Coastal Command, and in 1944 squadrons such as No. 811 NAS equipped with Fairey Swordfish played a part in protecting the Normandy convoys from being attacked by U-boats.

Several years into the war, the standard of aircraft recognition was still so poor that to protect British and American planes over the Normandy area from being shot at by Allied AA gunners, aircraft were painted in 'invasion stripes', i.e. the wings and rear fuselage had black and white stripes painted to show clearly that they were Allied forces.

By 1944 the Royal Navy was well on its way to its war's end strength comprising 61 battleships and cruisers; 59 aircraft carriers; 846 destroyers, frigates and corvettes, all of which could be classified as 'escort vessels'; 729 minesweepers; 131 submarines; 1,000 minor naval vessels including trawlers and drifters adapted for patrols; and

3,700 aircraft. Many of the aircraft carriers were the small auxiliary or escort carriers, most of which were supplied by the United States under Lend-Lease.

The service included a number of types of vessel no longer in service today. The large battleships with their 14in, 15in or 16in guns, so useful for bombarding targets ashore, were augmented by the much smaller monitors, again with 15in guns but being smaller they also had a shallow draft, allowing them to operate closer inshore. Two of these were of wartime construction, HMS *Roberts* and *Abercrombie*, each of 8,123 tons displacement and with two 15in guns as opposed to up to eight on a battleship, and eight 4in guns that could also be used as anti-aircraft weapons as well as multi-barrelled anti-aircraft pom-poms, known as 'Chicago pianos' to the men of the fleet. Another two, HMS *Terror* and *Erebus*, dated from 1916 and were slightly smaller but still had two 15in and eight 4in guns. *Roberts* and *Abercrombie* were off the British landing beaches, while *Erebus* was off the American destination of Utah Beach.

The bombardment group consisted of the elderly battleships HMS *Warspite* and *Ramillies* as well as twelve cruisers and thirty-seven destroyers. In reserve were the battleships *Rodney* and *Nelson* with their 16in guns and three cruisers. The heavier-calibre guns did not simply fire a heavier shell, their range was also greater. Nevertheless, the last British battleship class introduced before the war was the *King George V* class with just 14in guns. A shell from a 15in gun weighed more than a ton and had a range of more than 20 miles.

It was important that the landing ships and landing craft should reach the part of the Normandy coast where they were due to land. Matters of command and control were simplified by the establishment of British and American sectors, with the British eastern sector having the beaches designated Gold, Juno and Sword, and the American western sector having Omaha and Utah. The American sector was west of the British, which also included a substantial Canadian force destined for Juno Beach. The disposition of the British and American sectors was dictated by the basing of the troops in England. Some argue that the Americans would have been better equipped to take the eastern sector and the British the western, but that would have complicated an already difficult and demanding convoy system for the landings. Swapping the troops around before embarkation would have avoided this but then created problems of a different kind, stretching transport and logistics resources at a time when everyone was preparing for the cross-Channel assault and even creating enough of a commotion to have put security at risk.

Not everyone could wait until the night of 5/6 June before crossing the Channel. Getting the mass of landing ships and landing craft to the right beach was no easy task. Once clear of the rendezvous the ships headed for the five invasion beaches but, as previously mentioned, guidance was necessary and this came from the crews of midget submarines, the X-craft. These usually had a crew of four – two officers and two ratings – and when used offensively they would all be divers, capable of fixing mines to the hulls of enemy warships. For NEPTUNE, the officers were drawn from among the best of the Royal Navy's navigators.

For the men aboard these small craft, they left what was then the Royal Navy's main submarine base at Gosport, HMS *Dolphin*, just across the harbour from the major naval base of Portsmouth, late on Friday 2 June. They cleared the Isle of Wight, towed most of the way by converted trawlers, and crossed the 80 miles to the coast of Normandy; once in position they submerged and spent the daylight hours sitting on the sea bed, just offshore. On Sunday night, the midget submarines surfaced and dropped anchor once on their marking position. Those aboard X23 watched as a lorry dropped off a crowd of German soldiers who then played a game of volleyball on the shore, unaware that they were being watched or of what the future held in store for them.

Lieutenant George Honour was aboard X23:

We hoisted our radio mast and got a signal that the invasion had been postponed, so then we had to retreat to the bottom again and wait until Monday night. That night we surfaced and received a message that the invasion was on. So we went back to sit on the bottom and at about 0430 on Tuesday, 6th June, we surfaced again, put up all our navigational aids: 18-foot telescopic mast with a light shining seaward, a radio beacon and an echo sounder tapping out a message below the surface. This was for the navigational mine-layers used to guide the fleet to pick up as they brought the invasion in.

Our particular operation for D-Day was called 'Gambit'. When we looked it up in the dictionary, much to our horror it said the pawn you throw away before the big move in chess, which didn't encourage us too much.

Not everyone could wait until H-hour before landing on the beaches. The troops arriving aboard the landing craft would need to be shown the way off the beach and not spend time exposed to German fire on the beach. The Royal Navy Commandos were given the task of landing to set up signs and indicators for the main assault force. One of their landing craft was hit before it reached the beach with the ramp blown down so that it dropped below the bows, leaving those aboard unable to use it and having to leave the craft by the stern, dropping into the rough seas. None of them were too pleased as they had spent weeks training for the landing on windswept beaches in Scotland. On coming ashore, they were met by the discouraging sight of bodies being swept in and out with the waves and hastened to seek shelter in the sand dunes.

Reaching the beaches was an ordeal in itself. The Germans had placed obstacles along the coast: tetrahedral steel posts with shells and mines attached. A number of landing craft had been modified with twenty-four 60lb spigot bombs so that they could blow up the beach obstacles at half-tide. Immediately behind them came the landing craft tank carrying tanks with flails, which would clear the beaches of any mines to allow infantry to follow them ashore. The landing craft heading for the beach obstacles sailed in under a heavy destroyer bombardment, but at H-hour minus one minute the bombardment lifted, the landing craft let go their spigot bombs and within seconds the air was rent with massive explosions.

It seems that not all the beach obstacles could be cleared in time for the landing force. Able Seaman Ken Oakley was a Royal Navy Commando preparing to go ashore with the beach master, a naval officer who would take charge of operations ashore and ensure that the beaches were cleared quickly, the priority being to dismantle 'Rommel's asparagus' (half-sunken wooden poles, each with an unhealthy 88mm shell on the end). 'Rommel's asparagus' was, of course, also used in his attempt to close off the possible glider landing-grounds.

All around the sea was one mass of craft, landing craft of all kinds, shapes and sizes. A lot in our immediate area were LCAs because we were going for the initial assault. There was a good feeling as we went forward, except that most of the army was seasick. I wasn't very happy myself. However, when we got within sight of the shore we were getting splattered with light gunfire, nothing very heavy at this moment. Finally, we got within sight of the stakes, the dreaded stakes, with the shells and mines on, which protected the beaches. Our coxswain did a marvellous job. We were headed straight for this stake and I could see the 56lb shell lashed to it. In just the last second, he missed it. He got it just right. He steered us in between the stakes and got ashore without touching one of those shells. At the order 'Down ramp', we were all surging ashore. We were in a few inches of water. All around were craft beaching and chaos and more gunfire was pouring down on us. We ran, under fire, up to the top of the beach where we went to ground, about a hundred yards from high water. People were going down and screaming and crying all around us. As we hit the sand at the top of the beach we took stock of our bearings and realised that we had landed almost exactly in our correct positions.

The landing craft infantry (LCI) sailed towards the beach in tight circles and when they closed on the beach, they peeled off one at a time and rammed their bows onto the beach with the next LCI coming alongside the previous one. Some of the landing craft had been hit by German artillery fire and were ablaze, often with many casualties aboard. After the rough seas, many must have been longing to reach the shore.

Other ships, including converted merchant vessels as well as landing craft, were fitted with artillery rockets to clear the beaches and also put the defences under pressure. All this, of course, was in addition to gunnery. Destroyers at the time were generally fitted with a main armament of 4in guns, although a few of the more modern ships had 4.5in versions. Cruisers had 6in guns with 4in ones as a secondary armament. One of these was HMS *Danae* and on her bridge was Captain J.H.B. Hughes, a Royal Marine:

Just before dawn, those of us on the bridge of HMS *Danae* had a tot of the most superb 1812 brandy from a bottle laid down by my great-grandfather in 1821, sent to me by my father with the comment, 'You may find this of some use in the near future.' We then commenced the operations for which we had been trained, namely engaging and knocking out three enemy batteries. At about 1000 we closed the beaches to knock out the opposition to the landing forces in the Ouistreham area. Our open 6inch and twin 4inch guns went into independent fire, the guns being laid, trained and fired by the crews stripped to the waist. This was real

'Nelson stuff'. We knocked up a fantastic rate of fire. X and Y*
guns were firing at least 19 rounds per minute on occasion. We
all joined in, jumping in to relieve the exhausted crew members
where we could. It was exhilarating beyond description and even
my thirteen-year-old boy bugler fired Y gun with the lanyard
while the captain of the gun, a corporal, leapt to get more charges
into the breech.

Then it all came to a halt and we sailed to Portsmouth for re-
ammunition.

HMS *Danae* had been in Greenock when the plans for the landings
had been finalized. Her commanding officer assembled her ship's
company in their respective divisions on the quarterdeck in freezing
cold weather to tell them of her role. He commented that they had
'the honour to be expendable', to which someone in the ranks of the
stokers' division promptly commented: 'Fuck that for a lark!'

Another rating aboard one of the ships in the bombardment force
commented: 'Cor! I'm sorry for those poor bastards on the other side.'
The Germans might not have seen the invasion fleet coming, but they
certainly heard it when it arrived. The bombardment started before the
landing craft went in and crept ahead of the troops once they were
ashore. There seem to have been no reports of 'friendly fire' casualties
once on the beaches.

The naval bombardment started at 0530 and the landings commenced
at 0630, by which time the bombardment moved away from coastal
targets and headed inland.

There was a sense of improvisation even in this, the largest
amphibious assault in history and with first call upon the resources of
the British, and although the Americans had much to do in the Pacific,
there was no doubt that this was their biggest effort in the Atlantic.
The naval commander in the eastern sector was Admiral Philip Vian,
whose flagship was the light cruiser HMS *Scylla*. Aboard the ship,
the volume of messages to be decoded and encoded meant that extra
officers were required but there was no space to accommodate them.
The result was that they were sent every other day from Portsmouth
aboard MTBs and stayed working aboard for forty-eight hours before
being returned to Portsmouth.

---

*'X' and 'Y' turrets, the two closest to the stern, were manned by Royal Marines rather
than naval gunners on British warships.

Despite the best efforts of the minesweepers, by the time Operation NEPTUNE officially ceased on 30 June, 59 ships had been sunk and another 110 damaged, many by pressure mines. Nevertheless, despite a storm that wrecked one of the two Mulberry Harbours – that at St Laurent serving the US forces on Utah and Omaha beaches – 850,279 men, 148,803 vehicles of all kinds and 570,505 tons of supplies had been landed.

Once the initial landings had been made, the major warships were back to continue bombarding enemy-held territory. Ships were routinely rotated out of the Normandy coastal waters and back to Portsmouth or even Plymouth to re-arm and if necessary refuel. This fire could be so devastating that on one occasion Rommel authorized the movement of a Panzer division away from the coast to a much safer location further inland. Even the armour of a tank was not proof against a 15in shell.

Throughout June 1944, more than 70,000 shells were fired by the Royal Navy at German shore targets. Naval shellfire is more constant and wearing than that of land-based guns as the mechanized handling equipment means that a warship gun can fire six times as many shells in a given period as a land-based artillery piece and often the shells are much heavier.

The German Commander-in-Chief, Army, West, Gerd von Rundstedt, reported later:

> The enemy had deployed very strong naval forces off the shores of the bridgehead. These can be used as quickly mobile, constantly available artillery, at points where they are necessary as defence against our attacks or as support for enemy attacks. During the day their fire is skilfully directed by . . . plane observers, and by advanced ground fire spotters. Because of the high rapid-fire capacity of naval guns they play an important part in the battle within their range. The movement of tanks by day, in open country, within the range of these naval guns is hardly possible.

Another German report discovered later noted that:

> Even more disastrous than the material effect was the morale effect of the rapidly and precisely firing naval guns. Even when not reinforced by simultaneous air bombing, the drum fire inspired in the defenders a feeling of utter helplessness, which in inexperienced recruits caused fainting or indeed complete

paralysis. The supporting fire of warships was extremely accurate and made the movement of strategic reserves impossible within the 20-mile range of their guns.

So that was it. The constant hammering of exploding shells all around them kept many Germans imprisoned within their shelters and concrete gun emplacements.

However, the Germans weren't the only ones to suffer. Those aboard the ships got no rest until they withdrew to refuel and re-arm. The firing and recoil of a heavy gun on board a warship sends sound and shock waves right through the ship. The battleship *Nelson* had nine 16in guns spread over three turrets – the heaviest calibre in the Royal Navy at the time – and these each fired a round once every minute on the night of 12/13 June, bombarding Caen. Those aboard the bombarding ships demonstrated great endurance. They also had to be ready for action at a moment's notice at any time of day or night. Some of the officers did not take off their clothes for several days; some reports suggest for as long as seventeen days. It was tiring, but it says much about the poor state of the defenders and the weakness of the *Kriegsmarine* that the Germans never tried to take advantage of their weariness. Hitler had, of course, brought home his battle-cruisers *Scharnhorst* and *Gneisenau* with the heavy cruiser *Prinz Eugen* earlier in the celebrated Channel Dash of February 1942.

The Allied navies continued to shell for as long as necessary and as long as there were enemy targets within range. On 30 June US troops seized the port and city of Cherbourg, one of the great Channel ports. Elsewhere, the Allied armies took Caen on 9 July, followed by St Lô on 18 July and Avranches on 25 July, finally allowing the bombardment fleet to leave the Normandy coast, their work done. Seizing ports helped and was necessary, but capture often marked the start of considerable work to clear a port and its approaches of mines, while the Germans had usually been careful to sabotage many of the port installations.

Friendly Fire
While NEPTUNE ended on 30 June, the Royal Navy's involvement did not and the service continued to patrol the waters off the coast of Normandy looking for mines, while E-boats and U-boats were not forgotten. The campaign had seen relatively few naval casualties, a tribute to the use of overwhelming force and a reflection of the weak state of the German *Kriegsmarine* and Luftwaffe. The Germans were,

after all, by this time on the defensive in Italy and the south of France as well as in Normandy and on the Eastern Front.

What happened next was all the more distressing because it did not come as a result of an engagement with the enemy but was a clear case of 'blue on blue' or 'friendly fire'. On 27 August two of the Royal Navy's minesweepers were sunk and a third had its stern torn off after an attack by rocket-firing Hawker Typhoon fighter-bombers from the RAF's 263 and 266 Squadrons.

The Royal Navy's First Minesweeping Flotilla was operating off the French coast in the region of Cap d'Antifer when it was decided to move it to a new area and details of the change were sent by signal to all interested parties. Later that day, another naval officer came on duty and decided to send the flotilla back to its original area of operations; again a signal was sent, but somehow the area naval headquarters was not included among the recipients and therefore could not notify the Royal Air Force. As a result, when Allied radar spotted five ships sweeping in line abreast at noon on 27 August, they were immediately assumed to be a German formation. Not having received the signal detailing the change, the Flag Officer, British Assault Area (FOBAA) agreed that any ships must be German. Two of the vessels, HMS *Hussar* and *Britomart*, were larger than most minesweepers and had served as sloops on convoy escort duties. From the air they seemed large enough to be small German destroyers. A Polish airman flew over the ships in a Spitfire and reported that they seemed to be Allied vessels but gave the wrong position. FOBAA then attempted to contact the officers controlling minesweeping but couldn't get through as the lines were down. FOBAA then called for an anti-shipping strike and sixteen Typhoons of the RAF's 263 and 266 Squadrons were ordered into the air. As he approached the flotilla, the strike leader thought that he could see Allied ships so he radioed questioning his orders, only to be told to attack. He subsequently queried his orders twice.

At 1330 the attack began. Sweeping out of the sun towards the first ship, *Britomart*, the Typhoons started strafing and firing anti-tank rockets, deadly against the thin-plated hulls of minor warships. In less than two minutes the ship had lost its bridge and was listing heavily, while another, *Hussar*, was on fire. Those on board the ships immediately assumed that the aircraft must be those of the Luftwaffe and *Jason* signalled that she was under attack by enemy aircraft, but as the aircraft raced away the distinctive D-Day black and white 'invasion stripes' could be seen and another ship, *Salamander*, fired recognition flares, forcing the hapless leader of the strike to query his orders yet again, for the fourth time. Yet, he was again ordered back into the attack and at 1335 dived down again towards the warships, hitting *Britomart* once more and strafing *Jason* while rockets went into both *Salamander* and *Colsay*. Despite a large white ensign and a Union flag being draped over the stern of *Jason* as she fired further recognition flares, a third attack followed at 1340, hitting *Hussar* which exploded and *Salamander*, whose stern was blown off by rocket strikes. As the crippled *Salamander* drifted shoreward, a no doubt bemused German artillery battery with 9.2in coastal guns opened fire, forcing *Jason* to launch her small boats to tow *Salamander* out of danger.

This was the Royal Navy's worst friendly-fire incident of the Second World War, with 117 officers and ratings killed and another 153 wounded. The whole incident was covered up and those involved sworn to secrecy on threat of prosecution; the events only came to light in 1994 when the then Public Record Office, now The National Archives, released the papers.

The three officers responsible for this appalling and unnecessary loss of life and valuable ships were court-martialled, but two were acquitted and the other severely reprimanded. No doubt had the strike leader disobeyed his orders, he would have been dealt with far more severely.

Beyond Normandy

The Normandy landings did not mean that the war in Europe against Germany was over, not even for the Royal Navy. The Russian convoys still had to be run, and there was much to do even as the Allied armies moved across Europe. Seizure of the port of Antwerp was vital as the supply lines from the French Channel ports became extended. This was initially hampered by the need to capture the Dutch island of Walcheren, which blocked access to the port. After valiant attempts by Canadian troops to take Walcheren across a causeway linking the island to the mainland, it had to be taken by a seaborne assault with covering fire from the battleship *Warspite* which needed to be towed into position by a tug.

On 1 November at 0554 the three Royal Marines Commandos of the British 4th Special Service Brigade attacked from seaward at Westkapelle in Operation INFATUATE I, accompanied by troops of the No. 4 (Belgian) and No. 5 (Norwegian) Commandos from Brigadier Peter Laycock's No. 10 (IA) Commando. No. 4 Commando with French troops in support then crossed from Breskens to attack Flushing with support from No. 155 Infantry Brigade in Operation INFATUATE II, aided by a heavy naval bombardment from the crippled battleship HMS *Warspite*, two monitors including HMS *Roberts*, and other naval vessels, despite many of their landing craft being sunk by heavy fire from German coastal batteries. The crossing was made mainly in Buffalos, which one Royal Marine present described as being 'like tanks with no tops'.

The run ashore was not easy, as Captain J. Linzel of No. 10 Commando recalled.

> This operation had more impact on me. The objective was to clear the seaway to Antwerp. We went to Belgium, where the No.4 Troops Brigade and the No.10 Commando were billeted. We were an attached unit of 14 men. We entered our LCT's Buffalo's amphibious vehicles to go to Walcheren where we experienced heavy German artillery. Our vehicle got hit direct by a grenade, setting our flamethrowers and ammunition on fire. This was a chaos. Our burning Buffalo was pushed into the sea and I can remember that together with 10 other men I ended up in another Buffalo and landed at Westkapelle. We experienced some serious fighting there and a lot of the Brigade were killed. It took us 3 days to capture the German dyke at Vlissingen, there were about 300 casements.

Frederick Weston was a sergeant in No. 41 Commando Royal Marines:

> We were in the open, unlike D-Day, so we saw everything as we went in. It was very heavily defended, we manned gunboats to take these on and we also had rocket ships that shot off scores of shots at a time. We'd also been told that there could be fixed flame-throwers on this part of the beach, so that was something to look forward to. We managed to get on all right and got into the village there, and saw their strongpoint at the base of a lighthouse. We got cover in an old house and found the old hands in there getting a brew of tea going. As we were pretty wet and miserable at the time, we had a quick cup of tea.
> Unfortunately our troop commander was killed when we reached their strongpoint. It was a very sad occasion for us, it seemed like they were giving themselves up and then one man

decided not to, and that was the end of our troop commander. It made us all very angry.

This was one thing that most fighting men could not accept: enemy troops surrendering and when approached to be taken prisoner, shooting their exposed would-be captors. It says much for the discipline of the Royal Marines that they did not shoot the Germans, or at least the man who betrayed their trust.

Two days of street-fighting followed before the regional capital Middleburg could be seized and the Germans surrendered there on 5 November. Nevertheless, some resistance continued in the north of Walcheren and it was not until 8 November that this ended.

Tragedy now awaited the Allied navies at Ostend.

Even by spring of the following year, most of The Netherlands was under German control, including the major naval bases of IJmuiden and Den Helder, acting as bases for E-boats. The E-boats posed a major threat to the steady stream of shipping crossing the southern North Sea and as always, the best defence against E-boat attacks on the northern flank of the Allied convoys was to provide motor gunboats or motor torpedo boats as escorts or on patrol to ward off E-boat attacks before they could get within reach of a convoy. Two MTB flotillas were based at Ostend – the Royal Navy's 55th and the Canadian-manned 29th – with a mobile base unit to service the vessels. These two units had been fighting alongside each other since June 1944. The 29th had eleven 72ft 6in MTBs, while the 55th had the larger Fairmile 'D' boats. Most British MTBs and MGBs had petrol engines rather than the safer diesel alternative, meaning that accidents involving fuel vapour-induced explosions and fires were relatively common.

On 14 February 1945, there were no fewer than thirty-one MTBs of all kinds as well as other small craft gathered in the harbour at Ostend, with many of the MTBs moored alongside one another. Many of the crew members had been granted shore leave, but others were busy preparing for that night's patrols.

Among those preparing for the patrols were four of the Canadian boats of the 29th MTB Flotilla. Of these, *MTB464* was carrying out an armament check at sea when one of its engines cut out due to water in the fuel system. This was a common problem as one of the tankers supporting the MTBs had pumped water-contaminated fuel ashore. The base maintenance staff were too busy to provide assistance and simply suggested that the MTB's crew pumped water from their fuel tanks into buckets and then disposed of the contents over the side. Before long, a strong smell of petrol spread throughout the harbour. Many noticed this but no one reported it or took any action.

What happened next was a major fire, but what actually ignited it remains unknown. One witness was Ken Forrester, serving aboard one of the Royal Navy's MTBs, *MTB771*, in the 55th Flotilla:

> It was a rest day, and half the crew had been taken on a sightseeing trip to Bruges for the afternoon. It was around 3 o'clock in the afternoon. I had volunteered to make the tea and went up on deck to go to the potato locker which was just below the bridge. Before I got there I saw flames and smoke rising from the middle of a group of MTBs that were berthed in a large lock entrance some 30 yards away. Our boat was tied up to the wall with two others of our flotilla tied alongside us. The tide was low which meant that our torpedoes were below the level of the seawall. There was a raised gangway over the torpedoes bypassing the 0.5in turret. This gangway was level with the top of the wall. On seeing the fire I ran to the forward hatch–the crew's quarters–and yelled out *Fire!* Ran to the stern of the boat, took hold of a fire hose that was permanently rigged and ran unreeling it as I went. I was just passing over the gangway that was level with the wall when the boat that was on fire blew up with a huge *Woomph* noise. There was a rush of seething hot air which blew me over. The next thing I remember was picking myself up on the dockside with burning debris everywhere covering the quayside and all of our boats. Our own boat had been protected somewhat with being shielded by the dockside. I was still dazed, realised I'd lost my shoes and beard mostly singed off. I had blood running down my face by that time. Someone was running past me, so I ran while pandemonium was going on. Ammunition was exploding, torpedoes going off, pieces of flaming boats everywhere.

It seemed as if the entire harbour was ablaze, with torpedoes and other ammunition exploding, fuel tanks rupturing and exploding, adding their contents to the fire.

Some 36 members of the Royal Navy were killed with the loss of 7 boats, while the Royal Canadian Navy lost 26 personnel and 5 boats.

Taking the South of France

It had originally been intended that the Normandy landings would coincide with landings in the south of France, forcing the Germans to divide their forces. Another advantage of this two-pronged attack was that it would also put pressure on German forces still fighting in Italy who risked being cut off should the Allied landings result in an advance eastwards into northern Italy. No matter what the advantages of such a co-ordinated assault may have been, it soon became plain that insufficient resources were available to land in two places at once. The original plans for the Normandy landings had been on a much smaller front with fewer landing beaches than were eventually used, with a broader front seen as being less vulnerable to a German counter-attack. This was not all. The Normandy landings were not happening in isolation. American forces were moving across the Pacific and the demand for landing craft and landing ships plus supporting fire from battleships and cruisers was such that the south of France would have to wait.

It could be argued that, even if Stalin only saw land battles as constituting a 'front', then the Normandy landings had provided a 'second front', but in the Pacific there was a 'third front' and even a 'fourth front' as the United States Army conducted landings in the southern zone and the United States Marine Corps in the north, steadily advancing towards Japan, and even this is to ignore the fighting in Burma.

This global demand for resources also explains why so many of the warships engaged in supporting the Normandy landings came from the Royal Navy. The United States Navy was otherwise engaged; nevertheless, it did well to provide the support given off Normandy.

Operation Dragoon

The landings in the south of France were originally code-named ANVIL, possibly because the planners saw the landings in Normandy and in the south of France hammering the German occupiers into shape!

The south of France did not compare with Normandy. The Germans had left a substantial part of France unoccupied and under Vichy control partly to avoid overstretching their occupation forces. Even after they occupied Vichy territory following the Allied landings in North Africa in late 1942, the resources were not available to build a 'Mediterranean Wall', and indeed the Atlantic Wall itself was far from complete.

Landings in the south of France had been delayed by the need to devote further resources to the campaign in Italy. The landings at Salerno had not produced a fast enough advance, and those at Anzio had been even more disappointing. These problems and the strong German resistance at Monte Cassino had delayed entry into Rome until just before the Normandy landings. The scale of the landings in the south of France almost make it seem like a sideshow compared to North Africa, Sicily and Normandy, but even so the resources expended were considerable.

The seaborne operation was under the command of Vice Admiral Henry Hewitt, USN. He led a fleet of 500 landing and 200 escort vessels to put ashore Lieutenant General Alexander Patch's US Seventh Army between Cannes and Toulon on 15 August 1944. Hewitt had three American battleships as well as one each from the Royal Navy and the French *Marine Nationale*. There were also 9 escort carriers, 25 cruisers and 45 destroyers.

Little resistance was met and within a few days both the major naval base at Toulon and the important port of Marseilles were in Allied hands. The Luftwaffe mounted little resistance and before long the Supermarine Spitfires from the British escort carriers and the Grumman Hellcats from their American counterparts found themselves providing ground-attack missions in support of ground forces. This had not been entirely unexpected and some naval air squadron commanders had been granted time to fly with RAF squadrons flying ground-attack sorties in Italy.

Operations were helped by the fact that there were more escort carriers than at Salerno and there was plenty of room to manoeuvre, while the escort carriers could be rotated out of operations for refuelling off Corsica, avoiding the dramas caused by the shortage of fuel off Salerno. After 24 August the Germans were clearly withdrawing and, being out of range for the carriers, air-to-ground operations were taken over by the USAAF.

Chapter 19

Returning to the East

The naval war in Europe continued, as did the Atlantic and Arctic convoys, and there was also some mopping-up of enemy forces in the Adriatic as well as minesweeping operations around many of the newly-liberated ports. Nevertheless, the main body of the Royal Navy, and especially the larger ships, were ready for a return to the Far East for operations against Japan.

Many senior officers in the United States Navy had strong reservations about the return of the Royal Navy to what was 'their' theatre of war. Some saw the British role as being centred on the reconquest of Burma, at best. Others felt that the United Kingdom was solely interested in reclaiming its colonies, especially Malaya, the financially most important and viable of them all. There was also the feeling that they could finish the war against Japan themselves, which was probably true, but in fact the British contribution would prove to be worthwhile and not insignificant.

Reasons for the British to return to the Far East were many. Some felt that after having had such strong American assistance in the war against Italy and Germany, as well as so much Lend-Lease equipment, the Americans were owed support. There were also political reasons as they did not want to be seen as having abandoned Australia and New Zealand, and as much of the territory overrun by the Japanese was British – not just Burma but also Hong Kong, Malaya and Singapore – they wanted to be able to take the Japanese surrender in these territories. In fact, comparing the post-war record of the British colonies with those of The Netherlands or France suggests that in the longer term the British desire to be involved was the right one. Obviously, having been occupied by Germany, the Dutch and French were in a far weaker position, especially the Dutch as not only were they numerically weaker, much of their country was not liberated until Germany surrendered.

There were many practical difficulties to be resolved including communications and liaison, and this could be difficult enough in any large force, even a single navy. For example, in the Battle of Leyte Gulf, parts of the United States Navy were not where they were expected to be. In fact, the same could be said about the Imperial Japanese Navy whose organization began to fall apart during the battle.

There were difficulties on the American side, for having amassed a massive fleet, their supply and support systems were under considerable pressure, not helped by the speed of the American advance across the Pacific and the distances involved. A condition was laid down that the Royal Navy could not expect any use of USN facilities in the Pacific theatre.

Two of the senior American naval commanders, Chester Nimitz and Ernest King, felt that the British lacked the experience of mounting massed air attacks from carriers, despite the Fleet Air Arm's attacks on the *Tirpitz*, and the means of supporting a fleet far from its bases. There was some reason to doubt the ability of the British to assemble a balanced fleet that was also modern and adequate in strength, as this was why the Royal Navy had lost so many important ships early in the war. British ships tended to be short on range and eye-witnesses attested to the Royal Navy's slowness in refuelling at sea compared to the USN. Some idea of the distances involved can be gained from the fact that the journey from Japan to Singapore was about the same as Southampton to New York.

Undaunted, the Royal Navy started to resolve these problems. Simonstown in South Africa was already a suitable base, with South African Air Force airfields available for aircraft disembarking from the carriers as they entered port. There were also facilities, less sophisticated perhaps, in Kenya near Mombasa. Ceylon provided a forward base with naval air stations ashore and there were others in southern India. Australia became another important basing area for the new British Pacific Fleet which could use both Sydney and Brisbane, both with air stations ashore.

Not all senior American officers were opposed to British involvement and the prospect of having additional ships and aircraft appealed to this group. Liaison officers were exchanged and some of the problems of co-operation were resolved, initially by ensuring that the Royal Navy operated in one area and the United States Navy in another; another case of deconfliction. This did not mean that there was no co-operation and British, Australian and New Zealand ships did from time to time operate with the Americans and under their overall command. Locally, many American officers did all that they could to help.

Joint Attacks

Co-operation on a small scale was attempted at first, so that the two navies could get used to one another. During spring 1944, the USS *Saratoga* was attached to what was then the British Eastern Fleet, her aircraft joining those of *Illustrious* for the early raids on Sabang with the two ships forming the core of Task Force 70. It was a useful target, on a small island off the northern end of Sumatra, with a harbour and airfields vital to the Japanese war effort in Burma. It was also the baptism of fire for the new high-performance fighter-bomber for the Fleet Air Arm, the Vought Corsair.

This was not the first example of co-operation between the two navies. Apart from the North Atlantic convoys and the landings in North Africa, Sicily, Italy and France, the shortage of flight decks experienced by both navies had resulted in some unusual compromises. One of these was that HMS *Victorious*, second ship of the successful *Illustrious* class, spent much of the winter of 1942–43 being refitted at the Norfolk Navy Yard before being loaned to the USN with the temporary name of USS *Robin*. She was released back to the Royal Navy when the USS *Essex* arrived, lead ship of the *Essex* class and America's idea of a fast aircraft carrier, although with a wooden flight deck.

The ability of American industry to ramp up production meant that the *Independence*-class light carriers converted from the *Cleveland*-class light cruisers were probably not needed, bearing in mind that they were accompanied by mass production of escort carriers, known as auxiliary carriers to the Royal Navy. They were indeed as often as not more like 'auxiliary carriers' than escort carriers as many served as aircraft transports or maintenance carriers and, most important of all, many were used to provide cover for Allied landings, mainly in the Pacific but also off Salerno and the south of France. Those in the Pacific were mainly used by the United States Marine Corps, providing close support for troops landing on the many islands that lay along the route to the Japanese home islands.

The first attack on Sabang was made on 19 April 1944 with Corsairs escorting Barracudas, an aircraft that had seen action in Europe, notably against the *Tirpitz*, but would prove ill-suited to tropical conditions. Operating under the command of Admiral Sir James Somerville, the British Eastern Fleet was to be a thorn in the side of the Japanese. That first raid was unexpected by them and was devastating, despite the poor performance of the Barracuda. Fortunately, these aircraft were soon exchanged for the more capable and reliable Grumman Avenger and both ships were able to mount a second successful strike in May against an oil refinery outside Surabaya on the island of Java, with the loss of just one aircraft.

Operating together quickly exposed weakness in British organization. The British carrier air group was smaller than that of the Americans, but the Fleet Air Arm had to learn the importance of a fast turnaround of aircraft on the flight deck and in the hangar. Fortunately, these lessons were learned very quickly.

Completely integrated carrier operations by the two navies took some time and some adjustment. The signals used by the deck landing officer (DLO), more usually known as the 'batsman' as he used large bats (and lights at night) to signal to approaching aircraft, had to be changed as certain signals used by the two navies had exactly the opposite meaning. As the USN was the larger navy by this time, it was the American signals that were retained. There were other changes as well, some of them introduced many years earlier, such as the American idea of having a crash barrier, a net stretched across the flight deck to stop aircraft that missed all the arrester wires from crashing into those parked forward; however, this was a mixed blessing as aircraft hitting the net often stopped so abruptly that the pilot was badly injured.

One change that was forced not by the need to operate with the United States Navy but to avoid aircraft being mistaken for Japanese was to change the colours of the identification roundels on British aircraft. Officially these were red, white and blue from the centre moving outwards, although the white middle ring was omitted when camouflage was used. Because Japanese aircraft had a large red roundel, it was decided that British military aircraft would use a pale blue centre and a dark blue outer ring on their roundels, again without the white circle.

The Fleet Air Arm was allocated a number of particular targets. One of these was Palembang, with oil refineries and port facilities on the island of Sumatra, where the Japanese were subjected to heavy aerial attacks throughout December 1944 and January 1945. The most important attack on the island was Operation MERIDIAN I on 24 January 1945 with aircraft from no fewer than thirteen naval air squadrons flying off the carriers *Illustrious, Indefatigable, Indomitable* and *Victorious*.

As the war progressed eastwards and ever closer to Japan, a British Pacific Fleet was formed under the command of Vice Admiral Sir Bernard Rawlings but operating under USN direction. The British Pacific Fleet was given a US task force number, becoming Task Force 57 when the US fleet was known as the US Fifth Fleet and Task Force 37 when the designation changed to the US Third Fleet. This unusual, possibly unique, situation was created because command of the US Pacific Fleet alternated between two officers: it was known as the US Third Fleet when under the command of Vice Admiral 'Bull' Halsey and the Fifth Fleet when under the command of Vice Admiral Raymond Spruance. The task forces also changed their designations depending on who was in command. When not in command, each of the admirals and their staff were ashore planning the next series of operations.

While the concept of the naval air wing had evolved in 1943, in 1945 the Royal Navy changed these to carrier air groups.

The new British Pacific Fleet was assigned to operate against the Sakishima Gunto group of islands through which the Japanese were ferrying combat aircraft to Okinawa, and did much to cut the volume of Japanese reinforcements. This was the BPF's contribution to Operation ICEBERG, the attack on Okinawa, between 26 March and 25 May 1945. Landings on Okinawa started on 1 April and despite initial resistance being light due to a breakdown in Japanese communications, fierce and prolonged fighting followed ashore, while the aircraft carriers were all subjected to *kamikaze* suicide bomber attacks.

Operations against the Japanese involved additional hazards for the naval aviator. The Japanese never felt bound to observe the rules of the Geneva Conventions and if shot down the outlook for aircrew was grim. Many squadron commanders wore uniforms of a lower rank as some means of protection against interrogation and torture, and to avoid providing a propaganda coup for the Japanese.

Formidable was struck by her first *kamikaze* on 4 May, which had found the carrier relatively lightly protected as the battleships that could provide a dense curtain of anti-aircraft fire around the ship were away bombarding coastal targets. The attack came at 1131 with the flight deck crowded with aircraft ranged for launching. While the ship only suffered a 2ft dent in the flight deck near the base of the island, eight men were killed and forty-seven wounded. It was small consolation that it could have been even worse but for the fact that the medical officer had moved the flight deck sick bay from the air intelligence office at the base of the island as the AIO was the scene of most of the casualties.

Even worse was to follow. On 9 May, *Formidable* was struck again. The *kamikaze* hit the after end of the flight deck and ploughed into the aircraft ranged there. A rivet was blown out of the deck and burning petrol poured into the hangar where the fire could only be extinguished by spraying, with adverse effects even on those aircraft not on fire. Seven aircraft were lost on deck, with another twelve in the hangar. The ship later refuelled and obtained replacement aircraft. Nine days later on 18 May, an armourer working on a Corsair in the hangar deck failed to notice that the guns were still armed and accidentally fired them into a parked Avenger which blew up and started another fierce fire, destroying no fewer than thirty aircraft. Despite this terrible setback, the ship was again fully operational by the end of the day.

In the closing days of the war in the Pacific, the Fleet Air Arm was striking at targets in the Tokyo area when it earned its second Victoria Cross, but again, posthumously. On 9 August, Lieutenant Robert Hampton Gray, RCNVR, was leading a strike of Corsairs from *Formidable*'s Nos 1841 and 1842 Naval Air Squadrons to attack a destroyer in Onagawa Wan when he came under heavy anti-aircraft fire from five warships. He pressed ahead with his attack, even though his aircraft was damaged, and succeeded in sinking the destroyer before his aircraft plunged into the harbour.

Even with hindsight, it seems strange and very unsatisfactory that the Fleet Air Arm was granted just two VCs in the entire war.

The Escorts Arrive
Earlier, a small number of the Royal Navy's escort carriers had found their way to the East. Many of these were to act as aircraft transports and as maintenance and aircraft repair ships, but some of the first were deployed on convoy escort duties. HMS *Ameer* maintained anti-submarine patrols in the Indian Ocean through which convoys from the United States passed on their way to the Gulf, then known as the Persian Gulf, carrying supplies for the Soviet Union. *Ameer* was present off the coast of Burma when Ramree Island was attacked by the Royal Navy and the Royal Indian Navy in January 1945, a few months before the combined amphibious and overland attacks that liberated Rangoon. Landings on the island were aided by *Ameer*'s twenty-four Grumman Hellcat fighters of No. 815 NAS so that the island was available as a springboard for the landings in Rangoon.

Operation SUNFISH on 11 April 1945 saw Force 63 attack Sabang and Oleh-Leh in the Netherlands East Indies, led by the battleships *Queen Elizabeth* and *Richelieu* together with the cruisers *London* and *Cumberland* with the latter leading the 26th Destroyer Flotilla, as well as the escort carriers *Emperor* and *Khedive* with No. 808 NAS with

Grumman Hellcats. On 16 April, Force 63 attacked Emma Haven and Padang.

Many of the British warships were in Trincomalee in Ceylon on 8 May 1945, which marked VE Day in Europe. For those in the East, there was little to celebrate as the Allies fought their way through fierce resistance towards Japan, fully expecting to have to invade. On 14 May, Ultra intelligence warned that the Japanese cruiser *Haguro* and her destroyer escort were at sea having left Singapore, while the Nicobar Islands had been evacuated by a Japanese supply ship. The following day the escort carrier *Emperor* launched a strike of four Grumman Avengers of 815 NAS against the cruiser and her escort but one aircraft was shot down, although its crew were saved. A second strike, also of four aircraft, was launched but one had to return with engine trouble. Two of the remaining aircraft spotted five destroyers and spent some time trying to establish whether they were British or Japanese, eventually deciding that they were friendly which was fortunate as they were part of the 26th Destroyer Flotilla, also trying to find the *Haguro*. The remaining aircraft started looking for the downed crew but had been given the wrong search co-ordinates, and running low on fuel found first the supply ship escorted by a submarine and then the *Haguro* and her destroyer escort. The pilot signalled his findings and returned to the carrier with just ten minutes' fuel left.

Emperor launched three more Avengers, which found the cruiser and dive-bombed her, achieving a direct hit and a near miss. The return flight of 530 miles was the longest attacking flight from any British carrier during the war and the only time that a major enemy warship at sea was dive-bombed by the Fleet Air Arm. While *Haguro* was only slightly damaged she attempted to return to Singapore, but after dark was finally cornered by the 26th Destroyer Flotilla and sunk by gunfire and torpedoes in the entrance to the Malacca Straits early on 16 May.

The first of the new light fleet carriers arrived in the Pacific just as the war was ending and did not see action; however, they did see the surrender of the Japanese in Singapore and Malaya and then brought home many British prisoners of war from the Japanese POW camps.

Chapter 20

A Balanced Fleet

The Royal Navy in 1945 was a different service from the one that had gone to war in 1939. Manpower had actually peaked in mid-1944 and had already begun to fall but the number of ships was at its peak in 1945, as detailed earlier in Chapter 18.

This was a modern navy and a well-balanced fleet, possibly more so than at any time in its history. The irony was that the two oldest aircraft carriers, *Furious* and *Argus*, had survived the war while all the other pre-war aircraft carriers had been lost. By this time, these two veterans were no better than hulks. In fact, those ships that had served through the war were almost all in dire need of a heavy refit as not only had they taken battle damage, but routine refits had been neglected because of the pressure on the Royal Navy to keep as many ships at sea as possible, while its three main bases were also subjected to heavy aerial attack. One man who joined *Illustrious* after the war recalls seeing much evidence of the damage done to the ship off Malta and then again while undergoing emergency repairs in Malta.

Yet, even at the war's end, new ships were joining the fleet. One of these was the last battleship of the Royal Navy, HMS *Vanguard*, with eight 15in guns in four turrets. Serious consideration had been given to converting the ship before completion as an aircraft carrier, but this would have been a costly operation and the end result would have been too narrow in the beam to make an ideal carrier. The question was, of course, why was anyone ordering a battleship at this time? However, tradition dies hard and for the navies of the day, possession of a battleship was seen as a necessary status symbol. Many minor navies, especially in Latin America, kept battleships for many years afterwards, while others – for example, the Dutch, Australian, Canadian and Indian navies – all preferred the 'modern' option of an aircraft carrier.

While none of the *Colossus* and the extension of this class, the *Majestic*-class, ships saw action in the Second World War, they were involved in the Korean War and two saw service in Operation MUSKETEER, the Anglo-French invasion of the Suez Canal Zone. More enduring was that having ordered these ships in large numbers, especially for ships of their size, many were immediately available for sale or transfer elsewhere. These two classes saw service with the navies of Argentina, Australia, Brazil, Canada, France, India and The Netherlands, and in some cases introduced these navies to carrier-borne air power for the first time.

As many as possible of the Lend-Lease auxiliary or escort carriers were returned to the United States but some were in no state to go back, with *Dasher* having blown up killing many of her ship's company and others sunk or so badly damaged that they had to be scrapped and another, *Biter*, was loaned to the French as the *Dixmude*. *Nairana*, one of the few British conversions, was loaned to the Dutch as the *Karel Doorman*, the irony being that the want of air cover had seen the loss of the admiral of this name with his ship in the Battle of the Java Sea. The Dutch subsequently received a *Colossus*-class light fleet carrier, *Venerable*, and after returning *Nairana* to the Royal Navy their new ship was named *Karel Doorman*.

As the Royal Navy was run down from its wartime strength, the naval bases around the world filled up with redundant escort vessels, especially corvettes. Other ships were sold off. While many of the escort carriers returned to the United States were converted to merchant vessels, strangely few of those operated by the USN were converted. The Royal Navy kept one of the British conversions, the *Pretoria Castle*, for many years as a trials ship.

There were some problems with personnel, with those of the wartime 'hostilities only' category expecting to be released as soon as the war ended, but this was impractical. Nevertheless, the Royal Navy did not suffer the indiscipline, almost amounting to mutiny, that affected many Royal Air Force bases, especially in the Indian subcontinent.

One naval pilot, a lieutenant commander, managed to switch from the RNVR to the regular service, but was then disappointed to find himself demoted to lieutenant and left waiting for weeks for a new posting. Nevertheless, when he eventually did retire many years later it was as a captain. Less fortunate were those caught in training as pilots or observers when peace was declared. While still not commissioned as this did not come in wartime until flying training was completed, they found themselves posted to be trained as aircraft engine mechanics and all hopes of early commissioning lost. Worse, on being posted for training, their superior 'officer potential' led to extra harsh discipline being imposed on them until the newspapers found out about it.

The Post-War Navy

In contrast to the situation earlier in the century, the post-war Royal Navy included many national servicemen, although less than the Royal Air Force and far less than the British Army. Of those who did find themselves undertaking national service with the RN, many were Merchant Navy personnel whose national service had been deferred until their training was completed.

A substantial Royal Naval Reserve and Royal Naval Volunteer Reserve were both maintained for many years until eventually these two categories were merged into a single Royal Naval Reserve. As the future of the Royal Navy was planned by an Admiralty committee known as the 'Way Ahead Committee', flying training for reservists was dropped, and eventually as the service contracted and national service ended, the RNR was mainly tasked with minesweeping. Other cuts saw the last battleship, *Vanguard*, first as the headquarters of the RNR and then eventually scrapped. *Warspite* had been withdrawn for scrapping soon after the war had ended and showed her displeasure by breaking her tow and ending up beached in St Michael's Bay in Cornwall; *Vanguard* did the same, but off Southsea.

The wartime aircraft carriers eventually were scrapped, except for *Victorious* which underwent a massive rebuilding to emerge with a half-angled flight deck and three-dimensional radar in the late 1950s, but she too was scrapped a few years later after a fire while under refit. Nevertheless, by the mid-1960s the Royal Navy had five aircraft carriers and two commando carriers. The latter were equipped with helicopters and could take a Royal Marine Commando brigade wherever it was needed; a legacy of the Suez campaign when the Royal Navy flew off the first heliborne assault.

Naval bases were cut. While the former RAF base at Hal Far in Malta was transferred to the Fleet Air Arm as HMS *Falcon*, the 1970s saw the Royal Navy's presence run down and the base eventually closed as the Royal Navy left Malta after more than 170 years. Other major bases that were abandoned included Singapore and later Hong Kong after the territory was handed over to the Chinese People's Republic. Today, only Gibraltar remains of the overseas bases and there is no longer a Mediterranean Fleet or, even in its much-reduced state, a Home Fleet. The various overseas squadrons and stations have all gone. Chatham was the only one of the three manning ports to close but it was followed in the 1990s by Rosyth. Today, the Royal Naval

Reserve also has all but disappeared and its various 'divisions', small outposts around the coast, have gone.

Naval aircraft also changed. The first generation of jet aircraft such as the Supermarine Attacker was soon followed by the de Havilland Sea Venom and Armstrong-Whitworth Sea Hawk, but in the 1960s there was a major step forward. Starting with the Blackburn Buccaneer and then joined by the American McDonnell F-4M Phantom, carrier-borne aircraft suddenly became comparable with those based ashore. No longer was there a significant performance gap between aircraft designed to take off from ships and those based ashore. Both aircraft were also to see air force service.

The threat from low-flying aircraft also ended with Airborne Early Warning (AEW) aircraft such as the Fairey Gannet, a development of the Royal Navy's last fixed-wing anti-submarine aircraft, while this role passed to increasingly powerful and effective anti-submarine helicopters such as the Westland Sea King and later the Agusta-Westland Merlin.

The 1970s almost saw the end of the aircraft carrier with the previous decade having seen replacements, known as CVA.01 and CVA.02, for the Royal Navy's two largest carriers, *Ark Royal* and *Eagle*, cancelled. *Ark Royal* and *Eagle* were modified, with the former able to operate McDonnell Douglas F-4M Phantom fighters, and their lives extended. A complete end to British fixed-wing naval aviation was avoided when the Hawker Siddeley Kestrel vertical take-off aircraft appeared and this evolved into the British Aerospace Sea Harrier, while the concept of the 'through deck cruiser' emerged as a cut-price light fleet aircraft carrier. The discovery that a Sea Harrier had a much greater range or warload when using short take-off aided by a ramp known as a 'ski-jump' settled the shape of British naval aviation, and also that of Spain and Italy, for some years.

The ski-jump was not the sole British contribution to carrier aviation. British naval officers had invented the angled flight deck that allowed aircraft to land and take off at the same time, and allowed a pilot landing to go round for another attempt if necessary. The mirror-deck landing system was another of these inventions that helped aircraft to land, while the steam catapult enabled ever-heavier naval aircraft to take off safely.

In the end, three ships of what was known as the *Invincible* class were built. The conversion of the *Centaur*-class carrier *Hermes* as an interim 'Harrier Carrier' and the delivery of the first *Invincible*-class carrier meant that the Royal Navy was able to recover the Falkland

Islands which had been invaded by the Argentine Republic in 1982. Unfortunately, only two of the *Invincible*-class ships, *Illustrious* and *Ark Royal*, were kept in commission and then the Sea Harriers were scrapped, although of a more up-to-date mark than those that had rescued the Falklands. After that the remaining carriers were withdrawn, although *Illustrious* received a temporary reprieve as a helicopter carrier. In the meantime, the remaining Harriers were jointly manned by Fleet Air Arm and RAF personnel as 'Joint Force Harrier'.

The number of escort vessels also fell sharply from more than 182 in 1958: first to around 80; then to 40; to 25 in 2008; and eventually to just 19 today. Escorts were no longer steam- or diesel-powered but powered by gas turbines and gradually all escorts had a helicopter landing platform and hangar with some of the Type 22 frigates able to carry two helicopters. In the interests of economy and extending range, later escorts were powered by diesel and gas turbine propulsion.

Mines are no longer swept, not even hunted and then swept, but instead are found by sonar with a remotely-controlled submersible used to destroy the mine. Meanwhile, mine countermeasures vessels (MCMVs) as they are now known are no longer built of wood but of glass-reinforced fibre.

The biggest change has been the introduction of the nuclear-powered submarine, of which the first in Royal Navy service was named *Dreadnought*. These vessels were initially all 'fleet' submarines or 'hunter-killers', meaning that their main role was to counter Russian missile-carrying submarines, but later the responsibility for Britain's nuclear deterrent was passed from the RAF to the Royal Navy and four intercontinental ballistic missile (ICBM) *Resolution*-class submarines were introduced to carry Polaris missiles. There should have been five boats of this class but, with the nation ever more concerned about economics than defence, the fifth boat was cancelled. When Polaris was replaced by a more potent missile, Trident, the *Resolution*-class boats were replaced by the *Vanguard* class, also of four vessels.

The rank structure has also changed. The rank of commissioned airman or gunner that replaced the warrant officer rank was abolished in the mid-1950s and those holding this rank became sub-lieutenants, but change is often reversed and after the introduction of fleet chief petty officers, the rank of warrant officer has returned. At the other end of the scale, with all three services abolishing five-star ranks, there is no longer a rank of admiral of the fleet. Indeed, given the continued run-down of the Royal Navy, one wonders how much longer a First Sea Lord will be able to justify the rank of admiral?

At present the Royal Navy has the two largest aircraft carriers it has ever operated, the *Queen Elizabeth* and the *Prince of Wales,* under construction but there are no plans to operate both ships and in any case, there are insufficient escort vessels for both to put to sea safely in a potentially hostile environment. For the first time in history, the French *Marine Nationale* has more ships than the Royal Navy.

Bibliography

Akermann, P., *Encyclopaedia of British Submarines 1901–1955* (privately published, 1990)

Chesneau, R., *Aircraft Carriers of the World, 1914 to the Present* (Arms & Armour, 1992)

Cunningham, Admiral of the Fleet Viscount, of Hyndhope, *A Sailor's Odyssey* (Hutchinson, 1951)

Gelb, Norman, *Desperate Venture* (Hodder & Stoughton, 1992)

Hickey, D. and Smith, G., *Operation Avalanche: Salerno Landings, 1943* (Heinemann, 1983)

Hobbs, David, *Aircraft Carriers of the Royal and Commonwealth Navies* (Greenhill Books, 1996)

Ireland, Bernard, *Jane's Naval History of World War II* (HarperCollins, 1998)

Keegan, John, *The Price of Admiralty* (Hutchinson, 1988)

Kennedy, Ludovic, *Menace: The Life and Death of the Tirpitz* (Sidgwick & Jackson, 1979)

Kilbracken, Lord, *Bring Back My Stringbag: A Stringbag Pilot at War* (Pan Books, 1980)

Laffin, J., *British VCs of World War 2: A Study in Heroism* (Sutton, 1997)

Mallman Showell, J.P., *The German Navy Handbook 1939–1945* (Sutton, 1999)

Moore, Captain John, RN, *Escort Carrier* (Hutchinson, 1964)

O' Hara, Vincent, Dickson, W. David and Worth, Richard, *On Seas Contested: The Seven Great Navies of the Second World War* (Naval Institute Press, Annapolis, 2010)

Padfield, Peter, *Dönitz: The Last Führer* (Victor Gollancz, 1984)

Poolman, Kenneth, *Armed Merchant Cruisers* (Leo Cooper in association with Secker & Warburg, 1985)

— *Escort Carrier: HMS* Vindex *at War* (Secker & Warburg, 1985)

— *The Sea Hunters: Escort Carriers v U-boats 1941–1945* (Arms & Armour, 1982)

Preston, Antony, *Aircraft Carriers* (Bison, 1979)

— *Destroyers* (Hamlyn, 1977)

— *History of the Royal Navy in the 20th Century* (Bison, 1987)

Roskill, Captain S.W., RN, *The Navy at War, 1939–1945* (HMSO, 1960)

— *The War at Sea, 1939–1945*, Vols I–III (HMSO, 1976)

Sturtevant, Ray, and Balance, Theo, *The Squadrons of the Fleet Air Arm* (Air Britain, 1994)

Thomas, D.A., *Battles and Honours of the Royal Navy* (Leo Cooper, 1998)

Thompson, Julian, *Imperial War Museum Book of the War at Sea, 1939–1945* (Imperial War Museum/Sidgwick & Jackson, 1996)

Van der Vat, D., *Standard of Power: The Royal Navy in the Twentieth Century* (Hutchinson, 2000)

Vian, Admiral Sir Philip, *Action This Day* (Muller, 1960)

Winton, John, *Air Power at Sea, 1939–1945* (Sidgwick & Jackson, 1976)
— *The Forgotten Fleet* (Michael Joseph, 1960)
— *The Victoria Cross at Sea* (Michael Joseph, 1978)
Woodman, R., *Arctic Convoys* (John Murray, 1974)
Woods, G.A., *Wings at Sea: A Fleet Air Arm Observer's War, 1940–1945* (Conway Maritime, 1985)
Wragg, David, *Royal Navy Handbook 1939–1945* (Sutton [now The History Press], 2005)
— *The Fleet Air Arm Handbook 1939–1945* (Sutton [now The History Press], 2001)
— *Malta: The Last Great Siege, 1940–1943* (Pen & Sword, 2003)

Index